Preston Fidler beautifully integrates the twin missionary tasks of language learning and gospel communication. I highly commend *1000 Cups of Tea: Gospel Fluency Across Cultures*.

David Garrison, author, *A Wind in the House of Islam* and *Church Planting Movements*

This is the book that I have waited through 50 years of cross-cultural missionary service for someone to write. Language fluency is at the very foundation of missionary service. Clear and understandable communication of the gospel is the very heart of missionary service. Preston Fidler has effectively built that bridge between acquiring language fluency and communicating the gospel so that hearers understand, believe, and live the good news of Jesus Christ. His use of the scriptures throughout the book is outstanding. The book is technical but practical, theoretical but inspirational, faces realities of life but spiritually grounded. Every believer is called to communicate the gospel so that all who hear can understand and can respond. Certainly, every cross-cultural missionary should make *1000 Cups of Tea: Gospel Fluency Across Cultures* essential reading.

Sam James, author, *Servant on the Edge of History* and *The Making of a Servant*

These days evangelism makes a lot of people nervous. It can be difficult to have meaningful conversations about spiritual truth in our own language; but when we're attempting to communicate the goodness of the gospel in another language, the challenge is amplified exponentially. In *1000 Cups of Tea: Gospel Fluency Across Cultures*, Preston Fidler comes alongside those of us who may be discouraged in language learning or intimidated by the call to share the gospel cross-culturally and illuminates a path forward. This accessible, practical guide is the fruit of decades of experience learning to speak the gospel fluently. His sincere love for people and his passion for the hope of the gospel shines on every page.

Tina Boesch, author, *Given: The Forgotten Meaning and Practice of Blessing*

1000 Cups of Tea: Gospel Fluency Across Cultures provides an eloquent and passionate description of how effective and fulfilling ministry can be when it is built on relationships made possible by cultural understanding and fluency in the language of the local people. Here is the motivation: God is already at work in the world. We are called to engage with the people of the world, whom God loves; to recognize the activity of the word of God in the lives of the people we meet and to live out God's love through our relationships with them. *1000 Cups of Tea: Gospel Fluency Across Cultures* is not only for overseas workers but also for those who want to live out the gospel in any community, but struggle to cross boundaries of language, ethnicity, belief systems, or prejudice.

Carol Orwig, SIL International

1000 Cups of Tea: Gospel Fluency Across Cultures meets a critical need that I experienced numerous times during 30 years serving as a cross-cultural missionary. I was a language learner three times with different languages and learning systems. Later I informally coached dozens of language learners and eventually I assessed and made recommendations to language programs in numerous countries. This book gets it right! It is not enough to know how to buy vegetables or say "hello." Learning language is about sharing good news and that should be integral from the beginning. Insightful and encouraging! This book should be read repeatedly by everyone who is learning a language for gospel purposes.

Don Dent, Director, Kim School of Global Missions, Gateway Seminary, SBC; author, *The Ongoing Role of Apostles in Missions: The Forgotten Foundation*

1000 Cups of Tea: Gospel Fluency Across Cultures is an excellent account of a Christian cross-cultural worker that truly does the long-term work of language and culture learning so that Jesus would be known and glorified among the nations. Through reading Preston Fidler's relatable prose, heartfelt exhortations, and thought-provoking discussion questions, the reader is able to envision the humility, sacrifice, servanthood, and joy that comes with a lifetime of language learning and gospel ministry.

Natalie Mullen, Ph.D., Institute for Cross-Cultural Training, Wheaton College

I wish I had read *1000 Cups of Tea: Gospel Fluency Across Cultures* 25 years ago! Preston Fidler's book gives struggling language learners a clear path forward, challenging us to take steps every day to speak God's word to others. We don't have to wait until we reach a certain language level or "test out" of full-time study. Whether you are a new learner or a veteran of overseas life, this book will help you see how language learning can be a joy filled, Scripture saturated process.

Sarah Alexander, Lead Writer, *Along the Silk Road: Stories, Reflections and Photography*

Preston Fidler's *1000 Cups of Tea: Gospel Fluency Across Cultures* is simply a book on imitating Christ - "The Word Became Flesh and Dwelt Among us and we beheld His Glory!" As Preston and Jenn's pastor, I can attest first-hand that they live "gospel fluency" by communicating and reflecting Christlikeness not just in words, but in deed and truth! Therefore, *1000 Cups of Tea: Gospel Fluency Across Cultures* will intensify your desire not just to be fluent in one's new language to share the gospel, but to be fluent in living the gospel, fluent in hearing and obeying the promptings of the Holy Spirit and fluent in the very language of God and His Kingdom! *1000 Cups of Tea: Gospel Fluency Across Cultures* will propel you to an even higher call of your faith in Christ, your faithfulness to the work and your willingness to imitate Christ in every area of your life!

Mike Fritscher, Pastor, Cottonwood Church

Learning a second language as an adult is one of the most profound ways to express genuine care for a person from another culture. *1000 Cups of Tea: Gospel Fluency Across Cultures* provides compelling inspiration for committing oneself to this arduous task for the sake of the eternal.

David Broersma, Associate Professor of TESOL and Linguistics, Lee University

1000 Cups of Tea: Gospel Fluency Across Cultures is down on the ground, in the trenches, uber-practical wisdom, borne from experience and toil. You may be a new language learner, laboring to get to the place of being able to share the gospel for the first time. You may be a seasoned vet trying to stay sharp so that the gospel will be even more clear to your friends. You may be a discouraged language learner, thinking about throwing in the towel. I urge all of you to read what Preston Fidler shares.

Dean Polk, Church Planting Team Leader, Central Asia

OK, I admit – it is hard for me to be excited when I read books on better language learning. Of course, the topic is crucial, but books on it are often dry and technical. Preston Fidler surprised me. While his book does show us a proven and effective way of language learning, it even more deals with our gospel motivation behind language learning. Fidler calls the combination of the two, *gospel fluency*. Unexpectedly, I found myself reading *1000 Cups of Tea: Gospel Fluency Across Cultures* as I would a devotional book. Thank you, Preston, for this fresh approach to cross cultural workers learning language. It's good and needed.

Winfield Scott, Church Planter since 1991, Central Asia

Drawing on decades of experience as both a cross-cultural church planter and a language coach for other cross-cultural workers, Fidler points us squarely back to the truth of God's word, reminding us that the glorious gospel that both saved us and compelled us to go is our greatest motivator and tool. This book is birthed out of years of work with people on the frontlines, helping them with both practical techniques and spiritual encouragement to let the joy of the gospel be the fuel for learning.

Josiah Daniels, MA Ed., Certified Bilingual Educator

Anyone who knows Preston Fidler knows he lives life as a learner, so that he can more deeply share the most important gift he has to give, the Gospel. The heart of *1000 Cups of Tea: Gospel Fluency Across Cultures* beats the same as the heart of its author. Packed with practical suggestions on learning language, how-to's for growing in understanding of the culture, and applications of evangelism and discipleship tools, this book could easily become a field guide for learning to live in a new country as ambassadors for the Gospel. More

importantly, Preston encourages and challenges the reader by presenting Biblical admonitions as to the "why", the motivation for learning language and culture. Every chapter is saturated with a plea for international workers to not settle for "getting by." Preston knows the hard work it takes to go deep in a new cultural identity, but he also knows the joy, and desires for his readers to experience that joy.
    Scott Williamson, Church Planter

    Are you a follower of Jesus who needs to remember how to "bask in the glory of the gospel"? Are you a language learner who needs to turn your duty into delight? Are you a Language Coach looking for ways to encourage your learners? Read this book! Preston has masterfully combined the mechanics of language learning with the joyous task of sharing the gospel message in a never-before done way to introduce to us the concept of *gospel fluency*. I will continue to mine the treasures in this book for years to come!
    Lisa Sandston, Church Planter, Language Coach

    1000 Cups of Tea: Gospel Fluency Across Cultures is not just a book, it's a helpful focus to describe the goal for Kingdom-focused language learners: Learning to converse the gospel in a new language. Preston Fidler invites us to make the gospel the core orientation of our lives, and he shows us how to do this as language learners in a new cultural context. When we faithfully persevere towards gospel fluency, God uses even (especially?) our feebleness and limitations to bring glory to himself. He reminds us that he is sufficient, and even grants new life to dead sinners through our gospel communication. The path to gospel fluency runs uphill but Preston inspires to keep taking the next steps towards the goal.
    REC, Trainer, IMB Pre-field Design Team

1000 CUPS OF TEA
GOSPEL FLUENCY ACROSS CULTURES

BY PRESTON FIDLER

First Edition

Copyright © 2020 by Preston Fidler

All rights reserved. No part of this book may be reproduced in any form on by an electronic or mechanical means, including information storage and retrieval systems, without permission in writing from the publisher, except by a reviewer who may quote brief passages in a review.

ISBN 978-1-7356042-0-6

Unless otherwise indicated, all Scripture quotations are taken from: The Christian Standard Bible. Copyright © 2017 by Holman Bible Publishers. Used by permission.

Front cover, logo, design, and artwork by Eric Schmidt
Copyright © 2020 All right reserved

DEDICATION
For Jenn

Table of Contents

Preface	i
Introduction	ii
1 | Gospel Fluency	1
2 | Eyes Wide Open	11
3 | The Gospel for my Lost Neighbor	33
4 | Simple Familiar Gospel Story	53
5 | Gospel Radius	69
6 | Responsive Listening	89
7 | LQ	117
8 | Deep and Wide	142
9 | Language 180	186
10 | 1000 Cups of Tea	210
11 | God Speaks My Language	234
12 | Pilgrims	256
Appendix 1	280
Appendix 2	284
Appendix 3	290
Appendix 4	297
Appendix 5	311
Acknowledgements	314
Endnotes	315

Preface

Imagine your excitement. You have spent months immersing yourself in the language of your new neighbors. You have pored over their vocabulary and grammar. You have made countless verbal blunders and butchered their pronunciation. But one day, you open the scriptures and for the first time you not only read, you *comprehend* their Bible. This new confidence sets off an avalanche of opportunities. When you meet with your language partner you no longer carefully craft your sentences; you *converse*. When you watch a local film, you *understand* the plot. When you visit your neighbors over a cup of tea, you discuss topics beyond family news, and you begin *sharing stories* from their Bible. Welcome to gospel fluency.

Introduction

People often ask me what it takes to become fluent in a new language. I tell them it takes a thousand cups of tea.

What does learning our neighbors' language have to do with sharing the gospel with them? The answer may seem obvious to some, less obvious to others, but the question is definitely worth asking as we consider what it means to obey the Great Commission. That's why I wrote *1000 Cups of Tea: Gospel Fluency Across Cultures*. The vision is simple: cross-cultural Christian workers need tools, but more than anything else they need a godly reason to learn the language. I endeavor to provide both.

"Few Christians would argue with the assertion that the church should take God's command to 'go and make disciples' seriously. Yet for those who have answered God's call and actually crossed geographical and cultural barriers, the task of learning to clearly communicate the gospel in another language can be daunting."[1] Daunting indeed! So many cross-cultural workers experience learning a new language as an insurmountable chore. Carol sums it up well:

> As a consultant for language and culture learning, I work with people from a number of different Christian organizations. Many of them have gone overseas with the motivation of spreading the gospel, but they are struggling with learning the languages of the people to whom they want to minister. They may not see themselves as "language people". They may find themselves in cultural contexts which seem strange or hostile to them and to the gospel. They want to *finish* language learning, so they can get on with the real work

of evangelism or church-planting or discipleship. It seems so long before they can get on with the real work!²

1000 Cups of Tea: Gospel Fluency Across Cultures reminds tired learners of the joy they can experience in sharing the gospel in their new languages, as they learn them. It exhorts new learners, as well as leaders who send them and work with them, that language learning is something we don't *have* to do *before* we share the gospel, rather something we *get* to do *while* we share the gospel. And it inspires a generation whom God is raising up from churches, campuses, workplaces, and homes throughout North America and across the world, to faithfully learn the languages of their lost neighbors so that they can fluently share the gospel with them, whether in Los Angeles or Mumbai.

1

Gospel Fluency

We proclaim him. (Colossians 1:28)

Toward the end of our first year in our new field, Jenn and I were trying to learn a new language, set up work, and at the same time were expecting our third child. We were busy, struggling language learners. One morning, I read through Matthew 8:5-13, the story of the centurion who asked Jesus to heal his servant. I could understand it but expressing my thoughts in my new language was a challenge. I read it in English, prayed, and wrote out my thoughts. I did the same in my new language, only much slower. It was pretty ugly, but it was a start. As I look back on it, I believe this was the first step toward sharing the gospel with my neighbor over tea later that day.

I had scribbled down a few notes in my new language that gave me some traction to say something meaningful about the story and stay in the conversation with my neighbor. I noted that the centurion was a man of military authority, that his servant was dying, and that he (the centurion) knew about Jesus. I also noted that he believed Jesus could save his servant. We may recall that the centurion came to Jesus and asked for help. Jesus then offered to go and heal his servant, but the centurion, because of his unworthiness, declined to have Jesus come to his home. He went on to say that he knew the meaning of authority. He himself had a boss, and he obeyed his boss. He had men under him to whom he gave orders, and they obeyed his orders. "I am not worthy to have you come under my roof. But just say the word, and my servant will be healed" (v. 8). This military man, who understood authority, recognized Jesus' supreme authority. Jesus had authority over sickness. The centurion had faith that Jesus could heal his servant right then and there.

Jesus was amazed at the centurion's faith. And because of his faith, Jesus healed his servant. Jesus then invited him to sit with Abraham, Isaac, and Jacob. In other words, Jesus invited the centurion into the Kingdom of God. This man who had faith that Jesus could heal his servant, was actually putting his faith in Jesus as Lord over everything. For without faith in God we cannot enter into his Kingdom. Those who do not have faith in Jesus – even though they say they are children of the Kingdom – will be cast out. Only those who have faith in Jesus as Lord will be invited into the Kingdom of God.

This explanation may sound simple, but this is about how it sounded in my new language. I kept things simple, partly because of my limited language ability, but mostly because presenting the gospel should never be complicated. I simply wrote about how God had spoken to me from his Word, so I could discuss the gospel from the text with my neighbor. I also wrote out a prayer.

> Jesus, you are Lord of all. I believe in you.
> You saved me from my sins. You gave me
> eternal life. I am not worthy of it. Thank you.

This prayer was from my heart. I wrote it out, first in English, then very simply in my new language. As I prayed through it, I envisioned praying it aloud with my lost neighbor.

Whenever we read the Bible, the word of God reaches our hearts, and we are reminded of the gospel. I remember what Jesus, by his love and by his power, has done for me, and I want to effectively communicate this in the language of my lost neighbors. I want my neighbors to know this good news, and therefore, I want to do my best to communicate it to them in their language. I want to see Jesus glorified in their lives as they are supernaturally transformed by the gospel. As we learn our neighbors' language, we can learn to proclaim the gospel to them, from God's word, through our witness, in our conversations, and as we pray. We are never just pursuing language fluency, we are pursuing what I am beginning to understand as *gospel fluency*.

With these scriptures and well-rehearsed notes in my hand, head, and heart, I met my neighbor for tea and I invited him to talk about the gospel. We read through the text together, my neighbor listened to me retell it, and we began to discuss it.

Conversations never go quite as planned in situations like this, so I have learned to be flexible and try to stay in step with what I sense God is doing. There is a certain balance between preparation, delivery, and stewarding a sympathetic awareness of the flow of conversation as it reroutes in a direction we may not expect, yet can anticipate, because that's how God works. God opens doors we may not even know are there.

I had been praying for my neighbor, asking the Lord for favor in our time together, that he would see the truth of the gospel through our conversation. My language was still so weak and I felt that I was in way over my head. I knew so little about his world and his culture. I wondered if asking some questions related to his life and the topic would be a good place to start. I believed God was doing something in his life and community. I tried to be engaging and specific, listen to the Lord, and do my best to listen to my neighbor.

In simple words, I asked about my neighbor's view of authority – in his own life, his family, and in his community. We talked about God and unseen powers, what we fear, and what we trust. I invited him to consider the truth that we learned from the Bible: that Jesus has authority over everything – sickness, evil, sin, and even death. We talked about the Kingdom of God, heaven, and what it means to have faith in Jesus.

We reached a place in the conversation where we were talking about the military and authority. I was eager to hear my neighbor's thoughts and personal experiences since I knew he had served in the military. To my dismay, his face went ashen. He became quiet. I didn't know what was going on, but we had obviously touched a nerve. He whispered of abuse he had experienced, mentioning something about his commanding officer, an evil person, forcing him to commit atrocities he wanted to forget, but couldn't. He sighed deeply. The conversation drew to a close. I had no idea what was going on in his heart.

We often face communication challenges and barriers such as these when we share the gospel in another language. Does our message make sense? Do our weak language skills create barriers to the gospel? I hadn't been in the country very long. I was just learning to share the gospel, and those first steps are never easy. But God is faithful, and his word is powerful. God is able to bolster the gospel message we faithfully proclaim. "Other men may preach the gospel better than I, but no man can preach a better gospel" (George Whitefield).

When we feel the tension between the conviction to share the gospel with our lost neighbors, and the inability to do so adequately in their language – at least in our own estimation – we need to remember that in situations such as these we can easily lose sight of the underlying victory and purpose of our cross-cultural witness. We risk losing a fresh and vibrant word from the Lord when our efforts to express a daily witness succumb to the pressure of performance and the fear and frustration of potential failure.

Therefore, may we agree with Paul, "Even if I am untrained in public speaking, I am certainly not untrained in knowledge" (2 Corinthians 11:6). Cross-cultural life and ministry can be brutally humbling, requiring a certain endurance that can only be sustained by strength in our Lord, not in ourselves. In addition to the normal stress of cross-cultural life, we carry an extra burden, the duty to learn to speak well in another language, so we can share Christ well. Will we ever be good enough to truly communicate the gospel in our new language? Do we depend on Christ's strength in and through us, in this process? What may normally shut us down in weakness may just become the pivotal strength of our testimony, bearing vibrant witness to the gospel of Jesus Christ.

The next morning at 3 a.m., my phone rang. It was my neighbor. He had just had a dream about his military experience. His commander was once again ordering him to do something terrible. He was angry and afraid. Suddenly, a higher commander appeared beside him, assuming complete command and bringing peace and complete authority to the situation. My neighbor woke up and he immediately knew this new commander was Jesus, the one with supreme authority. I rejoiced in hearing this news and had the awesome privilege to lead my neighbor to faith in Christ that day!

God surprised me. He reminded me that the path toward *gospel fluency* is a humble journey of many faithful steps. I often look back at that experience when I face communication challenges. I had been faithful with what little I had. God had multiplied it. He is the one who bears spiritual fruit. We are just laboring for him. But we want to be skilled laborers.

What I'm talking about here is not merely language learning. Rather, it is a fresh look at the joyful fruit of proclaiming the gospel in another language to our lost neighbors, why many of us struggle with this, and how we can find victory in our cross-cultural gospel witness. How do we move from surface, rudimentary religious conversations and overused memorized texts, to clear and personal gospel presentations? Using the Bible, how can we successfully prepare, practice, and proclaim the gospel in the language we are learning? How can we become fluent in the discourse of the gospel, as we present it, discuss it, and invite our lost neighbors to respond to it?

Language learning is a life-long journey. We should never stop learning. The truth is, the more we learn, the more we realize how much more we have to learn. However, we should never be deceived into thinking that effective, clear, specific gospel proclamation is beyond our grasp to pursue right here and now.

So many of us embark on learning a language with noble intentions only to reach a basic conversational level, yet over the years never really make much progress. We sink into a mediocre existence of occasional cross-cultural ministry, never reaching the ability to share as we would have hoped in the language because we don't have the skills.

It doesn't have to be this way. The pursuit and practice of *gospel fluency* is attainable, and within a shorter amount of time than many of us may think. With the right understanding, heart-attitude, mind-set, and skills, we can all get there on a well-lit path.

So then, what is *gospel fluency*? We can describe it as the personal practice of proclaiming the gospel to our lost neighbors in their languages. Through the lens of the Great Commission, we understand in a fresh way that the gospel for all peoples really is the gospel for our lost neighbor. We come face-to-face with the joyful labor of learning to communicate the gospel story in our neighbor's heart language. As we operate within the limitless radius of the gospel, we can anticipate that God's word will reach into and transform lives, just as it did ours, affecting every aspect of our human condition.

As we listen and share the gospel with neighbors, again and again, over a thousand cups of tea, we are filled with hope because we truly believe in the transforming power of the gospel in our lives, and in theirs. Every day, we remind ourselves of the gospel. And it's from this place – out of this overflow, this life-giving hope – that we enter into the joyful ministry to which God has called us: to share the gospel with our lost neighbors.

As we learn the language of our neighbors, *gospel fluency* becomes our worthy pursuit and overshadows the toil of language learning. When communicating the gospel to our unreached neighbors becomes our cross-cultural focus, and when proclaiming the gospel becomes our language-learning purpose, our passions and sentiments grow in a Godward direction. Our aims and efforts no longer simply point us toward fluency in the language and culture, though that is happening; rather they point us toward fluency in the gospel.

When I think of *gospel fluency*, I am often reminded of Andrew. After retirement, Andrew came to live in my city with a strong call and desire to proclaim Christ to the nations. As his language coach, I arranged a tutor for him. Andrew never learned much language. Yet Andrew's hunger for the word of

God defied gravity. He read a book of the Bible every day. Literally. He was saturated in the gospel, sharing with everything that moved.

Andrew would gather with a few of his English-speaking neighbors, ask them to bring a friend or two, and then he would read and share from his Bible and have them read along in Bibles he brought and passed around. Andrew had a vibrant testimony and an insatiable desire to share Christ with his lost neighbors.

I wonder, sometimes, what I could have done differently, as Andrew's coach, to help him learn the language, to tap into that abiding desire he had to share his faith, to help him reach language fluency so he could have had the joy of practicing *gospel fluency* in his new language. Maybe some of us are like Andrew. We're going to share our faith whether we learn the language or not.

We need to remember this isn't an "either-or" option, it's "both-and." We don't have to put our gospel proclamation on hold while we learn the language. We *get* to share our faith *while* we learn the language; better put, we *get* to learn the language *while* we learn to share our faith in the language.

Years ago, a 22-year-old guy moved to an Asian mega-city and had no idea how to learn the language in order to share his faith with his neighbors. The alphabet was tough, but he figured it out, and within a few days he was reading street signs. Then a local brother challenged him to read John 3:16 and patiently helped him recite the verse aloud.

Was this a good language learning method? No, it wasn't. Was it effective preparation for sharing the gospel? Not really. But it did ignite a spark. In fact, that young man was so encouraged by the apparent "success" of reading through one verse, which he didn't even really understand, he began to do anything and everything he could to learn the language –

listen, speak, read, and write; ransack as many words, phrases, and sentences as he could get his head around; create conversations in the language with everyone he knew and met; eavesdrop, take notes, listen to songs, record sermons – so that he could eventually understand John 3:16, and so that he then could meaningfully share the gospel with his neighbors.

That young man was me, and what I lacked in direction, I made up for in desire. As Great Commission servants of Jesus we have this obligation, this fundamental desire to share his Word, "an intense fire in [our] hearts, trapped in [our] bones" (Jeremiah 20:9) to proclaim the gospel to the lost around us in their language, so that they can understand it. I want to help fan this desire into a roaring flame through some encouraging, purposeful, and effective language learning perspectives and practices, which will help us go the distance in our Great Commission calling.

We all have it within ourselves to learn the language with purpose, but we just need some help to get there, to actually do it. Perhaps that's why I want to reach out to learners like Andrew and my 22-year-old self, to help us move beyond what is keeping us from fluency, allowing us to learn, know, and practice what it means to proclaim the gospel in the language of our lost neighbors. *1000 Cups of Tea: Gospel Fluency Across Cultures* therefore aligns the mechanics and practice of language learning with our call to proclaim the gospel in that language. Language learning and gospel proclamation together form the essential daily practice and greater understanding of *gospel fluency*.

Reflect and Respond

1. Consider this statement: We share the gospel from the overflow of God's grace in our lives.

2. Describe a recent experience where you personally evangelized or discipled someone.

3. Have you ever shared the gospel with someone from another culture?

4. Describe or envision sharing the gospel with your neighbors in their language.

5. Take a moment to pray for your neighbors. Pray for opportunities to share the gospel with them.

2

Eyes Wide Open

Look, I tell you, lift up your eyes, and see that the fields are white for harvest. (John 4:35 ESV)

I first met Elias at an art exhibition where some of our friends from church were showing their work. At a break in the show, Zephir asked Elias to join us for tea. Recently retired, Elias shared how he and his wife were in search of something more. With no formal art training, his paintings were simple and beautiful. "Why art?" I wondered aloud. Elias did not consider himself a religious man, but he talked of a longing for deeper meaning in life, beauty, joy, and love. Art gave him a medium in his search, a way to communicate something significant where words failed.

As we drank tea, Elias shared more of his story with me. I wanted to share the gospel with him, but I wondered how successfully I could do this – in his language – in such a way that Elias would finally be able to hear the truth he had been seeking.

First Samuel 3:19 says the Lord was with Samuel and fulfilled everything he prophesied, or literally, "He let none of his words fall to the ground." That was my prayer as I began to introduce the gospel to Elias, in his language, the language I had been learning.

Beginning in Genesis 1 and 2, we looked at what the Bible said about the beautiful fellowship man had with God in the garden, and how God created a paradise on earth in perfect harmony, with no sin and no pain. Elias and I both marveled how everything God had created by a single spoken word was perfectly good, and God said it was good.

We then read about sin entering the world in chapter three. That's the world we live in now. We have inklings of the paradise we lost and we know there must be a God out there who loves us. That's why Elias paints.

We continued reading as I shared with Elias more from the gospel of God. I realized that it wasn't my words alone, nor my ability, that got through to Elias. It was God who was speaking to Elias through his word, just as it was God who gave me the ability to present the gospel to him. And that made all the difference.

A Shift in Perspective

The gospel is good news. It was good news for Elias. It's good news for all of us. The gospel is the story of God's redemptive plan of salvation for this lost and sinful generation. It's the story of God bringing us back into right relationship with him. It's our majestic hope in this life and throughout eternity.

The gospel is the good news of salvation through Jesus Christ, and the Bible is God's message of salvation. *1000 Cups of Tea* introduces us to the practice of learning language and culture from the perspective of and through the practice of proclaiming the gospel in the languages we are learning, so that our lost neighbors can hear the gospel in their heart language.

We are called to what sometimes seems an impossible task. In Matthew 28, Jesus commissioned us to proclaim and teach the gospel to all peoples. As we are called, we go. And as we go, we learn language and culture because God calls us to proclaim the gospel across cultures, to people of every nation, tribe, people, and language. I coach language learners who follow this call. For so many of us, we enthusiastically embark on this language learning journey only to lose our way somewhere between the phrases and sentences, or perhaps somewhere in the paragraphs, if we are lucky. We struggle to sustain a clear focus on our goal of reaching a level of interpersonal discourse fluency sufficient to proclaim the gospel. After many months of learning his new language, Tom summed it up well, "Language is hard...so I spent all week praying for English to become the heart language of all [my neighbors] ;-)..."

Let's be honest. Language learning is hard. Communicating the gospel in another language is even harder. To be fair, in our own strength, it's impossible. "Language is like a cracked kettle on which we beat out tunes for bears to dance to, while all the while we long to make music that will melt the stars" (Gustave Flaubert).

I thought of Elias' search. So often the task of language learning is seen for its limitations, a necessary drudgery, a means to an end, a burden to those of us who long for the ability to understand and proclaim the truth of the gospel in our new language.

Gospel fluency represents a shift in our perspective on language learning in cross-cultural Christian ministry. Language learning no longer focuses on just words and paragraphs, rather on relationships, and communicating the gospel with lost neighbors. When duty becomes a delight, burdens become a springboard. We find joy in hearing and speaking the gospel to ourselves in the language we are learning, as our daily manna, and in sharing the gospel with our neighbors, as our daily ministry.

I sympathize with the disciples who in John 4 returned from buying bread and were surprised to see Jesus talking with a Samaritan woman. They couldn't figure out what Jesus was doing, so they just told him to eat something. I'm sure that's what I would have said, too.

> Just then his disciples arrived, and they were amazed that he was talking with a woman. Yet no one said, "What do you want?" or "Why are you talking with her?"
>
> Then the woman left her water jar, went into town, and told the people, "Come, see a man who told me everything I ever did. Could this be the Messiah?" They left the town and made their way to him.
>
> In the meantime the disciples kept urging him, "Rabbi, eat something."
>
> But he said, "I have food to eat that you don't know about."
>
> The disciples said to one another, "Could someone have brought him something to eat?"
>
> "My food is to do the will of him who sent me and to finish his work," Jesus told them.
>
> "Don't you say, 'There are still four months and then comes the harvest'? Listen to what I'm telling you: Open your eyes and look at the fields, because they are ready for harvest." (John 4:27-35)

Jesus shifts our perspective. The disciples were thinking about bread. Jesus was thinking about souls. Like the disciples, my thoughts are usually on the next daily task, and that may even include learning a new word in my target language. My "food" is so often just about me and my small world. Jesus' food was to do God's will. He invited his disciples to lift up their eyes and see not grain, but souls white for harvest. Picture Jesus' disciples literally lifting up their eyes to see a whole Samaritan village – yes, non-Jews, foreigners – coming down the street toward them, eager to hear more about the living water Jesus offered the woman. Likewise, Jesus calls us to *lift up our eyes* (v. 35). So often as language learners we find our attention reduced to just getting the next word or phrase. Jesus calls us to a new perspective on learning a language and reaching out to our lost neighbors with the gospel.

Years ago, I led a church planting team among an unreached people group. Each of us had experienced a lot of resistance to the gospel as we learned language and shared our faith. About eighteen months along, we came together for a weekend of prayer and fasting. Toward the end of the weekend, we gathered in a circle, each of us taking turns to teach the gospel to each other in the language. To be honest, I don't remember exactly why we did this, but it turned out to be one of the most encouraging, unifying, and catalyzing moments we ever experienced as a team.

We each prepared and presented the gospel from various passages in the Bible, and then affirmed each other and prayed for each other in the language. I remember one young man, a gifted preacher, sharing from the book of Genesis in simple and yet profound words how "the Lord was with Joseph." As he told the story of Joseph, he reminded us from God's word that God is with us and that, "God always keeps his promises." As he repeated this phrase, in its powerful simplicity, it brought great encouragement to us all, especially to our national partners who had gathered with us – God truly is with us and indeed always keeps his promises.

When Jesus calls us to preach the gospel to the nations, he promises to be with us and to equip us. He provides us with the food to do his will. That begins with renewing our minds and our perspectives, as we consider the process of the language learning task. Ours may seem an enormously difficult task to communicate God's message to rebellious and stiff-necked people in very challenging and seemingly impossible circumstances. Throughout scripture and throughout Christian history we encounter those whom God called, who likewise struggled with personal fear and inability to communicate God's message. Ultimately, they fulfilled their God-given tasks, not because of their personal ability, but because of the power of God within them.

Moses

In Exodus 3-4, God revealed himself to Moses from a burning bush, commissioning him to lead the nation of Israel out of their bondage in Egypt. God promised his presence to guide Moses as he spoke with Pharaoh. Moses was afraid. He doubted God.

> But Moses replied to the LORD, "Please, Lord, I have never been eloquent – either in the past or recently or since you have been speaking to your servant – because my mouth and my tongue are sluggish" (Exodus 4:10).

As language learners, we can identify with Moses' doubts. In our communication struggles, it's easy to forget that God is with us and is ministering to us and through us by his presence. Fast forward to another revelation of God's glory upon Moses as he descended from Mount Sinai. Notice the amazing contrast.

> As Moses descended from Mount Sinai – with the two tablets of the testimony in his hands as he descended the mountain – he did not realize that the skin of his

face shone as a result of his speaking with the LORD. When Aaron and all the Israelites saw Moses, the skin of his face shone! They were afraid to come near him. But Moses called out to them, so Aaron and all the leaders of the community returned to him, and Moses spoke to them. Afterward all the Israelites came near, and he commanded them to do everything the LORD had told him on Mount Sinai. When Moses had finished speaking with them, he put a veil over his face. But whenever Moses went before the LORD to speak with Him, he would remove the veil until he came out. After he came out, he would tell the Israelites what he had been commanded, and the Israelites would see that Moses' face was radiant. Then Moses would put the veil over his face again until he went to speak with the LORD (Exodus 34:29-35).

What made the difference? God's presence was with Moses in both circumstances. But this time, the lingering effects of God's presence brilliantly radiated from Moses' face, reflecting the glory which he had experienced while on the holy mountain with God. Moses had been in God's presence, enveloped by the cloud of his glory for forty days and nights (Exodus 24:18) when he originally received the Ten Commandments. And he was again in God's presence for another forty days and nights (Exodus 34:28) when God had him rewrite them. We cannot infer, therefore, that had Moses spent more time with God at the burning bush his face would have shone. So then, how did the glory of God come to reflect on the very skin of Moses during this final descent, and why was this significant?

The most obvious and astonishing answer to this is that Moses simply asked God, "Let me see your glory" (Exodus 33:18). And what's more astonishing is that God did just that, though only partially. For God said, "You cannot see my face...and live" (33:20). In what is arguably one of the high-water marks of God's glory in the Old Testament, God physically positioned Moses within the crevice of a rock, covered him with his hand until he passed by, and then removed his hand so that Moses could see only his back (33:21-23).

> The LORD came down in a cloud, stood with him there, and proclaimed his name, "the LORD." The Lord passed in front of him and proclaimed:
> The LORD – the LORD is a compassionate and gracious God, slow to anger and abounding in faithful love and truth, maintaining faithful love to a thousand generations, forgiving iniquity, rebellion, and sin. But he will not leave the guilty unpunished, bringing the fathers' iniquity on the children and grandchildren to the third and fourth generation.
> Moses immediately knelt low on the ground and worshiped (Exodus 34:5-8).

Do we bask in the glory of the gospel? As glorious as Moses' transformation seems, let's remind ourselves that unlike Moses, whose face radiated a fading glory of the old covenant, we host the never-fading presence of God through the gospel.

> We are not like Moses, who used to put a veil over his face so that the Israelites could not stare at the end of what was fading away, but their minds were closed. For to this day, at the reading of the old covenant, the same veil remains; it is not lifted, because it is set aside only in Christ. Even to this day, whenever Moses is read, a veil lies over their hearts, but whenever a person turns to the Lord, the veil is removed. Now the Lord is

the Spirit, and where the Spirit of the Lord is, there is freedom. We all, with unveiled faces, are looking as in a mirror at the glory of the Lord and are being transformed into the same image from glory to glory; this is from the Lord who is the Spirit (2 Corinthians 3:13-18).

The presence of Christ in our lives compels us to proclaim the gospel. We are being transformed into his likeness, from glory to glory. We host his presence in our lives at all times, even as we proclaim him to our lost neighbors. "A saint shines on men when God has shone on him" (C.H. Spurgeon).

Do we enter into gospel conversations with doubt and fear of our personal weakness, or with faith and courage, confident in the power of God, and in the message of the gospel? Our language and culture fluency may be weak, but our faith in Christ is strong. As we share Christ with our neighbors, the presence of Christ in our lives changes everything. It also changes how we enter into the encounter. Our only hope in communicating the gospel to our lost neighbors is in the transformational power of God's word and the presence and glory of Christ in and through our lives. Paul reminds us of this earlier in the same chapter:

> Such is the confidence we have through Christ before God. It is not that we are competent in ourselves to claim anything as coming from ourselves, but our adequacy is from God (2 Corinthians 3:4-5).

Jeremiah

Jeremiah received a dramatic call as a prophet to the nations (Jeremiah 1:5). He, like Moses, also protested, "Oh no, Lord GOD! Look, I don't know how to speak since I am only a youth" (1:6). He, too, doubted his ability to communicate

God's message. But God responded with a call that went against everything Jeremiah felt about himself.

"See, I have appointed you today over nations and kingdoms to uproot and tear down, to destroy and demolish, to build and plant" (1:10).

God led Jeremiah to preach a message of judgment and utter destruction; a message that was very difficult to preach, and equally hard for people to hear.

> Therefore, look, the days are coming – this is the LORD's declaration – when this place will no longer be called Topheth and Ben Hinnom Valley, but Slaughter Valley. I will spoil the plans of Judah and Jerusalem in this place. I will make them fall by the sword before their enemies, by the hand of those who intend to take their life. I will provide their corpses as food for the birds of the sky and for the wild animals of the land. I will make this city desolate, an object of scorn. Everyone who passes by it will be appalled and scoff because of all its wounds. I will make them eat the flesh of their sons and their daughters, and they will eat each other's flesh in the distressing siege inflicted on them by their enemies who intend to take their life (Jeremiah 19:6-9).

The Lord's message through Jeremiah reminds us of hell itself, devoid of hope. The people's reaction described in the first part of the next chapter was predictably harsh.

> Pashhur the priest, the son of Immer and chief official in the temple of the LORD, heard Jeremiah prophesying these things. So Pashhur had Jeremiah the prophet beaten and put him in the stocks at the Upper Benjamin Gate in the LORD's temple (Jeremiah 20:1-2).

We must take into account Jeremiah's faithfulness to the message of God, harsh as it would seem. He suffered greatly for his obedience to preach a message he didn't even want to preach, and one that no one wanted to hear. Just released from the stocks, bruised and bloodied from the beating, Jeremiah bitterly complained,

> You deceived me, LORD, and I was deceived. You seized me and prevailed. I am a laughingstock all the time; everyone ridicules me. For whenever I speak, I cry out, I proclaim, "Violence and destruction!" so the word of the Lord has become my constant disgrace and derision (20:7-8).

However, it's the next thing Jeremiah says that brings great comfort to me. Though he suffered greatly in his calling to preach a hard message devoid of any apparent hope, his hope and trust remained in God alone.

> I say, "I won't mention him or speak any longer in his name." But his message becomes a fire burning in my heart, shut up in my bones. I become tired of holding it in, and I cannot prevail. (20:9).

Memorize this verse! Unlike Jeremiah, we have a message of great hope and gladness. Ours is not a message of destruction. God has called us to proclaim his salvation for all peoples. The sad and perplexing mystery why anyone would reject this good news is overcome by the glorious mystery of the gospel – why God would ever love us enough to save us from our sins! So, it is this gospel we proclaim. We are compelled. Like Jeremiah, the word of God is a fire in our bones. We are weary of holding it in.

The message of the gospel compels us to learn the language. Our confidence is in God and in his message out of the gospel, which he has given us to live out and to proclaim. God ignites our hearts with the power of the gospel. The good news of God's salvation consumes our lives. "God, I pray thee, light the idle sticks of my life and may I burn for thee. Consume my life, my God, for it is Thine" (Jim Elliot).

Peter

Unlike Moses and Jeremiah, Peter actually walked with Jesus in real life. He knew the very author and subject of the gospel in flesh and blood, watched him, ministered alongside him, learned from him, marveled at his authority, and testified of his glory. He was also filled with grief and shame from denying Jesus (Luke 22:62). Peter then experienced this life-changing encounter with his risen Lord.

> When they had eaten breakfast, Jesus asked Simon Peter, "Simon, son of John, do you love me more than these?"
> "Yes, Lord," he said to him, "you know that I love you."
> "Feed my lambs," he told him. A second time he asked him, "Simon, son of John, do you love me?"
> "Yes, Lord," he said to him, "you know that I love you." "Shepherd my sheep," he told him.
> He asked him the third time, "Simon, son of John, do you love me?"
> Peter was grieved that he asked him the third time, "Do you love me?" He said, "Lord, you know everything; you know that I love you."
> "Feed my sheep," Jesus said (John 21:15-17).

This moment of restoration and reinstatement changed Peter forever. Throughout the book of Acts, we see that this encounter ushered him into an incredible ministry of spiritual fruitfulness, authority, wisdom, faith, miracles, love, and power. In all that he did, he loved God and fed his sheep. Filled with the Holy Spirit, Peter had entered into his calling; he knew his apostolic identity in Christ.

Yet in the wake of this dynamic ministry, Peter experienced an unexpected shift in his spiritual understanding that caused him to pause and really consider the breadth of God's purposes for his life and for the world around him, introducing him to a totally new dimension of his calling. God was calling Peter to preach the gospel to those he was still unable to view in his mind and heart as recipients of God's grace – to non-Jews, outsiders from other cultures. This was, again, life changing for Peter.

> He became hungry and wanted to eat, but while they were preparing something, he fell into a trance. He saw heaven opened and an object that resembled a large sheet coming down, being lowered by its four corners to the earth. In it were all the four-footed animals and reptiles of the earth, and the birds of the sky. A voice said to him, "Get up, Peter; kill and eat."
> "No, Lord!" Peter said. "For I have never eaten anything impure and ritually unclean."
> Again, a second time, the voice said to him, "What God has made clean, do not call impure." This happened three times, and suddenly the object was taken up into heaven (Acts 10:10-16).

After the third time, we read that while Peter was wondering about the meaning of the vision, some men who had traveled several days in search of Peter arrived at the gate of the home where Peter was staying, having been sent by a man named Cornelius.

Cornelius was a God-fearing Gentile. An angel of the Lord had visited him and had instructed him to send for Peter (Acts 10:1-8). So, Cornelius sent his men in search of Peter and while they were on the way, Peter had his vision. This was all a part of God's remarkable plan.

Something indeed had shifted in Peter's mindset, in his spirit, as a result of this vision from the Lord. Peter had been called to love God and feed his sheep, but Peter was still unable (unwilling?) to consider Gentiles as God's sheep. He had never thought about loving them and feeding them, until he had this vision on the roof.

Peter asked the men at the gate why they had come. When they explained that they had been sent by Cornelius to search for him, Peter invited them in, and the next day he traveled with them to meet with Cornelius.

They arrived at Cornelius' house, and Peter heard Cornelius' testimony, his desire to follow Christ, and about the visit from the angel. Peter responded, testifying how God had changed his heart, opened his mind, and shown him his heart for the nations. This was an incredible breakthrough for Peter, a new and fresh understanding of God's purposes and calling for his life – to love God and feed his sheep, from every fold, every nation.

> Peter began to speak: "Now I truly understand that God doesn't show favoritism, but in every nation the person who fears him and does what is right is acceptable to him" (Acts 10:34-35).

Peter brought the word of the Lord to Cornelius. Cornelius and those in his household believed in the Lord Jesus Christ and were baptized (10:48). Through all this, the realization that only God could have done this was the most significant for Peter. Only God could have orchestrated this whole series of events culminating in the salvation of Cornelius and his household. Only God could have changed the heart of a stubborn Jew who then became his unexpected witness to the Gentiles. God had done it in Peter's heart, on the beach. And he did it again, while Peter was praying on a roof, and then again in a Gentile's home. This was Peter's testimony, a testimony to chosen exiles, living among the nations, found in the introduction to his first letter.

> Peter, an apostle of Jesus Christ: To those chosen, living as exiles dispersed abroad in Pontus, Galatia, Cappadocia, Asia, and Bithynia, chosen according to the foreknowledge of God the Father, through the sanctifying work of the Spirit, to be obedient and to be sprinkled with the blood of Jesus Christ (1 Peter 1:1-2).

J. Hudson Taylor

I have been crucified with Christ, and I no longer live, but Christ lives in me. The life I now live in the body, I live by faith in the Son of God, who loved me and gave himself for me.
(Galatians 2:20)

Hudson Taylor is most remembered for the immensity of his Great Commission vision, faith, and supreme contribution to the task of taking the gospel into inland China, a task he personally described as "worth living for and worth dying for."[3]

His life and ministry in China provide us with such an amazing expression of what it means to live out the Great Commission in the middle of immense adversity. There he buried four of his eight children along with his first wife.[4]

A letter to his mother describes some of the intense pressures and challenges with which he struggled every day.

I have often asked you to remember me in prayer, and when I have done so there has been much need of it. That need has never been greater than at present. Envied by some, despised by many, hated by others, often blamed for things I never heard of or had nothing to do with, an innovator on what have become established rules of missionary practice, an opponent of mighty systems of heathen error and superstition, working without precedent in many respects and with few experienced helpers, often sick in body as well as perplexed in mind and embarrassed by circumstances – had not the Lord been specially gracious to me, had not my mind been sustained by the conviction that the work is His and that He is with me in what it is no empty figure to call "the thick of the conflict," I must have fainted or broken down.[5]

In 1900, during the height of the Boxer rebellion, the China Inland Mission, which Taylor led, lost more members than any other group: 58 adults and 21 children were killed.[6]

In the wake of this tragedy, Taylor held tightly to the promises of God when all else seemed hopeless. "I cannot read, I cannot pray, I can scarcely even think – but I can trust."[7]

One might think this would have been a good time for Hudson Taylor and his CIM colleagues to give up and go home. They didn't. Instead, experiences like this brought Hudson Taylor to a deeper, more radical, and complete dependence on God than he had ever known possible. "Complete surrender" became his secret to sustaining a fruitful and long-lasting ministry in the middle of raging challenges and adversity – that he personally described as the "exchanged life" (Galatians 2:20). In other words, it wasn't the outer circumstances or accomplishments that concerned him, rather his inner life in Christ.

John Piper said of Taylor's life, "This new yieldedness was so powerful and so sweet – so supernatural – that it rose up like an indictment against all vain striving."[8] Taylor himself described the results of spiritual surrender this way, "Work is the outcome of effort; fruit, of life."[9]

As I read my tea-stained 1987 paperback edition of *Hudson Taylor's Spiritual Secret* (originally published in 1932), what stands out to me is not what Hudson Taylor *did*, but who he *was* in Christ. It was his humble, enduring, singular devotion to Christ characterized by overwhelming, enduring peace, and "soul rest" that sustained his life-long vision to reach every unevangelized province in China with the gospel. It was Taylor's own son and daughter-in-law, as the writers of this little biography, who offer this amazing portrait of the normal everyday life of this servant of God as they traveled with him. Don't let the formal nature of this account distract you from noticing the deeply personal and powerful influence Hudson Taylor's life in Christ must have had not only on him, but also upon all those around him.

> It was not easy for Mr. Taylor, in his changeful life, to make time for prayer and Bible study, but he knew that it was vital. Well do the writers remember traveling with him month after month in northern China, by cart and wheelbarrow, with the poorest of inns at night. Often with only one large room for coolies and travelers alike, they would screen off a corner for their father and another for themselves, with curtains of some sort; and then, after sleep at last had brought a measure of quiet, they would hear a match struck and see the flicker of candlelight which told that Mr. Taylor, however weary, was poring over the little Bible in two volumes [presumably, English and Chinese] always at hand. From two to four A.M. was the time he usually

gave to prayer; the time when he could be most sure of being undisturbed to wait upon God. That flicker of candlelight has meant more to them than all they have read or heard on secret prayer; it meant reality, not preaching but practice.[10]

This is good news and more than likely a fresh perspective for those of us who, like Taylor, often face adversity in our all-too harried "changeful" cross-cultural lives and ministries. We need to remember that it is God who calls us to this perspective and into this practice, this "inner-life" expression of complete surrender, yieldedness, faith, and fruitfulness – where striving ceases, Christ becomes all in our lives, his word comes alive in our minds and hearts, and then overflows to those around us, even in our new languages and cultures. "The living God still lives, and the living Word is a living Word, and we may depend on it."[11]

How do our personal lives reflect the testimonies of these servants of God? When we honor the call of God to go to another culture, and to learn another language, we need to remember that when God called Moses, Jeremiah, Peter, Hudson Taylor, and so many others, he transformed their lives in the process. God revolutionizes our hearts and beckons us to *lift up our eyes* just as Jesus called Peter and the other disciples to do at the well (John 4:35 ESV). He shows us things we would never have otherwise seen. We become aware of people around us. Unlike never before, we see those from other cultures who speak other languages. We become mindful of the message of the gospel we must proclaim. As God did a miracle in Peter's heart leading up to his encounter with Cornelius, so God is at work in our hearts, and in the lives of those around us. Even now, God is pursuing the hearts of those we may not even know yet, whose languages we may not even speak yet.

Toward Gospel Fluency

"If you are ever drinking at the Fountain with what will your life be running over? – Jesus, Jesus, Jesus!"[12]

My friend Rob shared of a time he and his two young boys were at a cafe near their home not long after they began learning their new language. "I noticed a very conservatively dressed man watching us from behind the counter. He didn't show much emotion, and I thought he was probably annoyed with us or suspicious. I knew he wasn't someone who would be open to talking with me."

Rob then did what probably most of us wouldn't do. As he and his boys finished their juice, he approached the register to pay, and then greeted the man in his new language. Rob described what happened next and how it changed his perspective.

"The man immediately gave me a huge smile and said, 'Hello. How are you?' I was really convicted of my quickness to judge this man by what I saw. While Yusuf speaks very little English, he has been very happy to see us and has been patient and encouraging as I fumble through child-like conversations in his language. I pray for opportunities to share with him. Recently, we were able to talk some about prayer and faith...at least I think we did :)"

As Rob shared this story, he reminded me how easy it is for us to get busy with the details of life and the different roles we play. But, when we intentionally put ourselves among the lost, God provides opportunities to share the gospel. We just need to learn to walk by faith, and not by sight, trusting the Lord to guide us to those he chooses, not just to those who we think are easy to talk to. How intentionally do we enter into our communities – walking by faith and not by sight – to reach them with the gospel?

My goal in this book is to introduce the practice of gospel fluency in our new languages early on. I want to dive into what it means to delight in language learning through the lens of the Great Commission and to love our lost neighbors by sharing the gospel with them. I want us to discover what it means to reach and exceed conversational fluency through cultivating a practice of evangelism and discipleship as we become fluent in the gospel in our new languages.

So how do we become fluent enough to share the gospel in the language of our lost neighbor? How do we get there? It's a process. Our first goal in this process is to reach *basic conversational fluency*, when we are no longer tethered to rote words and phrases and can begin to actually interact in meaningful and creative ways with people at a basic level. More specifically, it's at this level that we come within range of understanding and telling simple familiar gospel stories.

I consider this the breakthrough point in our language learning. If we can get to a point where we can understand and tell simple, familiar gospel stories, we have a very specific and powerful reason to keep learning. Moreover, as we gain fluency in simple gospel story comprehension and presentation, we are on a great path toward sustained *discourse fluency*. This is when we truly begin to practice *gospel fluency* at deeper and broader levels.

Discourse fluency is the ability to describe, narrate, explain, and persuasively discuss meaningful topics of interest, with minimal or no preparation, through speaking, dialogue, and responsive listening. *Gospel fluency* is the practice of discourse fluency using redemptive content.

Let me say it this way: *Gospel fluency* begins most earnestly when we reach the point where we can understand a simple gospel passage from the Bible in our new language, and the gospel we understand in our new language feeds our minds and souls.

My best personal *preparation* for gospel fluency involves daily reading of Scripture in my new language, and thinking hard on it, in prayer. I have realized that I cannot rely only on memorized texts from last week's seminar if I want to be fluent in the gospel in my neighbor's language today.

My best personal *practice* of gospel fluency is teaching the Bible to key people God brings into my life and having them teach it back to me. In this way, I learn the language and the culture, how to teach in the language, and how the gospel is changing their lives simultaneously as it is changing mine. This is also one of the main ways I practice obeying the Great Commission (Matthew 28:18-20).

Making a habit of daily proclaiming the gospel to my lost neighbors takes deliberate personal preparation and practice, as well as prayer and faith. God opens doors we may not even know existed as we prayerfully prepare, practice, and proclaim the gospel to our neighbors every day.

I personally need to practice this better, and live with this as a greater daily anticipation. I can testify that I am always astounded by God's marvelous grace, as he daily invites me into his presence and allows me to participate in the gospel for all peoples beginning right here, right now, as I lift up my eyes.

Reflect and Respond

1. Reflect on this statement: I was reminded of the gospel this morning as I read God's word and prayed.

2. Based on your response, describe your desire or vision to personally share the gospel with your lost friends or neighbors today.

3. Prayerfully consider this statement as you think about relationships with neighbors: God weaves our lives into the fabric of other people's lives for his glory.

4. Take a moment to pray that God would open your eyes to see more of what he's doing in your life, through your life, and in the lives of those around you today.

3

The Gospel for my Lost Neighbor

...he asked Jesus, "And who is my neighbor?" (Luke 10:29)

It is no accident that in Luke 10 as we read Jesus' response to the question, he tells a story of a Samaritan foreigner reaching out to a Jew. Jesus is helping us understand what it means to proclaim the gospel to our neighbors as we cross ethnic and language boundaries. This is a prelude to the Great Commission. We must seriously consider that just as we are all called to obey the Great Commission and proclaim the gospel to all peoples, we are also called to personally bring the gospel to our lost neighbors in such a way that they can understand and receive the gospel. We choose to learn the language of our neighbors so that we can share the gospel with them. It's just that simple. I often ask myself these questions:

- When was the last time I shared my faith with my lost neighbors?

- When I ask myself that question, am I convicted? Filled with compassion?

- Do I have a regular practice of proclaiming the gospel to my neighbors?

- What am I doing in my life to be fluent in the gospel for my neighbors every day?

- How much time do I spend in God's word in my new language every day?

- Do I remind myself of the gospel in my new language from God's word every day?

- How does this affect and reflect on my daily witness to those around me?

Jesus meant to redefine how many of us think of what it means to be a neighbor. The Samaritan, Levite, and priest all passed the same road and saw the same man stripped, beaten, and left half-dead. But only one reached out to him as a neighbor and responded to his needs – a foreigner. In fact, we know from the story that this Samaritan went to great lengths to care for this man. What efforts do we expend to reach out to our lost neighbors? Do they know the good news? Will we be the ones to tell them? Do we even know their language?

We need to begin to connect the dots between learning the language of our lost neighbors and sharing the gospel with them. What is our current practice of evangelism where we live right now? In the languages that we use every day? At home? With our neighbors, whomever they may be? At work, at school, near home, away from home? This is our essential task – to share the greatest news ever with our neighbors. This is where gospel fluency begins.

When we talk about personal evangelism in any context, at home or abroad, we need to ask: Are we aware of our neighbors, and do we have an awareness of how much they need the Good News? Do we desire to share the gospel with them? Where are the eyes of our hearts for the harvest, this harvest that is within the radius of our personal lives? We're talking about personal evangelism. But, at a fundamental level, we're talking about more than that. We're talking about a personal awareness of the gospel in our lives, and what it means to truly love our neighbors as ourselves, and that sharing the gospel with them really is loving them.

If we are not already walking in our calling – as those who behold and testify – we may find that we ultimately lack the desire to press on deeper and wider in the language. Why is that? The problem is fundamentally not about our desire to obey the Great Commission. We desire to obey it. We may just need to be reminded of the joy of the gospel.

I introduced this chapter with the question: When was the last time I shared my faith with a lost person? But, as I reflect on recent conversations with language learners in tough places, maybe there is a prior question: Do I delight in sharing the gospel?

Because if I do, chances are I will also delight in learning the language. I regularly have conversations with beginning language learners about the priority of the gospel, even when our lives feel so dominated by the challenges of learning language. Simply put, for each one of us our essential calling is to make disciples of all peoples, and this begins with evangelizing our lost neighbors at home right now. I've heard this called the *main task* or the *main thing*.

When we see the common aspects of the practice of gospel fluency with our neighbors in any place, whether familiar or foreign, I think we're beginning to arrive at our fundamental motivation. I was recently asked to compare and contrast the practice of gospel fluency in our home language and culture with that of our new language and culture.

I see no distinction. And I want this to be clear to church planters, churches, students, and everyone on our teams. As we practice gospel fluency in our home cultures, among our neighbors, right here and now, there's a good chance that when we get into our new places and languages, we'll reach discourse fluency because our motivation to share the gospel is as high in our new language as it has been in our first language. However, the same is true that if we don't live to share the gospel regularly at home, then chances are we won't have the motivation to reach fluency in our new language.

> ...if your goal is to learn a language, you'll probably fail...if your goal is to know people – to deeply love people, to be involved in their lives – then success in language learning is predictable. If your goal is to be deeply involved in a network of relationships with people, then language learning will almost be spontaneous. It will not be a goal in itself – it will rather be a means to an end.[13]

Those who regularly share their faith in their first language have tremendous motivation to learn their second language precisely because their attitude to share the gospel precedes their interest in learning the language. In other words, those who regularly delight in sharing their faith with their neighbors now, will probably continue to practice this as they learn their new language. They are successful language learners because they already practice gospel fluency. "At the end of the day, the biggest obstacle to evangelism is Christians who don't share the gospel" (Albert Mohler).

Glitter it with the Gospel

Dan supervises learners in really tough language settings. Over coffee one day we were talking about what we wanted for these learners. Dan said he wanted them to reach basic conversational fluency. I agreed. We talked about ways they might be able to learn some gospel stories, share their testimonies, and find ways to practice. I thought out loud,

"How can we help them learn to be savvy, respectful, wise, and aromatic with the gospel in their conversation?"

I'll never forget Dan's response: "We need the language of the humble, the gospel of humility...talk about your marriage, how much you love your wife, and glitter it with the gospel."

Just that phrase, "glitter it with the gospel," made me see things in a different light as I thought of these learners and their tough learning situations. As a coach, I honestly couldn't think of much I could offer these learners. But I could remind them of our delight in the gospel, our source of joy, even as we learn language. I wrote this as a word of encouragement to them:

> Don't focus on learning the language. Focus on the light of the gospel, in and through your life, as you consider the people around you. When your goal becomes the language, watch out that it doesn't become a barrier instead of a bridge, something that leads to confusion rather than clarity. Relentlessly examine and re-examine your perspective and language learning practices. We should always place the gospel before us in all circumstances and use whatever means, whatever language, whatever preparation we have, to communicate the gospel.
>
> I want to emphasize this: never assume that gospel proclamation is a rote presentation. It is almost always, at least for us as learners, as guests, as bridge-builders, something that "glitters" the conversation, a touch of yeast or leaven that works through a whole batch of dough. God multiplies our simple words, our testimony, our witness, our loaves and fishes. Use the language we have, whatever we have prepared, to present the gospel with "gentleness and respect" (1 Peter 3:15 ESV).

We are called to proclaim the gospel. We behold God's glory, and we tell what we behold. We need to learn to operate in our calling as we learn the language. When the gospel for our neighbor becomes our language learning focus and our purpose, then our language learning becomes delightful, satisfying in every way. Let's get this right. We want to learn the language well, but for the right reasons and with the right conviction. Our focus is not on learning the language; our focus is on becoming fluent in the gospel.

The response I received from one of these learners sums up the point of this chapter pretty well:

> As I've processed this lately, and been praying for opportunities to share, boldness to share, and the ability to be clear when sharing, I've seen the Lord giving me a fresh love for language learning which I think is an answer to the prayer for clarity when sharing. He has also been answering those prayers about opportunities as well which has been a great encouragement.
>
> In the recent days, the Father has started to turn this language pursuit from duty to delight. For once, I've actually started to think of this as a hobby, a pleasurable activity, and so the idea of pulling out my Quizlet flash cards or charting some verbs while on vacation doesn't seem like such a violation of protocol. I can already see the balance this perspective creates in my life in which so much of the stress that relates to language learning begins to subside.
>
> I'm thankful that the Father in his grace is working on my heart in this way at this point in our term as opposed to me arriving at a "language burn-out" state. I've really come to see how much of first term is about a paradigm shift.

This learner went on to say how he was inspired by guys who have "modeled excellence in not just pursuing language, etc., but also have fought to keep the focus on the *main thing* when it's so easy to become caught up in learning and the platform."

When we begin to realize that our purpose is not about performance, but rather living in true awareness of the gospel in our lives, and learning how to live it out, how to glitter it, and how to proclaim it among our neighbors, in all areas of our lives, that's a good shift.

> I will not be content until I can minister in [my new language] similar to how I would be able to in English. I know this is a lofty goal. But the gospel, as well as deep spiritual truths and doctrines, best communicates in the heart language of a people. I firmly believe this. This is what drives me. Not [an organizational benchmark]. For the [organization] didn't send me here. God did (Sam, second-year learner).

I am often asked what the best ways are to determine language learning aptitude. How do we ensure people actually have the capacity to learn a language? My response places the emphasis on attitude, not on aptitude. If people love their lost neighbors enough to share Christ with them today, they will sustain the ability and determination, for that same purpose, to learn the language tomorrow.

We get to do this!

What makes a successful language learner? Aptitude plays a part. But attitude plays a bigger part. Are we not thankful that we have the resources to be able to learn our neighbor's language? Do we not deeply desire to reach a level of fluency so that we can share the gospel? Fellow language learners in Christ, we get to do this! I caution us against an entitlement attitude that expects and therefore only reaches minimum standards. This is a tragic perspective. Our minimum standard should be our baseline for really taking off in our learning and ministry. We get to do this! By God's grace we get to learn to share our faith in another language and reach out to our lost neighbors!

If we have a habit of regularly sharing our faith now, we will continue to do so as a part of our language learning practice. And this passion, this practice, will drive us – not to learn the language, but to proclaim the gospel to our lost neighbors in their language. And we will be thankful for every class we attend – every word we learn and use – that puts us on this path toward fluency. I truly believe this grateful attitude – this *thankfulness* – is the best litmus test for determining our long-term language learning capacity and success.

Our purpose is to tell the good news, and that purpose is what compels us to learn the language so we can tell it. If we are walking in our calling, regularly telling the good news to those around us, our language learning becomes a part of that joyful process of gospel proclamation.

> Language learning is one of the hardest things I've ever done. What was the game changer for me? I had "hard language" with no "ministry joy," It was torture. But when I found ministry joy in the hard language progress, it was no longer torture. It was rewarding (Greg, first-year learner).

We start with what we know, mistakes and all. Our weakness is God's strength, and as we take the next faithful step, we know that the gospel is true and sustains our testimony by the power of his word and Spirit.

We endure the challenges of language learning setbacks when we don't "feel" the progress. But with every gospel story we tell, and every passage we explain, we find joy in inviting people to follow Christ.

Let's not confuse our goal. Our goal is not competence in learning the language. Our goal is fluently proclaiming the gospel. What do I mean by this? One language learner recently told me that her entire first four-year term was being overshadowed by a proficiency level she was told to reach. I responded with this word of encouragement:

> Please do not let language proficiency goals distract you from your overall goal – the ability to proclaim and teach the gospel in your new language. Everything we do in language learning is to become fluent in our interpersonal communication of the gospel. Our first goal, therefore, is to get to the point where we can begin to do this. This means more than working through a single prepared presentation. It means working through multiple simple gospel passages. We must learn to tell them and explain them simply, and dialogue about them informally. We must be able to talk about how the gospel impacts our lives, in simple words of testimony. This is gospel fluency, and rest assured that this gospel fluency goal most certainly correlates with proficiency levels we are trying to reach.

Language learning is no easy task. Nor does it lend itself to quick results. It requires endurance, patience, humility, discipline, faith, and wisdom. The task of language learning has the capacity to strip us of our confidence, purpose, and desire. It is easy to lose sight of the goal. "Run in such a way to win the prize" (1 Corinthians 9:24).

Have you ever done something that is so difficult – though you love it and have a passion for it, it is just so hard to do? Proclaiming the gospel in another language is hard. It's insanely hard. I've heard getting to the gospel in a conversation described as "seven seconds of insanity." Ratchet that up a few notches when trying to do it in another language.

1 Corinthians 9:15-27

We are called to do hard things. Sometimes our biggest challenges are really our greatest opportunities. (Tim, veteran co-worker)

Paul worked hard to effectively proclaim the gospel to all peoples (see Acts 14:11-18, Acts 17:16-34, and Acts 21:37-40). Paul was determined to do everything he possible could to make the gospel personally accessible to his lost neighbors, whomever they were, in all walks of life. We see this clearly expressed in 1 Corinthians 9:15-27. In his own defense, Paul willingly made no use of his rights as an apostle. He had no reason to boast. No obligation was placed on him to preach the gospel. He preached it free of charge, anticipating with great hope an eternal reward.

> For my part I have used none of these rights, nor have I written these things that they may be applied in my case. For it would be better for me to die than for anyone to deprive me of my boast! For if I preach the gospel, I have no reason to boast, because I am compelled to preach – and woe to me if I do not preach the gospel! For if I do this willingly, I have a reward, but if unwillingly, I am entrusted with a commission. What then is my reward? To preach the gospel and

offer it free of charge and not make full use of my rights in the gospel (1 Corinthians 9:15-18).

Reminiscent of the fire of God's message in Jeremiah's bones, Paul was driven by an intrinsic desire to preach – "woe to me if I do not preach the gospel!" (v. 16), boasting in the status of his situation, denying his rights as an apostle, demonstrating an open-hearted passion and willingness to proclaim the gospel, no matter the cost. Though putting himself under the same obligation as those who exercised their rights as apostles, Paul made no use of these rights in order to exemplify a stewardship he willingly embraced. He made himself a servant to all, that he might win more. Paul worked hard to make *himself* accessible to all people, so that the *gospel* would then be accessible to all people.

> Although I am free from all and not anyone's slave, I have made myself a slave to everyone, in order to win more people. To the Jews I became like a Jew, to win Jews; to those under the law, like one under the law – though I myself am not under the law – to win those under the law. To those who are without the law, like one without the law – though I am not without God's law but under the law of Christ – to win those without the law. To the weak I became weak, in order to win the weak. I have become all things to all people, so that I may by every possible means save some. Now I do all this because of the gospel, so that I may share in the blessings (1 Corinthians 9:19-23).

Paul put himself under an obligation to reach all people with the gospel. He made difficult life choices. He resolved to make himself "a slave to everyone" (v. 19), in order to identify, communicate with, and actually become "all things to all people" (v. 22) – to Jews, to those under the law, to those without that law, to the weak – beautifully articulated in the singular purpose, "that I may by every possible means save some" (v. 22).

As we consider Paul's example, we need to ask ourselves what it will take to reach our lost neighbors with the gospel. What life choices do we need to make as we pray, go, preach, enter new communities, adapt to new cultures, and learn new languages? We share this same obligation, this calling, but does this mean we always have the desire or will to do what it takes to share the gospel at every moment? Likely not. I think this was what Paul was driving at here. The work is hard. There will be days we may lose heart, grow weary, or suffer pain. However, we still have an obligation. And even if we don't live by this obligation – as Paul testified – we are compelled by an inner calling from God to proclaim the gospel, whatever it takes. Paul's calling was greater than his identity as an apostle, stronger than any rights attached to that identity, and more persuasive than any emotion or personal will he could muster to bolster his preaching. He was bound by his calling. He practiced spiritual stewardship. He was compelled to preach the gospel at all costs.

This is good news for us. We have the same command to follow. Indeed, we can identify with Paul as we enter new communities, adapt to new cultures, and learn new languages in order to reach our lost neighbors with the gospel. God entrusts us with a specific stewardship in which we are called to proclaim the gospel in the languages and in the cultures of our lost neighbors in such a way that the message of the gospel is clear, accurate, and natural in our witness. This is undeniably hard work. Paul compared the intensity of this work to that of a boxer in training, and an elite runner in competition. These examples bring to mind hard training, self-control, intense workouts, focused practice, and an insatiable will to win.

> Don't you know that the runners in a stadium all race, but only one receives the prize? Run in such a way to win the prize. Now everyone who competes exercises self-control in everything. They do it to receive a perishable crown, but we an imperishable crown. So I do not run like one who runs aimlessly or box like one beating the air. Instead, I discipline my body and bring it under strict control, so that after preaching to others, I myself will not be disqualified (1 Corinthians 9:24-27).

It would seem that we're left hanging at the end of this passage with an impossible task. Who are we kidding? Everything about this work is hard. Is this what it takes to reach the least-reached with the gospel? Can we engage them with the gospel? Can we even learn their language and culture? It would seem we are faced with an impossible challenge. If that's where we are, we are right where God wants us.

The task of becoming fluent in the gospel in another language and culture can at times feel impossible. While learning the language itself may often feel excruciatingly slow, "three steps forward and two steps back," the amorphous challenges of adapting to a totally new and foreign culture often exhibit the deep-bone pain of identity loss and shift in the midst of bewildering and overwhelming change. We need the truth to wash over us during these moments, to remind us that even though we are weak, Christ is strong, and that it is only through his power we are sustained.

We are called to proclaim the Good News to our lost neighbors, and this pursuit compels us to learn their languages so we can meaningfully communicate it. Perhaps we see the need for gospel fluency, but have a hard time getting started or making progress. Maybe we perceive insurmountable barriers. I've seen learners suffer severe setbacks and discouragement, to the point of giving up, feeling unable to learn and use their new languages in ministry. We may try to convince ourselves that learning a new language is not worth it, that it's not necessary, that it takes too long, or that somehow we just need to do something else to bypass the chore of learning the language so we can get to the gospel.

How urgent is the task of personal evangelism? How urgent is the task of language learning? Until we can connect the dots between these two questions, we will tend to let language learning slide as other urgent items come across our desks or into our lives. Sure, these things need to get done, and we need to do them. But at what price?

Do we carry a debilitating burden to share the gospel because of language barriers we are unable to overcome? Our burden to speak with integrity – to effectively proclaim the gospel in the language we are learning – is nothing short of an act of bold faith, godly courage, and high risk. What if we get it wrong? What if we do not say what we intend, or say what we do not intend? Isn't it strange how this same high calling compelling us to master the language so we can effectively proclaim the gospel – this sense of duty to steward the gospel well – can at times paralyze us from continuing to learn?

Why is this? The truth is, we have to first speak poorly before we can speak fluently in any new language. While this can be discouraging, there is hope. God honors our faithfulness as we courageously proclaim the gospel, even in our poor expression. God's word transforms our lives and the lives of our neighbors. "The Bible is supernaturally inspired by God to conform you and me into the image of Jesus Christ, and that is our greatest need" (David Platt). It is God's word that is powerful, not ours. God works through our imperfect speech as we proclaim the gospel, whether in our mother tongue or in our new language, in miraculous and redemptive ways we cannot begin to comprehend.

Fellow language learner – encourage your brother and sister to press on. God will speak through our feeble words – our weakness. We know we do not have the fluency of native speakers, and probably never will. So why put forth the effort? Because our effort is one of faith: that God will actually use us, that he has called us, and through our gospel witness, he demonstrates his mighty strength and salvation.

We must maintain a Godward perspective as we learn language. This can be challenging, especially as language learning can be so mentally and psychologically debilitating, as well as culturally stressful. When we find ourselves in stressful situations, trying to use the language and understand people around us, the temptation is to retreat rather than engage. We must remember our calling. Remember, it is God who strengthens us in our language learning pursuits for his glory. We can indeed, with all integrity, take faithful steps to make progress: reasonable progress, noble progress, progress that bears fruit which endures. This is honoring to the Lord, and he will multiply our efforts according to his power at work within us, for his glory.

"Just tell me the gospel again and again."

This was my colleague Richard's daily motto and has become mine. Richard and I would meet with a couple of local brothers to read through Scripture and pray together each week in the local language. One of the things I learned from each of these brothers was how much we each need to hear the gospel. It was our ambition to speak the gospel into each other's lives when we met. It was such a personally enriching and deeply encouraging time in the Lord together.

Richard knew several languages, and he was more fluent in some than others. He would return from teaching in one where it "flowed like water" and then get back into the language we used together for our guys' time, which often didn't flow as well. Yet I never recall a moment when that distracted us from drinking deeply from God's word together.

We would take a book of the Bible and work through it together. We would remind each other of the gospel. So many times I recall Richard saying something like, "Would you look at that?" and we would down-shift and talk through the text, considering how God was calling us to respond. Are we not continually astounded by the beauty of the gospel, and God's marvelous wonderful grace in our lives? "Keep it simple, accessible. When we are in first gear, we get to see everything" (Richard).

Lydia loved sharing her faith with her neighbors, and she did a great job learning the language so she could do this. She reached a point where she was able to have many life-changing heart-to-heart conversations. One evening I got a call from Lydia describing a recent fruitful conversation with her good friend M.

Lydia compared it to an experience so wonderful, it just takes your breath away. She first asked, "Have you ever skied down a slope at the end of the day after a fresh snowfall?" And then said, "Well, multiply that by 1000, and that's how I felt when I knew what I was saying was reaching M's heart."

Nothing remotely compares to this joy. This is the joy of the shepherd who found the lost sheep! This is the joy in the presence of God's angels when one sinner repents!

Dave is starting his third language. It's not easy, but he's motivated to learn. Like Lydia, Dave has a passion to share his faith. Dave has a fire to share his faith. And that fuels his language learning. Recently, he wrote,

During our last couple years in [a previous location], I remember thinking at one point 'I can't remember when I've last gone a day without sharing some Biblical truth with someone.' It's been much more difficult to do that here but finally, in the past couple of weeks, I feel like I'm at a point language-wise to do that. I still don't have natural opportunities to share every day that I'm out but probably more than half. Hopefully, as I continue to grow in language and find better ways to ask better questions that will naturally lead to spiritual conversations, I will have more opportunities to share and will be able to share better.

Not long ago I had the privilege of meeting with a team doing ministry in a large city. Josh, the team leader, gave a word of personal encouragement, "I used to share the gospel every day back home. Since arriving here, I felt that I'm just learning the language. But today…today is different. Today I experienced something I haven't experienced in a long time, like a memory from the distant past, another life."

Josh went on to describe the joy of communicating the gospel in his new language with a neighbor. And it was more than just a few sentences. That was important for him to emphasize, and I'm glad he did.

Josh said what made the difference was that he just had to entrust both his language abilities and his language limitations to the Lord. He talked about how he practiced telling a simple Bible story, how he learned to relate his testimony to it, and how he worked and worked on communicating them fluently. By the time he told them, even though there were some mistakes, it was understandable. And the point is, he did it. And he has also found someone to help him work on making it better.

I was inspired to help others follow Josh's example. I recently shared with a group of team leaders doing ministry in other languages, who were also supervising language learners, "I challenge you, and I want you to challenge your team, to dig deep into the word of God, in your new language, every day, as much as possible." Here's what I exhorted them to consider:

> Read one simple passage. Get one simple take-away. Work on one simple testimony. Get help from people who are one or several steps ahead of you. Have at least a part of your daily personal Bible study and prayer in your new language. Then with a Bible in your hand, and the word of God in your head and in your heart, rise from your knees to share the gospel with your lost neighbor.

Soon after, I met with a few learners to work through this three-step process:

> **Step 1:** Personal study. Read it multiple times in the language. As you do this, work toward 100% comprehension. Pray for insight and clear simple expression. Take notes, stay on topic.
> **Step 2:** Practice with a trusted friend. Practice re-telling the passage to your teacher or to a friend. Engage in a short dialogue about the topic. Get feedback and tips to improve your presentation and dialogue skills. Record it for review.
> **Step 3:** Listen and review. Listen to the recording. Say it again with your friend and others so they can hear your improvement.

The results? More people began to experience the insatiable joy of telling the gospel story in the language of their calling. They realized that this was within their reach, that it didn't have to take a long time to get there. We just accelerated this process with some good language learning practices. Easy, right? Far from it. It was hard work. But it was a labor of great joy because of the results.

This three-step process has become the framework for some of the most fruitful ongoing language learning practices that we practice and promote. We've adjusted it some to include intentional gospel proclamation and teaching opportunities with lost neighbors as an essential part of Step 3. We call this Language 180. Each step may take 60 minutes, totaling 180 minutes, each day, to complete. This is time well spent in direct ministry and ongoing learning. Language 180, or something like it, should be a long-term goal for new learners, and a well-honed practice for the rest of us. Richard summed it up well:

> Learn to communicate the Good News at every step of language learning through gospel-centered relationships and gospel language content. You need to *learn* gospel content but you also have to *use* that content in order for it to stick. It takes deliberate practice. Build fluency as you learn ever more challenging gospel language pieces and share that gospel language with others who give you helpful feedback. Seek to improve as you learn from them how to do better. Rinse and repeat that cycle. Again, and again.

Reflect and Respond

1. Think about some of your neighbors who don't yet know Christ – perhaps those from your hometown, workplace, college, new city, or elsewhere. Make a list. Pray for them.

2. Consider how you can cultivate a heart of anticipation that God will provide insights and opportunities for you to share the gospel with them today.

3. Describe one way you can share the gospel today with your neighbors as you learn their language.

4. Do you delight in the gospel? And in sharing the gospel? How do you cultivate and sustain the joy of the gospel in and through your life?

4

Simple Familiar Gospel Story

Then children were brought to Jesus for him to place his hands on them and pray, but the disciples rebuked them. Jesus said, "Leave the children alone, and don't try to keep them from coming to me, because the kingdom of heaven belongs to such as these." After placing his hands on them, he went on from there (Matt. 19:13-15).

I love this story for many reasons. It is perhaps the shortest and simplest gospel story in the Bible. What's not to love about that? There is very little imbedded in the structure, and few characters. The plot is simple, the conflict identifiable, and the resolution profound and palpable.

This is also a story that is familiar to us all. People brought children to Jesus for them to receive his blessing. The disciples rebuked the people. Jesus then told his disciples to let the children come. He taught the disciples an important lesson about faith, that we must have faith as children to enter God's kingdom. And then he blessed the children.

But, perhaps my favorite reason for loving this story is that it reminds me of an evening not long ago when my wife led a young lady to the Lord. We were meeting with her family – the grandmother, her son, the son's daughters, their children, and the aunt of one of the daughters. We read through this simple story and I invited the family to respond. The young lady who had just come to Christ earlier that day, told her family that she was like one of those children. She thanked Jenn for leading her to Jesus. And she thanked Jesus for inviting her to come to him. We experienced the joy of hearing each person in that room share one by one from their hearts a new and fresh understanding of what it means to come to Jesus.

The gospel is not complicated. The New Testament is full of simple familiar gospel stories, just like this one, that speak of coming to Jesus in simple, childlike faith. We identify with these stories. We came to Christ in much the same way. And we get to tell these simple stories, including our own, when we share the gospel with people.

In Mark 10, a great crowd was following Jesus as he left Jericho, and a blind beggar named Bartimaeus shouted out to him, "Jesus, Son of David, have mercy on me!" Those around him rebuked him, telling him to be silent. But he cried out all the more, "Have mercy on me, Son of David!" Jesus called him. And those around him said, "Have courage! Get up; he is calling for you." And throwing off his cloak, he sprang up and came to Jesus (v. 50).

In Mark 2, Jesus was teaching in a crowded house. Four men brought a paralytic to him, but they could not enter through the door because of the crowd. As they were not able to get their friend in need to Jesus, they removed the roof from above where Jesus was teaching. When they had broken through, they lowered the mat on which the paralytic was lying (v. 4).

In Mark 5, a great crowd was following Jesus when a woman who had suffered from bleeding for twelve years came up behind him in the crowd and touched his garment, for she said, "If I just touch his clothes, I'll be made well" (vv. 27-28).

In each of these stories, people came to Jesus to receive healing and salvation. In each situation, they came while facing considerable physical and cultural opposition. They did not politely ask to see Jesus. They resisted opposition and found a way to him. They ran, they climbed, they pushed, they dug, they begged. This is how they came to Jesus – in childlike faith. If we ever wonder what Jesus meant by that phrase, here it is: unrefined, uninhibited, risky, unconventional, hope-filled, desire-filled, God-ordained, out-of-the-box faith. In each of these lives, Jesus explicitly and audibly recognized their faith. He forgave them and healed them because of their faith, and because he could. Isn't this how we come to Jesus? He is the answer to all of our needs. He is the giver of salvation. This is our testimony, too.

I love the immediate declarative thanks and praise, words of testimony that we hear from so many who came and received healing and salvation from Jesus. "When the woman saw that she was discovered, she came trembling and fell down before him. In the presence of all the people, she declared the reason she had touched him and how she was instantly healed" (Luke 8:47).

Of the ten lepers who were healed, one returned to Jesus. "He fell facedown at his feet, thanking him. And he was a Samaritan" (Luke 17:16).

As we share the gospel from these simple familiar stories, we can invite our neighbors with full confidence in the power of God's word, exhorting them to come to Jesus with this same kind of faith. People they know, communities they live in, even their families may try to dissuade them from coming to Christ. Beliefs, shame, fears, and doubts may all contribute to a lack of faith. But Jesus is calling them, as he calls us all, to follow him.

In Matthew 14, Jesus' disciples were in a boat on a lake. Jesus came toward them walking on the sea. The disciples were terrified. Jesus told them to have courage, and to not be afraid.

> "Lord, if it's you," Peter answered him, "command me to come to you on the water."
>
> He said, "Come."
>
> And climbing out of the boat, Peter started walking on the water and came toward Jesus. But when he saw the strength of the wind, he was afraid, and beginning to sink he cried out, "Lord, save me!"
>
> Immediately Jesus reached out his hand, caught hold of him, and said to him, "You of little faith, why did you doubt?" (Matthew 14:28-31).

Jesus caught Peter's hand as he was sinking. Peter was afraid. He doubted the power of Jesus. Doubt and fear are strong deterrents to faith. Peter was in way over his head, literally! We sometimes feel that way. I have seen eyes glaze over as I share the gospel. Fears rise. Doubts multiply. It's crazy, isn't it? When we invite our neighbors to come to Jesus in faith, it's a life-changing proposition. Flesh resists the truth.

We need to tell this story. We need to tell every gospel story: the unexpected salvation of Zacchaeus, the sobering response of the rich young ruler, the joy of the lost son who was found by his father, and the polarizing anger of his older brother. People need to know that the journey to Jesus is a strong call, that faith is real, and though sin and flesh are crouching at the door, redemption is at hand.

The beauty of these stories is that they simply preach the gospel. The fundamental theme in each of these passages is that people did come, and that they came to saving faith in Jesus, by the grace of God. Each of these stories provides vibrant illustrations of faith, of people who came to Jesus in faith, and therefore came to faith in Jesus, We can point to these living examples as we invite and persuade our neighbors to do the same.

When people come to Christ where I live, they often talk about it like they are "coming home" into a relationship with God that they never thought was even possible. New believers testify where once there was fear and loneliness, now they have peace, joy, and know their Heavenly Father who actually loves them.

One of the most popular passages among new believers where I live is Matthew 7:9-11. I so often hear people say something like, "Did you know that our Heavenly Father loves us like this?" and then immediately read these verses aloud in renewed astonishment.

> Who among you, if his son asks him for bread, will give him a stone? Or if he asks for a fish, will give him a snake? If you then, who are evil, know how to give good gifts to your children, how much more will your Father in heaven give good things to those who ask him (Matthew 7:9-11).

Though these verses may not consist of an entire story or parable, they clearly display the gospel and the love of God in a beautiful word-picture of our Heavenly Father who captivates our hearts, invites us home, and gives us new life. I wondered how new believers here were so often drawn to these particular verses, and then I heard Kaya's story.

When I first met Kaya, he was a broken man. Recently divorced, his young son lived with his mother. Kaya himself had come from a broken home. His dad sank into serious debt to loan sharks while trying to finance his floundering construction business. He left Kaya's mother "for her protection," but Kaya soon discovered that was just an excuse. His father had been unfaithful and had remarried as soon as they divorced, leaving Kaya's mother penniless. The tragedy and pain of Kaya's broken childhood home was now repeating itself. Kaya had not seen his father in ages, nor had he seen his own son in months.

Kaya's despair turned to joy as he put his faith in Christ. For his whole life, Kaya had only known rejection, fear, and loneliness. God saved Kaya from his sin and rescued him from his despair. The way Kaya described it, God literally invited him "home" to his Kingdom, as his loving Heavenly Father.

As we met one day for Bible study and prayer, Kaya handed me a handwritten note with these verses from Matthew 7:9-11, along with this prayer, "Lord I want to inherit eternal life. May your Kingdom come and may your holy name be glorified! Forgive my sins. I am no longer lonely because of you. You are my Heavenly Father. I want to preach the gospel. I pray for my son. I pray he would also know your love."

I am thankful for these simple verses and for this simple prayer. In their profound simplicity, they opened my mind and my heart to better understand at least some of the life issues my neighbors, including Kaya, struggle with. I saw how God changed Kaya's heart and gave him hope in Christ. I continue to see how God is changing lives around me, one simple gospel story at a time.

We as language learners need to understand what it really means to tell *simple familiar gospel stories* as we learn our new language. As we learn to tell these stories, we don't learn them in a vacuum. We are simultaneously learning the basic *texts or discourses* of life going on around us, the back-and-forth of stories that define who we are before our neighbors and help us understand them. In other words, as we learn to talk with people, and as we learn to share the gospel, we are learning the basics of how to discourse in our new language.

A Thoughtful Pursuit of Discourse

Discourse is conversation, discussion, and dialogue; it's the meaningful topics we think about and therefore learn to talk about. Simple, direct, and concrete, the ebb and flow of our basic expression or discourse ability in our new language slowly begins to usher us into the fabric of our neighbor's lives.

There is a strong relationship between the ability to sustain a basic conversation in our new language on familiar topics, and the ability to understand and tell a simple familiar gospel story. We should never separate these two skills. Though one may be an *interpersonal communication skill* (dialogue), and the other a *presentational speech skill* (story), we cannot and should not develop one without the other. We are called to present the gospel. However, more importantly, we are called to converse the gospel. People will respond. We need to be able to understand and attend to their responses in meaningful ways.

We may be asking the question, "At what level can we tell a simple gospel story?" Or, put differently, "How long do we need to learn language before we can tell a simple gospel story?"

Rather than levels or time frames, let's consider discourse ability. What functional abilities do I need in the language – rote phrases? sentences? paragraphs? – to be able to tell a simple, familiar story? Understanding our functional ability in the language can help get us on the right track as we consider true progress.

Any meaningful language interchange we have with those around us is discourse. Discourse fluency starts at a very basic level. We begin with simple words and phrases, and progress to sentences, then paragraphs, and finally entire discourses. As this happens, our ability to dialogue improves. When we describe a picture, when we listen and respond to a story, or when we explain why a story from our lives or from the Bible is so important to us, that is all discourse. Discourse is the ability to speak, listen, and dialogue.

Speaking and hearing a new language begins with the most predictable and simple phrases and sentences. As we progress, we are able to speak, understand, and respond in broader and deeper ways to a growing number of familiar and unfamiliar topics. With growing complexity, our paragraphs become a rich discourse of stories, descriptions, and discussions on all topics of life.

As we look down this road of greater *gospel fluency*, we picture the ability to confidently and extemporaneously describe, narrate, explain, and discuss many simple and familiar topics that we have worked through. We are better able to see and grasp how we can begin to effectively teach the Bible to our friends and neighbors in their language.

As we imagine the ability to dialogue about these topics, we begin to see how our responses are no longer simple sentences. Rather they are robust paragraphs that allow us to engage in meaningful discussions with our neighbors. We can envision the outcomes of this teaching, the fruit of this ministry God has given us.

These represent the content and expression, the "nuts and bolts," of *discourse fluency*. These are what we need to be thinking about when we consider fluency in the language and, therefore, fluency in ministry.

For years I've used a helpful little chart to help direct learners to correlate ministry outcomes with language levels using the ACTFL scale.[14] We will not look at formal definitions; I want to focus on the discourse outcomes. As we look through the following descriptions, let's consider the functional ministry we could do at each of these language levels, and the discourse fluency we may need for each of these tasks.

Discourse Fluency and Ministry Outcomes

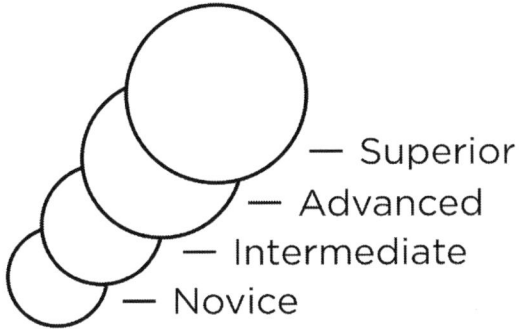

Novice

- Use phrases about God
- Distribute tracts
- Initiate relationships
- Share memorized words of blessing

Intermediate

- Pray for people
- Ask questions about faith
- Share testimony
- Tell simple Bible stories
- Weave in some basic truths

Advanced

- Read the Bible for meaning
- Ask deeper questions
- Pray more fluently
- Teach simple Bible study
- Lead and participate in basic discipleship

Superior

- Lead deeper discipleship
- Develop and instruct leadership training
- Participate in Biblical counseling
- Teach regularly

One of the things I like about this chart is that when we look at it, we immediately can see some things that we can do, or should be able to do soon. This is what I mean by functional ministry descriptions. We see these descriptions as things we can do, based on our language ability.

As a language coach and disciple-maker in her new language, Amy thoughtfully expanded the language tasks related to this chart simply by asking the question, "What can I do in church?" I love this question! *This* is the question we should all be asking ourselves as we pursue *gospel fluency* (see Appendix 2). We no longer learn a language simply to reach a level. Rather, we actively practice *doing* something eternally meaningful in the language with those around us and are therefore inspired to keep learning. Because the more we learn, the more we can do.

There is an interesting correlation between language level and how much one is able to actually do in the language at that level. At the *Novice* level, there is very little we can do in the language. Notice, though, that as we progress into the *Intermediate* level, and into each successive level, how much more we can do in the language. Notice how much more ministry we can engage in, how many more ministry outcomes we can expect.

Considering this, where on this chart would we actually reach the ability to understand and tell a simple familiar gospel story? Remember, this is not about reciting a memorized story, nor is it a story told in isolation of conversational ability on a range of familiar topics. It may be helpful to view this ability – the practice of understanding and telling a simple, familiar gospel story – as the fulcrum of our language learning, the tipping point with the capacity to infuse the rest of our language learning journey with joy. In a very real sense, the simple, familiar gospel story is that for which we are aiming, *and* from which we spring-board. It's the effectual turning point in our language learning that gives us the drive to keep going. If we get to a place where we can understand and tell simple familiar gospel stories, we muster the inspiration to keep learning. When we reach basic narrative comprehension and presentation abilities, this puts us squarely on the path toward sustained discourse fluency – that is, *gospel fluency*, giving us both the language skills and the spiritual acuity to proclaim the gospel in our new language.

I have tried to learn all I can from those who know how to tell simple, familiar gospel stories in their new languages. They are able to tell natural, accurate, and clear gospel stories precisely *because* they have learned to craft them well and practice them with diligence. Here are a couple of my favorite examples of fluent gospel story practices.

Story Crafting

Learn to craft a natural, accurate, and well-told Bible story.

One of the most effective ways to learn to tell a simple familiar gospel story in our new language is to learn to actually "craft" a Bible story.[15] Here's how it works. Story crafters begin with at least three different audio versions of the story. Using at least one accurate audio version of the Biblical text available in their new language, along with accurate informal narrations of the text, they listen to each audio seven times. They avoid writing things down. They try to construct the story in their minds. Then, they ask themselves these eight questions as they practice telling the story:

> What did you like about the story?
> What bothered or confused you about the story?
> What does this story show you about God/Jesus?
> What does this story show you about people?
> If this story is true, what should you do to obey God?
> How will you remember this story?
> Who will you tell this story to?
> What is the most important point of this story?

Story crafters follow this six-step process to craft natural, accurate, and well-told Bible stories:

1. Find the central image, message, or point of the story. Think about which action shows that most important point. Concentrate on this "most important point" as the theme of the story.

2. Visualize the story. Explore the feelings:

> Walk back through the story in your mind several times as different characters in the story. Close your eyes and put yourself in the scene. Walk through the story in your mind as if you're walking through a movie scene. Try to sense the smells, the feelings, the tastes, the emotions of the character. Ask the Holy Spirit to show you what he wants to through this activity.

3. Draw the story. Build the structure. Either storyboard it or draw it on a story arc that allows you to see the climax (the most important point) of the story.

4. Choose your words. Use words you know that your neighbors would use. For example, Matthew 14:26 says, "When the disciples saw him [Jesus] walking on the sea, they were terrified," but you or even your neighbors may have a word or phrase other than "terrified" to describe the fear the disciples felt, so use that word or phrase, instead.

5. Craft the story. Start trying to tell the story using the phrases you chose. Tell the story several times to yourself. Record yourself telling the story and listen to it.

> Don't write anything down. This sounds counter-intuitive, but you can check in your Bible every once in a while to make sure that you haven't missed anything. Doing this verbally is very good for your memory and your internalization of the truths of the story. It is awkward at first, but it is worth it!

6. Tell your story. Find members of your audience to tell the story to. Find ways to insert it into your conversation. Ask someone to help you learn the story by listening to you tell it to them. After you tell the story to your audience you can ask them to re-tell it back to you. Ask them the questions you asked yourself.

Good News Skeleton

Tell the Good News from your heart, from what you already know. (Meg)

Meg is a cross-cultural evangelist. She knows several languages and works hard to effectively share the gospel in all of them. She teaches others to do the same. For several years, she taught new language learners to memorize 150 gospel sentences, with varying rates of success. Since then, she has found better ways to help newcomers learn simple gospel stories in their new languages by using what language they already know. Meg described to me how she began using the Good News Skeleton.

> I kept thinking, how can people have something that is more doable? And I noticed also that memorizing things, if they got stuck on one part, it's like they couldn't even jump to the next sentence, or to a later sentence. They just got this 'deer in the headlights' look. So, I felt that having the 150 sentences was hard on people.
> I told people, "You can modify it, you can cut it down to fifty sentences. Do what you want to do. Change it to *your* vocabulary."
> But people didn't. It's like as soon as gave them a piece of paper with sentences on it, it was like it was gold and that they had to do it exactly like that.
> A team-mate of mine showed me a really good way to share the gospel using hand motions. I really liked it. It was very learn-able. It still felt pretty long. I wanted people not to memorize it. I got this idea to just have a skeleton. It's sixteen sentences. What I found is that I didn't give people the handout. First, we learn it in English. Then, in the local language. And we do it a little different each time. We don't have to say these magic memorized sentences. We can learn to tell the Good News from our hearts, from what we already know.

Meg then introduced me to the *Good News Skeleton with Hand Motions*, a simple, elegant gospel presentation and invitation that is best demonstrated and watched.[16] Here are the sixteen sentences.

In the beginning there was *God*.

God created the first *people*. They had a perfect relationship with God. But people disobeyed God, they *sinned*. People were separated from God.

Sin is a barrier – to be with God.

How can we remove sin?

Only God can remove sin.

God became a person and lived among us. That person was *Jesus*.

On the cross, Jesus took our sins and became the sacrifice. Jesus died, was buried, but on the 3rd day he rose from the dead.

Because of Jesus, a relationship with God is possible. I believed in Jesus, and my sins were forgiven.

According to the Bible, God's Spirit filled me.

Do you want your sins forgiven through Jesus?

Hand motions describe the highlighted themes. For example, God as the first theme is represented by our raised, outstretched right hand. We then clasp it with our other hand to represent God's original and intended relationship with people. As the story unfolds, because of our sin, that clasp is undone and replaced with a barrier we are burdened to carry (represented by a rock, cellphone, or something similar) which can only be removed by Jesus, God's chosen sacrifice. Can you picture it? Watch the video![17] These sixteen sentences, intentionally simple, form a skeleton, a framework with which we create a basic gospel presentation. As our language improves, we begin to discover how to build upon this skeleton.

For example, if we want to talk more about God, we can learn to describe who he is, his nature, that he is one. We can learn to talk about his purposes, holiness, justice, mercy, and love. If we want to talk more about people, we can work on saying how we were created in perfect relationship with God, that we sinned, and that we need a savior. Or about sin – our rebellion against God, what keeps us from his holy presence, our futile attempts to eradicate sin, and our need for salvation. Or Jesus – God who lived among us as a man, did great miracles, was completely sinless, obeyed God fully, became the guiltless sacrifice for our sins by dying on the cross, and who rose again as our living Lord.

The point is, we can and should begin sharing the basics of the simple, familiar gospel story early on. Then, as we learn more language, we can begin to slowly add descriptions and explanations. Practicing the Good News Skeleton or crafting gospel stories in our new languages has been incredibly motivating for me and so many other learners. Quite simply, we are motivated to learn more language – words, phrases, and stories – so we can share more of the gospel.

Reflect and Respond

1. Describe how you personally identify with the message of the gospel when you read the Bible.

2. What is one thing you can do to help you begin to more fluently share the gospel from simple familiar stories in the Bible?

3. Is there anyone who can help you with this; perhaps a language partner, national partner, team-mate, or neighbor? Take a moment to pray for that person.

4. Consider how you can begin to practice crafting gospel stories or using something like the *Good News Skeleton* in your new language with your neighbors.

5

Gospel Radius

But you will receive power when the Holy Spirit has come on you, and you will be my witnesses in Jerusalem, in all Judea and Samaria, and to the end of the earth (Acts 1:8).

Mehmet heard the gospel for the first time in our local house church in the town where we lived. I met with Mehmet several times after that and sensed his struggle with sin. He had a rough marriage but was stubborn and did not surrender his life to Christ. After we moved, I continued to pray for Mehmet.

Several months later I received a phone call from a friend who lived in our city of 18 million people, several hours from Mehmet's hometown. James shared with me that as he had been walking through a busy part of the city the day before, he had felt impressed to share the gospel with a certain guy sitting on a bench, and that guy was Mehmet. Mehmet told James that he had heard the gospel in his hometown from me. Once it all became clear to Mehmet that James knew me, it suddenly hit him, "How did God find me in this huge city?"

That evening the three of us met for tea. "This shouldn't be happening," I thought to myself. Only God could love Mehmet so much to pull this off. As we read and talked through the parables of the Lost Sheep (Luke 15:1-7) and the Lost Son (Luke 15:11-32), we marveled together at how much

God loves us, that he loves Mehmet, and *that* is the reason he pursued him all the way to the city. Mehmet had come to be with his girlfriend. Instead, in the middle of millions of people, God chased him down. That's just the way God works.

The radius of the gospel is limitless. It reaches all people in all situations and speaks to the human condition at every level. The buoyancy of the gospel sustains every conversation so that as we proclaim the gospel, we live it; and as we live it, we cannot help but proclaim it. When we open our eyes we see the Holy Spirit at work in people's lives as God woos them to himself, even in the so-called mundane.

We bear the gospel in simple powerful witness through the daily stuff of shared life, in homes, over tea, and at work. The discourse of the gospel should encompass the entire radius of our discourse ability in our new language, using everything we know in the language, covering all topics. As we begin to view our lives through the lens of the gospel, all conversations become those precious opportunities we are given to share the gospel with our neighbors.

Consider the multiple ways in which the gospel is woven into the fabric of so many conversations on diverse topics, stories and life situations throughout Scripture. We read over and over how Jesus, the apostles, and other witnesses ministered to those around them in all walks of life.

John 4 tells us that Jesus was leaving Judea and traveling through Samaria on his way to Galilee. He came to a town called Sychar, which was near Jacob's Well. Jesus, worn out from his journey, sat down at the well. A woman of Samaria came to draw water (John 4:1-26).

This is the backdrop to one of the most surprising gospel conversations we find in all of Scripture. Jesus initiates by asking this foreign woman for a drink. She was in shock; "How is it that you, a Jew, ask for a drink from me, a Samaritan woman?"

Forget the drink. Jesus immediately responded, taking her completely off guard again, "If you knew the gift of God, and who is saying to you, 'Give me a drink,' you would ask him, and he would give you living water."

When she asked about this living water, he surprised her with a knowing intentionality that once again, broke all the rules, "Go call your husband," he told her, "and come back here."

"I don't have a husband," she answered.

"You have correctly said, 'I don't have a husband,'" Jesus said. "For you've had five husbands, and the man you now have is not your husband. What you have said is true."

Jesus' discourse was full of the gospel, completely attentive, personal, full of compassion, direct, and to the point, while at the same time, wildly surprising. Do we have this kind of intentionality in our intercession, and in our gospel conversations? Do we really believe that the gospel is able to reach every crevice of a person's life? Jesus did. As crazy as this conversation was, it was definitely going straight to this woman's heart.

She responded in the only way she knew how, eerily reminiscent of conversations I regularly have with neighbors who like to take the conversation back to similarities and differences in our beliefs. "Sir, I see that you are a prophet. Our fathers worshiped on this mountain, but you Jews say that the place to worship is in Jerusalem."

Undeterred, Jesus responded with astounding, almost shocking, clarity, "Believe me, woman, an hour is coming when you will worship the Father neither on this mountain nor in Jerusalem. You Samaritans worship what you do not know. We worship what we do know, because salvation is from the

Jews. But an hour is coming, and is now here, when the true worshipers will worship the Father in Spirit and in truth. Yes, the Father wants such people to worship him. God is spirit, and those who worship him must worship in Spirit and in truth."

The woman said to him, "I know that the Messiah is coming (who is called Christ). When he comes, he will explain everything to us."

Driving this truth home, Jesus reached her heart, "I, the one speaking to you, am he."

Jesus proclaimed the gospel to this woman in ways that quite honestly blow my mind. It certainly wasn't culturally appropriate. And it represented incredible and miraculous spiritual insights into this woman's life and soul.

Jesus exemplified for us here, in an amazingly powerful and provocative way, exactly what it means to be fluent in the gospel. When God leads us to proclaim the gospel, he will empower us.

The Bible says the disciples were amazed that he was talking with a woman (v. 27). We read that the woman left the jar and went and told the men of the town about Jesus, "Come, see a man who told me everything I ever did!" (vv. 28-29), and they all came to meet with Jesus. This all feels very counter-cultural, yet so amazingly powerful. This is the power of the gospel as it reached the heart of this woman and radiated throughout her whole community.

Did Jesus in fact tell this woman everything she had ever done? To her understanding, he did. The gospel reached every meaningful recess of her heart. The gospel has the power to reach into our lives and expose everything we have ever done, felt, or thought. It has the power to reach everyone and meet every need in all circumstances, and through all cultures, no matter how surprising. This is the radius of the gospel.

Jesus was deeply satisfied to be doing this work of the gospel, "My food is to do the will of him who sent me and to finish his work" (v. 34). The will of God is for us to proclaim and teach the gospel. By the power of the gospel, God draws men and women to himself. We sow and reap spiritual fruit. Jesus said to his disciples, "Listen to what I'm telling you: Open your eyes and look at the fields, for they are ready for harvest" (v. 35).

What are we expecting in our ministry? Should we be ready for the unexpected? Jesus crashed into the common culture, inviting people – in strong encounters like this one at the well – to drink living water, and to respond to the truth of the gospel. He knew people – intimately. He knew their lives, communities, and cultures. He knew their problems, their pain, their sins, their secrets, their shame, their trappings, the deepest longings of their hearts, their deepest questions, and even the questions behind their questions.

The woman asked, "Give me this water," and Jesus responded, "Go call your husband." Everything he said to her peeled back the layers of deception, grief, shame, pain, sufferings, and deep longings... he nailed it.

"That's fine," we may say, "but I'm not Jesus. I don't really know my neighbors' deepest problems, pain, sins, and secrets." Perhaps as we begin to tap into tap into Christ's love for our neighbors, when we just love them with his compassion, we begin to know them less as we would and more as he does. We begin to see the gospel less from our own perspectives, and more from his, as the shepherd who seeks his lost sheep (Luke 15:4) or as the father who runs to embrace his lost son. "But while his son was still a long way off, his father saw him and was filled with compassion. He ran, threw his arms around his neck, and kissed him" (Luke 15:20).

It is absolutely impossible to ignore the simple, profound compassion that permeated all contexts of Jesus' ministry (Matthew 9:36, Mark 1:41, Luke 7:13, etc.), inviting him in so many amazing ways into the painful, sinful, grief-filled lives of those around him.

As Jesus was leaving Jericho, two blind men sitting by the road cried out for mercy. Though the crowd rebuked them, they cried even louder, "Lord, have mercy on us, Son of David!" (Matthew 20:29-31).

Jesus stopped, called them, and said, "What do you want me to do for you?" (v. 32).

Wasn't it strangely obvious to Jesus and everyone else (us included) that these blind men simply wanted to see? But Jesus still asked. He wanted to hear it from them. And I think this has a lot to do with the compassion he had for them.

"Lord," they said to him, "open our eyes" (v. 33).

Moved with compassion, Jesus touched their eyes. Immediately they could see, and they followed him (v. 34).

When we compassionately proclaim the gospel to our lost neighbors we begin to know them and love them as Jesus does. That's how Jesus lived, and that's how we should live, too. We are called to follow Jesus. We are called to proclaim the gospel. We are called to host the presence of God as we live and learn about life in our new language and cultural setting, and as we get to know our new neighbors.

Our lives truly intersect with the world around us, the world God called us to, in powerful and true ways, in ways that demonstrate spiritual integrity when we hone in on the gospel. Are we orienting the core of our lives to the gospel? Until we view the gospel as the center of everything in our lives, then our entire global and cosmic orientation remains faulty, worldly.

After his resurrection Jesus instructed his disciples to stay in Jerusalem. They asked him again about the restoration of the kingdom of Israel. Jesus then told them the Father's master plan for the kingdom, that by the power of the Holy Spirit they would be his witnesses in Jerusalem, Judea, Samaria, and to the ends of the earth. We stake our lives on the truth of this verse. This is our commission. This is the ever-widening radius of the gospel. This radius is both geographic and ethnic in nature. The following illustration represents Acts 1:8.

Acts 1:8

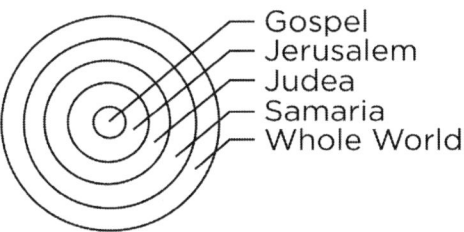

I believe this expanding radius of the gospel is also very personal in nature. As the gospel changes our lives, and as we are called to proclaim the gospel to our lost neighbors, and then to their neighbors, in and through just about every walk of life conceivable, we get a micro-view of this ever-expanding radius of the gospel. As the gospel is spreading to all peoples, it spreads from neighbor to neighbor, and from community to community. And we are personally responsible to be a part of that process.

Our neighbors are found in all domains of our lives. They may live in the apartment next door to us, or across the street. They may be people we work with or buy from. They may run the fruit stall or drive a taxi. We may learn to use specific language with each of them, as they do with each other. But, in every situation, every relationship, and through all conversations, we can build bridges to the gospel in these daily encounters.

The gospel is at the center of everything in this world that has eternal meaning, and this begins with our personal understanding of the gospel in our own lives: our personal testimonies. We can confidently, boldly, and joyfully proclaim what God has done and what he is doing in our lives, that he saved us and is saving us, and that he speaks to us every day from his word. Indeed, we must daily consider the revelation of the glory of Christ to us through the pages of Scripture. This is the gospel to us, for us, and for those around us. "The glory of Christ is actually blaring from the pages of the Bible. God is not only NOT giving you the silent treatment, he is practically yelling."[18]

We hear and speak the gospel through the amazing testimony of Scripture and the witness of our lives. And we are responsible for bearing that testimony before our neighbors. The gospel reaches our lost neighbors through our testimony of the gospel. We proclaim and teach the gospel to those who are lost, so that they may be saved. And they are responsible to tell their lost neighbors. This is how the gospel reaches the world. This micro-view of Acts 1:8 may look something like this:

Gospel Radius

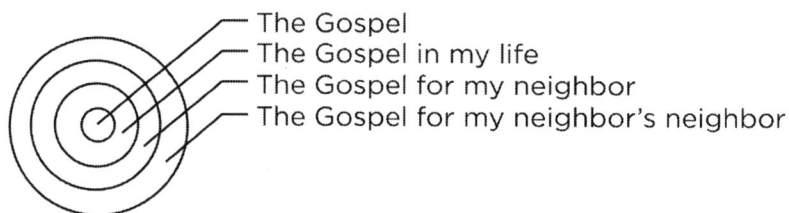

The concentric circles of identity and relationship begin with the gospel as core to all that has eternal meaning in the world. It is core to our identity and to our relationship with God. The gospel radiates from our proclamation of the word of God and from our testimony, reaching our neighbors through all life circumstances and situations. The gospel reaches into and redeems every part of our lives. The gospel is not just a concentric ripple. It is a vector that has the power to reach in and transform every part of our world and the world around us. Is it possible for us to be *that* aware of the ever-permeating effect of the gospel as we carry the very presence of God into all areas of the lost world God has called us to reach?

We are called to love our neighbors, which means we tell them the gospel because we love them. Where I live, that almost always means over tea, through shared life events, and usually involves family members and neighbors. I've heard this referred to as the *enlistive blessing of God*. I call it "the gospel for my neighbor's neighbor."

"Come and see," Philip answered (John 1:46). Andrew and Simon were brothers, and Philip and Nathaniel were friends, and they were all neighbors from the same hometown, Bethsaida. Jesus invited Andrew to come to his home. Andrew then invited Simon to meet Jesus, whom Jesus then named Peter. Jesus then called Philip to follow him. Then Philip invited Nathaniel to come and meet Jesus (John 1:35-51). Each invitation led to an invitation, which probably led to another invitation.

Mustard-Seed Gospel

He presented another parable to them: "The kingdom of heaven is like a mustard seed that a man took and sowed in his field. It's the smallest of all the seeds, but when grown, it's taller than the garden plants and becomes a tree, so that the birds of the sky come and nest in its branches" (Matthew 13:31-32).

I recently had tea with Metin and his contractor, Ziya, who is also one of the elders of our house church. Ziya remodels houses. Metin has several houses in the area and entrusts Ziya with all the work he does to them. Metin has cancer and probably doesn't have long to live. Ziya and I prayed for Metin as we drank tea. We prayed for healing. We prayed he would receive salvation through faith in Christ, the ultimate healing for his soul. I was so thankful that Ziya sees his business as a place of ministry to guys like Metin.

Jesus described the kingdom of God as a mustard seed. When planted, it grows into a tree in which birds nest. When we sow the gospel into the lives of our neighbors, we are communicating the living word of God that has a compounding spiritual effect upon their lives as they receive the word of God.

We are sowers of the word of God. We need to understand our identity within this paradigm as we learn the language and communicate the gospel. As we consider the gospel for our lost neighbors, we need to have a healthy understanding of our calling to personally take the gospel to them, to know their names, their situations, their languages, their cultures, and their communities, for the purpose of communicating the good news.

Whoever sows bountifully, reaps bountifully. Whoever sows sparingly reaps sparingly. There's a certain risk in sharing the gospel with new neighbors in uncharted conversations. We exercise faith as we consider the radiating and permeating effect of the gospel in all situations. It's usually easier to brush off potential opportunities that may seem off-topic, rather than pursue them right then and right there.

One of Ziya's employees is from an unreached minority ethnic group. Not long ago Melih had a serious accident at work requiring extensive surgeries on his hand. As he recovered at home, Ziya invited me to visit Melih and his mother. We shared the gospel with Melih and he translated into his mother tongue for his mom to understand. Ziya lives out the gospel as he works with Melih and the other guys. He is not just their boss. He in many ways is like their older brother. They listen, watch, and take it all in. Ziya is sowing seeds of the gospel into Metin, Melih, their families, and so many other neighbors at work and through his business.

One of the things I really appreciate about Ziya is that he is quite aware of the gospel at work in the lives of his neighbors, customers, and employees in everyday ways. He is learning to present the gospel and that's one of the reasons he invites me to come along. As I disciple Ziya, we pray for his neighbors, and we pray that we can share the gospel clearly and boldly with them. For Ziya, this means living and sharing the gospel at work and at home. He can't see it any other way. That encourages me to be more aware of the activity of the word of God in the lives of my neighbors in everyday situations. We see this in the ministry of Jesus.

Jesus dined with tax collectors and Pharisees. He broke bread with his disciples. He met people at their places of work. He talked with farmers and told them about the kingdom of God using farming analogies. He talked to rich people and challenged them to follow God by selling their possessions. He rebuked other rich people for their greed in comparison with the generosity of a poor widow. He blessed children, raised dead sons, taught people in their homes, and taught them in his home. He attended weddings, had late night discussions, and asked for water on a long hot day's journey.

How can we present and proclaim the gospel well in all circumstances? How can we view the centrality of the word of God in all seemingly tangential topics and discussions? How can we learn about life and culture around us so that we understand how the gospel is reaching our neighbors through the stuff of their lives?

I recently received a phone call from Ziya. He was on his way to our city to visit Metin in the hospital. Metin was close to death. His wife called for Ziya to come. They had no one closer they could turn to during this time of fear and grief. Ziya then called me. I was honored to join these precious friends at Metin's bedside as once again Ziya shared the hope and comfort of salvation in Jesus Christ with Metin and his family. As we talked and prayed over tea before leaving the hospital I was reminded of how only God could orchestrate all this because he loves us so much.

Bridges

What would be natural bridges to the gospel for every topic that I engage in? And how would I get to the gospel from that topic? (Josiah Daniels, co-worker)

When we think of the radius of the gospel, we need to understand that it has an all-pervasive effect on every area of our lives and the lives of our neighbors. Do we believe this? Do we live with this kind of expectation? Do we learn and practice language with this understanding? This takes faith, boldness, and creativity.

As we consider sharing Christ with our lost neighbors, how can we grow in our understanding of gospel-relevant themes, so that our gospel-sharing is conceptually more connected with where they are?

We are not just trying to build bridges to the gospel. We need to understand and believe that they are already there. We simply need to discover them and find ways to cross them. "Indeed, the Lord's arm is not too weak to save, and his ear is not too deaf to hear" (Isaiah 59:1).

Consider the common ground. What did we fear? What did we long for? What godly sorrow did we endure (2 Corinthians 7:10) that brought us to repentance? Ultimately, we find common ground where the Spirit of God is at work in the soil of our neighbors' hearts. The Bible describes four kinds of soils, referring to four kinds of people. Three soils produce no fruit. They hear the gospel but do not respond in repentance and faith. Only one soil produces fruit that leads to repentance and faith. The good news is that the gospel bears fruit in the rich soil of repentant souls (Matthew 13:8, 23). The transforming work of the seed of the gospel produces faith in this soil – in our lives, and the lives of our responsive neighbors. This is good news!

We have assurance of God's salvation. And because of this we personally identify with this soil, the soil of the soul who hears the word of God and repents, because we are also of this soil. Our testimony bears witness to the transforming power of the gospel in our lives. And we have great hope that God is at work in the lives of our neighbors who identify with our testimony. Our attention is to their heart-cry. When people are prompted by the Holy Spirit, when they are convicted by God's word, we see the fruit of deep interest in the gospel and begin to see the fruit of repentance. Those wooed by God to his kingdom, when they hear the gospel, may ask themselves, "Could this be true?" For this is good news. It is the deepest desire of our hearts, and theirs. "You want to know where God is working? Share the gospel and you'll find out" (Mark, co-worker).

My wife, Jenn, looks for all kinds of bridges to share the gospel with our neighbors, whether through art, crafts, music, or simple life stories. Recently, she created a wordless tract illustrating the tragic yet beautiful life and death of a young child – a child who could easily have been one of our neighbors' neighbor. As we've shown this tract to different people, reactions have ranged from weeping to sharing a personal experience. Everyone identifies with it in some way. It's amazing how one simple story made up of a few illustrations and no words (except at the end) has opened the door to so many amazing gospel conversations.

Color (not visible here) first appears in the tract as a red heart and red cross on the leaflet the little boy finds. As he reads it and believes, the little boy and everything around him become full color. All is radiant as Jesus receives the boy's soul into in his arms, while the boy's body remains a black and white shadow in the box. The tract concludes with these three gospel passages on the final page:

> For God loved the world in this way: He gave his one and only Son, so that everyone who believes in him will not perish but have eternal life (John 3:16).

> For by grace you have been saved through faith. And this is not your own doing; it is the gift of God, not a result of works, so that no one may boast. For we are his workmanship, created in Christ Jesus for good works, which God prepared beforehand, that we should walk in them (Ephesians 2:8-9).

If you confess with your mouth, "Jesus is Lord," and believe in your heart that God raised him from the dead, you will be saved. One believes with the heart, resulting in righteousness, and one confesses with the mouth, resulting in salvation. For the Scripture says, "Everyone who believes on him will not be put to shame." For everyone who calls on the name of the Lord will be saved (Romans 10: 9-11, 13).

Spheres of Influence

We have a finite number of people that we can invest in. Are we willing to lay down our relationships in our home community in order to create space for new connections, relationships, and identity, within our new language and culture community? (Josiah Daniels)

Our neighbors rarely evaluate Christianity by reading about it. They watch us. They talk with us. (Timur, national partner)

There are two simple facts that influence our ability to reach our lost neighbors with the gospel. These are simple, but important for us to consider: First, we need to know our neighbors, and allow them to know us. This means meeting them, and spending time with them. Second, we need to be able to talk with them. This means engaging them in all sorts of conversational topics, however mundane. These two essentials help prepare the soil for fruitful gospel encounters.

If we don't know our neighbors, chances are we won't be able to share Christ with them very well. We really need to get to know them. This means spending time with them. Let's stop there for a minute. Do we even have time for our neighbors? Are we prepared to make hard choices to spend time with them, in our new language, which may mean less time talking with our friends and family back home?

This may require significant lifestyle changes on our part. This may take effort for us to intentionally set aside time, to say "no" to our preferred social media and reach out to new friends in our new language, in their social networks, and face-to-face.

This takes deliberate effort. We really need to reach beyond just superficially knowing our neighbors. We need to show a genuine interest in their lives, their interests. We need to pray for our neighbors, ask God to show us how he is involved in their lives in big and small ways, and consider how we can share the gospel with them. "Therefore, whether you eat or drink, or whatever you do, do everything for God's glory" (1 Corinthians 10:31). No topic is too shallow to reach nor too distant to bridge to the gospel. No situation is beyond the wide radius of the gospel.

John Piper wrote a prayer in the form of a poem entitled "How to drink orange juice to the glory of God" where he says that everything in our lives – even the mundane – comes from God and gets its proper meaning from how it relates to God.

> Father, every good gift is from You.
> Even the ability to receive them is from You.
> We love to declare our dependence on You
> For the smallest and greatest things.
> Grant that nothing in our lives
> Will be disconnected from You.
> Make us conscious all the time that
> Everything gets its proper meaning
> From how it relates to You.
> May it be our joy to join our orange
> Juice – and everything else – to Your grace.
> With overflowing thanks, we pray, in Jesus' name.
> Amen.[19]

I love this prayer! If we think about it, everything in our lives truly relates to the gospel and we need to learn to "join our orange juice – and everything else" to God's grace. As we live in thanksgiving for God's grace in all things, we proclaim the gospel through all things to our neighbors.

It's easy to get into a rut talking only about a few things that we prefer to talk about, that we are comfortable talking about. Most of us tend to be this way. But if we push ourselves to talk about lots of things, generally our ability to speak or converse in our new language blossoms. We need to learn to talk about lots of things. We need to learn to talk about orange juice.

I had a friend in my city give me some great advice as I was learning the language. "Talk about anything and everything with people you are getting to know. If you show an interest in everything about their lives and talk about everything in your life, and don't hesitate to talk about God, it will become clear to you and your friends how God is at work in every aspect of their lives and yours."

This advice helped me be purposeful and keep moving forward in the language, enriching my relationships with people more broadly and deeply. How did I go about doing this?

I began to observe what was going on around me more intently, carrying a notebook, taking notes, and writing down questions that came to mind as I noticed things. This would help me be more prepared at any time with things to talk about, and questions to ask, as I had conversations with people.

I began reading things about the culture: articles, short stories, magazines, and current events from newspapers, even cutting out and using pictures as conversation starters.

I began listening more to the radio and following TV and online programs in the language, starting with the basics – headlines, a few words here and there – enough to launch me into conversations about specific topics.

It's amazing how asking open-ended questions on so many topics seems to touch everyone's life in some way. I found that following my friend's advice not only improved my language ability but provided great invitations into peoples' lives and opportunities to see God work in their lives.

Our lives intersect with our neighbors in multiple overlapping spheres or segments: work, school, religion, family, community. People buy, sell, care, host, converse, argue, love, play, cry, and laugh together. Life happens in community. We are family and we have family. We are neighbors and we have neighbors.

The New Testament refers to some of these spheres as households (Acts 16:31-34). We call them "life circles" where I live. These are the *liminal* "coffeeshop" spaces where neighbors meet, the intersections of life where the dynamics of community take place. Life happens here, and God takes us into these life spaces to be with people – our neighbors – to engage them, in big ways and small ways. God invites us into his redemptive work in their lives through this dynamic of life-in-community, however great or incremental, obvious or hidden.

C.S. Lewis exhorts us to a Godward perspective in our daily interaction with our neighbors, reminding us that indeed there are no ordinary people, just as there are no ordinary moments we have with them. Every person is an immortal, and every moment with them, truly, is a gospel moment. "There are no ordinary people. You have never talked to a mere mortal. Nations, cultures, arts, civilizations – these are mortal, and their life is to ours as the life of a gnat. But it is immortals whom we joke with, work with, marry, snub, and exploit – immortal horrors or everlasting splendors."[20]

We should never diminish the amazing redemptive work that God is doing in the lives of our neighbors as we engage them in daily life. We need to commune. We need to love deeply. And we need to learn the language of the mundane that may open doors to those grace-filled day-in and day-out orange juice experiences we share with our neighbors.

Reflect and Respond

1. Reflect on this statement: I didn't share the gospel today because it didn't come up in our conversation; we were talking about other things that weren't relevant to the gospel.

2. Respond to this question: How can the gospel be a part of every conversation?

3. How are you investing in the lives of your lost neighbors? Do you have time for them? Do you engage in many and varied conversations with them?

4. Take a moment to pray for opportunities to share the gospel with your lost neighbors through all walks and conversations of life.

6

Responsive Listening

More than half of the task of communicating the gospel in other languages and cultures is listening to the response of people when they hear the gospel, understanding their response so that we know that they are understanding the gospel, and then engaging them meaningfully with the gospel. (JB)

I am finding that even though I am starting to understand what people say, I often misunderstand what they mean. (Steve, first-year learner)

We're not speaking to brick walls. (Sean, co-worker)

Go, ask questions, and listen. (Bill, co-worker)

I watched and listened as Dinch shared his faith with Erol – Bible open, asking questions, inviting Erol to tell his story, finding points of connection, probing, and persuading Erol to a walk of faith in Jesus Christ. Dinch shared his faith regularly. He was eager to read Scripture, pray, and share his testimony with neighbors, tapping into their hunger for God.

On the ride home Dinch and I reflected on our conversation with Erol. Dinch helped me connect the dots between the gospel message and Erol's situation. Dinch seemed to have a knack for knowing how to reach into people's lives. Something he said made me think long and hard. Dinch told me the main reason he asked so many questions and dug deep with Erol on certain issues was because he wanted to be sure that he was understanding Erol, and that Erol was understanding him.

That's right – my national partner Dinch, in talking with Erol in their heart language, needed to make sure Erol had understood him. I had to have him explain to me what he meant. Dinch wanted to ensure the message of the gospel was clear, not just from his perspective, but from Erol's as well. He wanted to make sure Erol understood what he was trying to communicate. For that reason, Dinch said, he did his best to patiently and wisely attend to Erol's responsiveness. How did Erol understand the gospel from Dinch's witness? Dinch's aim was to clarify the gospel, as much as possible, for Erol's understanding, not just for his own.

I came away from that experience contemplating my level of language and gospel fluency in my new language. I thought I had been doing rather well. Dinch's convicting words set me back on my heels. Was I truly listening to my lost neighbors when I shared the gospel with them? Was I understanding their responses? Was I attending to their responses? Were they hearing the gospel, really?

We often think we are communicating more than we really are. The message of the gospel is communicated not only in the words we say. It is also, essentially, communicated in how we understand and respond to our hearers, as they hear the message, to be sure they understand the message. How can we better listen, understand, and attend to their responses to the gospel? How can we effectively understand and respond to our lost neighbors when they inquire about the gospel? This is the art and practice of *responsive listening*.

Responsive listening is more than just a surface understanding of what people are saying. We may think we understand people. But the truest test of comprehension is not in our passive understanding of what people say, rather in how honestly we verbally and non-verbally attend to what they say, responding meaningfully and appropriately. When we engage in gospel conversations with our lost neighbors, in their language, our helpful and instructive responses to their questions and thoughts will demonstrate whether we truly understand them. This not only demonstrates our language ability, but also provides evidence toward applying godly, prayerful wisdom to our responses.

We must learn to listen and respond to how people receive the message of the gospel. Otherwise, we risk misunderstanding what people are hearing, and therefore miscommunicating the message of the gospel. To listen with understanding and to respond with godly wisdom are precious jewels in our language learning, cross-cultural evangelism, and disciple-making; arguably more challenging to master than speaking, and in some respects more valuable.

Listening: The Fountain Head of Gospel Fluency

If anyone is thirsty, let him come to me and drink (John 7:37).

God speaks to us from his word and by his Spirit. We need to listen. Jesus invites us to drink deeply. Jesus went on to say that he who believes "will have streams of living water flow from deep within him" (John 7:38). We hear and attend to the word of God as it reaches deep into our souls and are compelled to tell the message of the gospel to those around us. I've heard this described as living out of the overflow of the gospel in our lives. This image beautifully captures a faith-filled posture of *responsively listening* to God's word.

This posture compels us to press in and listen, to tune-in, and attend to the message of the gospel. Our hearts and minds are quickened with sharper conviction, assurance, compassion, and authority. As we listen to God speak to *us* from his word and by his Spirit, we believe he is *also* ministering to our neighbors in ways that only he can do. God invites us to enter into this ministry through prayerful awareness and hope-filled anticipation.

And as we hear from God and trust that he is at work in the lives of our neighbors, we approach listening to our neighbors with a deeper awareness of God at work in their lives. We practice *responsive listening* right then and there, in those moments we engage them, hear from the Lord, and share the gospel.

Our speaking skills are sharpened when we enter any conversation with a heart to understand the perspective of our hearers. This requires sympathetic awareness and understanding. As we learn to attend to those around us, we develop a cohesive posture of listening and speaking that helps us engage our neighbors with the gospel. Language is a paradox: Our best posture of speaking is one that attends well. Our best posture of listening is one with a compelling message.

We have a couple at our house church who listens well. They listen. They pray. They ask questions. They offer encouragement and advice. They share Scripture. Then they listen more. I love watching them in action. They provide amazing counsel for many believers. But they do the same when they share their faith with non-believers. And it's amazing to see the response. People open up. They share their burdens. They receive prayer gladly. They are comforted because someone has heard their story. And they respond to the gospel.

Listening is a huge investment. It is diving into the deep end of our conversations and discussions. It is total immersion – in our own language, tiring; in another language, absolutely exhausting. It takes total intentionality, requiring undivided attention, interpreting, question-asking, confirming, hypothesizing, re-confirming, adjusting, exploring, and more listening. The more we hear, the more we realize how little we know of the person, and of the situation. We keep digging, learning more.

This kind of godly listening can be done in homes, over tea, in casual settings. People who may normally be somewhat closed to the gospel open up when they know someone cares enough to listen to them. This is often where people first really hear the gospel. Hearts soften and ears become attentive when people realize someone cares enough to listen and respond. One of the best ways to open up a flow of honesty and receptivity within our gospel conversations in our new language is to practice the art of listening, to make space to hear what people are really saying to us when we share Christ with them. I thought of Dinch and Erol. Listening really is the fountain head of gospel fluency.

The Gospel is a Lamp

Take care how you listen (Luke 8:18).

Shining the light of the gospel into lostness calls for a deeper observation, a practice of spiritual discernment, a habit of listening and responding. We, in our own strength, ultimately cannot discern how a person receives the word of God. Only the Spirit of God illuminates.

What is hidden will be made known, what is in the dark will be illuminated. As I understand the integrity of the gospel (Luke 8:16-18, Mark 4:21-25) we carry this lamp initially for our deeper awareness, to see and hear what we need to perceive and understand, to reveal what has been concealed, and to boldly proclaim the gospel with the godly and sympathetic compassion of Christ.

Responsive listening skills help us develop insights into the culture. This is huge within any dialogical context, but especially as we practice evangelism and discipleship in our new language. We develop insights into the culture. We begin to understand communication nuances and apply them with greater fluency.

Listening is hard work. Listening can be especially difficult cross-culturally in another language. Learning to listen and to appropriately respond is often more challenging than learning to speak. Learning to hear and understand heart-level issues, and then to respond to them with biblical and relational sensitivity, can be a painfully slow and difficult process.

Responsive listening is a skill that only comes through hours and hours with people in tough communication situations during which we develop listening skills and are able to practice responding to people in ways that are culturally meaningful, biblically sound, and full of godly wisdom.

As we are called to proclaim and teach the gospel, we are called to enter into our neighbor's lives and engage them in these conversations critical to the gospel, and critical to their lives. We are called to pray, teach the gospel, listen well, and respond with understanding, as people hear and respond to the gospel. How can we become fluent listeners in our new language? How can we learn to respond with anticipation and sympathetic understanding as the Holy Spirit works in people's lives?

As we proclaim and teach the truth, how can we seek to understand our neighbors and respond to their needs with sincerity and empathy? How can we effectively grapple with our bent toward conceptual rigidity and reach beyond our cultural myopia to truly understand our neighbors' view of the gospel in the reality of their own lives and situations? We must find a way forward toward greater fluency in our *responsive listening,* toward understanding and attending to their response to the gospel.

First Responders

What they wanted even more [than the help that we were prepared to give] was for someone, anyone, even a stranger who was still trying to learn their language, to sit for a while, or just stand with them, and let them share their stories.[21]

As I write this my wife is visiting one of the first neighbors we befriended when we arrived to our city many years ago. Suna's and Mahmut's youngest son was the same age as one of our boys and they became friends. Doctors found a tumor in Han's brain and Han soon passed away. We were devastated. We grieved with our friends, prayed for them, and sadly watched them sink into a dark place which nearly disintegrated their family. Suna has always been open to Jenn's friendship, almost like a beacon in the night.

Every time they meet for tea, Jenn engages as a first responder. She just knows Suna cannot continue to cope without Jesus, so Jenn reaches out, prays, listens, and responds. God has used this ministry to bring Suna to a place where hope begins. Jenn continues to meet with Suna, praying that God would fully bring Suna to a place of faith in Christ. "The person of the Holy Spirit gets us ready. He prepares us. He speaks to us even as we are conversing with our neighbors" (Jenn).

Engaging as a first responder means we are there, at the scene. And it also means we do what we can. We have no agenda. We come to listen. We empathize. We pray. We share words of comfort and the hope of the gospel. Often this is best expressed through the simple questions we ask – What happened? How do you feel? What's the most difficult part for you? – and, more importantly, how we choose to listen, just listen, as people respond.[22]

The Bible describes Jesus as knowing the thoughts of people's hearts (Luke 9:47). He had compassion, and he acted on it with godly understanding. One of our biggest opportunities is also one of our biggest challenges. When we respond to people in need, we will hear problems, issues, concerns, questions. When we share the truth and share in the ongoing life-changing effects of the gospel, in our lives and theirs, people's lives change. We must be attentive. We must be responsive listeners. This is hard work. This is the work of the gospel. "It's hard to believe in someone you don't know, but when you finally realize who God is, you won't want to follow anyone else" (Jenn).

People are hurting, desperate, and in pain. They need to know who God truly is. They need to recognize their need for his saving grace. They need to confess their sins. Behind the layers of sin and doubt, they long for the salvation, assurance, and hope that only the gospel provides. God calls us to listen and respond. But God doesn't leave us to ourselves.

When we attend to those responding to the gospel, when we seek to listen to them with understanding, we can trust that God is in the conversation. He knows our hearts, and he knows theirs. When we listen to others, we must first listen to God. He ministers to us through his word, by his Spirit. He gives us insight and understanding as we listen and respond to our lost and hurting neighbors. Our words – those we say, as well as those we hear – are powerful when they are expression of our hearts' intent, our will, our agreement, and our faith.[23]

Zephir tripped and fell right in front of Yuri's house on her way back from the market. Yuri and his invalid wife Nelli host a small house church in a village near our home. Zephir and her husband had recently arrived with their grown son and had not met their new neighbors. Yuri saw what happened and quickly ran out, helped her up, gave her a glass of water, and invited her in to rest and talk with Nelli who was lying on the sofa.

Nelli asked a few questions and it didn't take long for Zephir to open up about the grief she felt because of her son's addictions, and the personal emptiness she felt in her heart. Yuri told me that from the moment he came to Zephir's aid, he sensed the guidance of the Holy Spirit in their conversation, providing insight into what God was doing, right then and there, in Zephir's heart.

We listen to what God is saying to us through prayer, through his word. This plays out in how well we listen to those we engage. As we engage them with the gospel, we need to be aware of how God is involved in the heart-level communication; how he is wooing people to himself, and how he is using us in that process. We need to be spiritually attentive.

Zephir prayed to receive Christ that evening. And Yuri continues to spend time with her wayward son, mostly just listening.

Into the Unknown (Ethnography 101)

While Paul was waiting for them in Athens, his spirit was troubled within him when he saw that the city was full of idols. So he reasoned in the synagogue with the Jews and with those who worshiped God and in the marketplace every day with those who happened to be there (Acts 17:16-17).

Observation and inquiry were a profound part of Paul's strategy for ministry as he traveled to new places and encountered new cultures. In Acts 17, as Paul waited for his team to meet him in Athens, he was aware of the surrounding spiritual darkness. His spirit was disturbed within him. Not simply a reflection of his opinions, judgments, or assumptions, this was a deeper awareness that could have only come from God, from a certain spiritual sensitivity placed on his heart by God (Acts 17:16).

How did Paul respond to this spiritual darkness? Scripture says he walked into this unknown situation with eyes wide open. He prayerfully observed, listened, inquired, conversed, reasoned, learned, and taught. Every question he asked and every observation he made were bathed in prayer with keen awareness and faith-filled anticipation to introduce the gospel (Acts 17:17-34).

Though ridiculed and misrepresented – a risk we all face in situations like this – Paul was invited to speak more. God was opening doors. And through Paul's posture of ministry and learning, he was able to speak to the Areopagites at the point of their understanding. He preached the gospel to them based on what he understood they believed, an awareness that certainly emerged from prayerful observation and inquiry.

Paul's response to the sense of need God had put in his heart led him to this understanding. He entered Athens as uncharted territory. It was a foreign city with foreign beliefs. Aware of his surroundings and the spiritual realities they represented, Paul did not make off-handed assumptions. He wanted to get it right. He wanted to understand what was going on. We see that Paul prayerfully engaged. He watched. He asked. He listened. He learned. He brought people into the discussion. He reasoned with Jews, devoted Gentiles, people in the marketplace, and philosophers (vv. 17-18).

Paul introduced the gospel to the people of Athens with a keen sensitivity to their cultural vantage point, but also very aware that the gospel was new, strange, and in so many ways entirely counter-cultural to his audience.

Paul's invitation was like no other. He knew their hearts. He knew their quest to find true meaning. He knew their despair. They sought what they did not know. God used Paul to bring pagan philosophers into a deeper awareness of the "unknown" God for whom they searched. We learn from the passage that many walked away. But many believed.

Paul observed a completely foreign situation with godly discernment and responded to those around him with godly insight. As we enter into the cultural unknowns around us, we, too, are called to observe and respond with godly wisdom and insight as we engage the lost around us. "The purpose of a man's heart is like deep water, but a man of understanding will draw it out" (Proverbs 20:5).

As I passed his office on my way to work one day my accountant neighbor Hasan called me in to show me his broken fish tank. Sometime over the weekend while he was out and the office locked, his fish tank had mysteriously cracked from one side to the other and the water and fish had spilled out onto the new wood-paneled floor. Hasan reached down and showed me water damage that was already beginning to appear, shaking his head, concluding, "Someone vexed this office with the *evil eye*."[24]

The evil eye? Really? I confess, I was surprised and confused to hear this coming from a successful accountant. He couldn't have been more serious. "It is the look. Not what is seen, but what is looked at," as he proceeded to explain that obviously some of his neighbors must have been envious because of the new floor renovations. "Energy went from their eyes," pointing with his finger outward from the corner of his own eye, "and entered into this fish tank, causing it to crack precisely while I was gone," preventing him from being able to save the fish and keep the floor from being damaged.

Hasan had done everything he could to prevent this. He had strategically placed glass beads throughout the office, downplayed every compliment given about the fish tank and the new floor, and tried to make sure that no one – especially anyone jealous or angry –was able to release negative energy in his workplace.

Wow, what a complicated, fearful existence! It seemed Hasan's prime task in life was to protect against this ever-present evil. I began to notice just how pervasive this sort of practice was. People wore little pieces of glass resembling misshapen weird-colored eyes on their clothes, inscribed them onto objects, and pinned them on baby blankets. These eyes seemed to show up on every door, home, office, apartment, entry way, floor, sidewalk, store, decoration, piece of jewelry, and greeting card...they were everywhere! One thing was clear: my neighbors really wanted protection from evil.

Belief in this metaphysical malevolence, this evil, permeated everyday life. Accidents were attributed to the force of the evil eye: slips on the sidewalk, car accidents, sicknesses, broken fish tanks. Bad things happened to people because evil caused the bad things. Bad things were only avoided when protection against the evil causing the bad things actually worked.

This wretched fear-filled existence defined much of what my neighbors believed about the causes and effects of everything going on around them. I began to understand how people around me lived in fear, all the time. Their lives were consumed with trying to ward off the powerful effects of evil. But nothing could actually take away this fear. The fear itself seemed to fuel their vigilance to stay alive. Fear may have kept them alert to the ever-present threat of evil but robbed them of any peace they could ever hope to experience. And this was this world I had entered.

Getting to *Why* (Ethnography 102)

> *Evil eye*: An impersonal, amoral force responsible for misfortune, applied to objects both animate and inanimate, providing meaning to people's lives in the sense that it creates a cause-and-effect explanation, perhaps even an underlying connectedness between the metaphysical and physical realities of the universe.

My encounter with Hasan reminded me that things are not always as they seem, especially for those of us entering new cultures and learning new languages. Whether it was the fear of the evil eye, or some other deep belief or worldview that formed who my neighbors were, what they did, and what they believed, I wanted to do whatever I could to reach an understanding of those *whys* in their lives. Working definitions like this one (above) certainly provided a good starting point for me to roll up my sleeves and begin to navigate the beliefs, traditions, and practices that enveloped the world in which I lived. But it was in actual conversations with my neighbors where I could ask the honest questions that helped me get to *why*. Did my understanding even vaguely represent the reality in which they lived? If so, how then could I reach into that world and begin to discover the *why* beneath so much of the *who, what, when, where,* and *how* I was seeing and hearing all around me? Not surprisingly, conversations with Hasan and other neighbors about these realities led to many more "broken fish tank" stories. All I had to do was ask.

> Have you personally experienced the effects of this evil power? Can you describe your experience? Where and

when did it happen? How did it happen? Were you able to protect yourself from it? If not, could you have protected yourself from it? Can you avoid it? What works? What doesn't work? How does it work? What does it do for people? Do you believe it works as protection against evil, or is it just superstition? What do your parents believe? What about your grandparents? How long has this horseshoe been over this door? Is it traditional to use colored pieces of glass and horseshoes as protection against evil? How do you know when something bad happens because of evil? How do you feel? How would you protect yourself or others, such as your children or relatives, from evil?

"Years ago, as a child I was sick. We had no medicine. My parents and grandparents read the holy book and then blew on me. I somehow survived. We are now educated and have medicine, but I still do it all."

"From your eye comes energy. That's the evil. It's very real. And that's how it works. The first time you look at something, energy passes from you to that thing. If the energy in your glance is negative then it could somehow destroy whatever you look at, unless it was protected by a specific object or action."

"The reason that is there [pointing to a blue eye painted on a truck] is because that is exactly what people see when they first look at the truck. It protects the truck from envy. It protects the driver from accidents."

"We still like to give beads to one another as gifts, for sentimental reasons, but also to preserve the tradition of believing in cosmic protection, whether or not we truly believe it."

"It's tradition. It's just a little piece of glass on your clothing. It's like footballers kissing their shoes before the big match. I don't believe it actually protects us.

People like to use these little blue glass beads because they are pretty and traditional. But, let's not forget, belief and tradition are mixed. If people stop believing, then tradition dies. That's not good."

"My grandparents used to force me to wear a blue bead until I reached the age of ten. It's a tradition. Sometimes, I still put the blue bead on my son."

"This horseshoe has been over our door for 40 years. Do I believe it keeps the evil away? I don't know. Some people believe and some don't. It's tradition. It's good luck."

"Sometimes we don't want our kids to play on the street, so we say something like, 'There's a crazy person down the street!' and this will make them afraid and they won't want to go outside to play. Or, if our kids are eating candy before bedtime, instead of forcing them to spit the candy out, we might say, 'The ghost of your ancestors will get you if you don't!' Of course, we don't believe this, but they are influenced by it."

"I believe in evil, sure. But I don't think there is anything I can to do avoid it."

Responses like these emerged from many conversations with neighbors, helping me to understand just a little bit more about their fear of this metaphysical evil power, and the all-consuming burden they carried to protect themselves against it. I began to see how these beliefs and practices were deeply woven into the fabric of their lives and culture. When asked, some acknowledged the power of the evil eye, while others dismissed it. But it seemed everyone respected or at least practiced the *tradition* of believing in the power of the evil eye and doing all they could to protect themselves against it. Perhaps this near-universal will to sustain the tradition and practice of warding off the evil eye represented a deep-set fear that even influenced those who brushed it off as mere superstition.

I have come to these insights cautiously and carry them gently as I continue to ask questions in an effort to peel back the layers of this evil, fearful world in which my neighbors live. I realize how much more I have yet to uncover. Asking my neighbors open-minded questions starting with the surface realities of daily experience that can lead to deeper questions of belief and worldview helps me to better understand them. As I've said, I just ask the questions. They tell the stories.

Asking questions and listening to responses are some of the best ways to begin to understand how our neighbors think and feel. This all starts with the power of wonder. As we suspend our preconceived ideas and assumptions to more fully participate in the amazing newness of life happening around us, do we wonder, "What is this?" or "What could this mean?" with a heart and mind to really learn from our neighbors? As we engage them in basic *who, what, when, where,* and *how* questions on all life topics, do we anticipate hearing everyday life stories within the texture of their responses? Can we begin to envision the deeper *whys* that may define what they believe and how they think?

As we attend to that which is going on around us and really listen to what our neighbors are saying – their interests, concerns, passions, and beliefs – we indeed find opportunities to dive a little deeper, beneath the surface of basic conversations, to understand more of the *whys* that encompass the contexts of their lives. Our ultimate desire is to understand and to then engage the spiritual needs of our lost neighbors, waiting expectantly upon God's grace as we introduce the gospel and invite them to respond.

Not long after my conversation with Hasan about the fish tank I was asked to help at a youth camp where kids from all over the country came and brought their friends to hear the gospel. On the last night of the camp, one young man who had recently put his faith in Christ shared his testimony before the group. He like so many others had grown up surrounded by what he could only describe as a resident evil power that had consumed his life and home with fear. He had literally lived in constant fear his whole life. And then he talked about the gospel in his life; how he came to faith in Christ, and how God had miraculously taken away his fear and replaced it with peace, concluding, "Could this even be possible?" The whole room grew quiet. Young people throughout the room began weeping. What this young man shared that night ministered to every heart. This is one of the most amazing realities Christians in my part of the world can share with their neighbors. God removes our fear and gives us peace.

Navigating the unknowns of our new cultures and languages with suspended prejudice, careful observation, insightful questions, and attentive listening requires dedicated practice and prayerful awareness. I have tried to learn all I can from people I've seen doing this well. They know how to engage in meaningful gospel conversations precisely *because* they have learned to observe, ask questions, listen, and understand their neighbors and the contexts in which they live. They practice gospel fluency by demonstrating the power of listening. Here are a few of my favorite examples of fluent listening practices.

Question Approach Index (QAI)

Years ago, I was introduced to David Penny's *Question Approach Index*[25] which addresses the value of asking questions in our new languages and cultures both for learning purposes, and also for identity, community, relationship, and ministry purposes. This approach helps us understand how to become a good listener by becoming a good question-asker. The QAI offers ten reasons why we should ask lots of questions:

1. Using questions disciplines one to go slow, be respectful, and not jump to conclusions. Right from the beginning, it demands that we be a listener. It gives us a chance to learn more as we go, whether language, culture, truth, or other. Using questions nurtures a learner's spirit, letting us presume our target knows more than we do. It encourages us to be humble. It calls for a proper attitude.

2. Using questions protects us from declarative statements which can seem proud, aggressive, and presumptuous. It helps us avoid getting too far ahead of where our neighbors are and diminishes the likelihood of offensive remarks.

3. Using questions honors our neighbor's interests in the conversation, inviting them to take the discussion where it needs to go.

4. Using questions invites our neighbors to wrestle with and discover the truth themselves as they answer our questions. It allows them to go as far as they can while giving us the chance to lead them a little further in the truth by means of another question, *might it be...?*

5. Using questions forces us to determine what is worth asking, what is worth following up, and what should be the focus or direction of our inquiry as they guide and provide direction into conversations with our neighbors.

6. Using questions limits our words and helps us choose more carefully the best way to say something, what is of value and importance for the discussion and what is of greatest importance to the individual concerned. One can greatly influence a discussion with a few, well-chosen words.

7. Using questions puts a gentle burden of responsibility on the one who answers to demonstrate that he has sufficiently understood the areas being addressed.

8. Using questions helps our neighbors be more forgiving and understanding when we make errors or cultural blunders. This is essentially because the nature of a question-asker is less threatening, like the role of a learner or foreigner who still has much to learn. In short, being a question-asker gives us room for a few errors.

9. Asking questions offers a strong appeal without forcing our views upon anyone. We are called to persuade our lost neighbors to hear and respond in faith to the truth. Asking questions is a winsome way to do this.

10. Using questions allows our neighbors to redirect the conversation when it reaches a level they cannot sustain. Unlike the use of declarative statements, which can easily drive a conversation to an abrupt end or in an unhealthy direction – especially when using a new language – we are less likely to run aground with questions.

These are all great reasons for us as language learners to make a habit of asking questions. The more we ask, the more we get to hear responses. This, then, gives us great opportunities to practice our listening and our responsiveness to many topics and life situations. We want to learn to engage people in topics of deeper interest. Asking questions is one of the best ways to jump-start this learning process.

Using questions can be a great way to open the door to the gospel. In many languages and cultures people commonly respond to questions with questions. For example, a reasonably common response to a simple question such as "Where are you from?" may be "Where do you think I am from?" (communicated in a light-hearted manner, as in, "Guess where I am from!") In our part of the world, questions about faith are common, "Are you a Christian?" It makes a lot of sense to ask something like, "What do you mean by Christian?" This sort of interrogatory response can open the door to a gospel conversation. Jesus commonly asked questions to get people to think about eternity. "What will it benefit a man if he gains the whole world yet loses his life? Or what will a man give in exchange for his life?" (Matt 16:26).

Any 3

Any 3 is an evangelistic method developed by Mike Shipman using a rubric of specific questions designed to lead anyone to Christ, anywhere, anytime.[26] It's a five-step process that goes through a series of questions, responses, and transitions, leading up to the telling of the *First Sacrifice* and *Last Sacrifice* stories. *Any 3* begins in Step One with questions to help us get acquainted and connected with people. Questions such as "What is your name?" or "Where are you from?" often can transition to more specific questions related to responses. "Are you (Hindu, Muslim)?" In Step Two we may ask, "Most religions are alike, aren't they?" Responses at this point can begin to get more complicated. We may ask a transition question at some point, "In your religion, what do you do to receive forgiveness?"

Any 3 can quickly get us into great gospel conversations. The more language we know, the deeper and wider our conversations can go. *Any 3*, while typically not viewed as a listening practice or strategy for evangelism, in fact, is. The better we understand the conversations we are having, the deeper and wider we can go in sharing the gospel. Indeed, probably the one thing *limiting* our ability to effectively use *Any 3* is our ability to *understand* and appropriately follow-up on responses to our questions, especially as they go deeper and become more complicated.

Any 3 provides great opportunities to practice listening to those with whom we are sharing the gospel. Learners who are working on their listening skills have often found *Any 3* most helpful when they can first practice using it in a controlled setting with a language partner. This is a great way to become skilled in using the method, and also a great way to practice listening and responding to all kinds of answers to important gospel-oriented questions.

An alternative to practicing with a language partner in a controlled setting is accompanying a language or ministry partner in real-life *Any 3* evangelism settings. As we ask questions, and lead people through the discussion and inquiry, and into the sacrifice stories, we can be learning right along with our partners better ways to use the method, especially toward understanding people's responses to the questions. That is, as people respond, this may adjust how we attend to their responses. The best way to learn to do this is alongside a national partner who more fully understands the meaning of the responses, and can model how to better attend to those responses as we together learn to apply the method in meaningful ways.

Discovery Bible Study (DBS)

The method is simple; people are complicated.
(Joe, DBS practitioner)

I've had a bit more experience with the *Discovery Bible Study*[27] method than I have had with other methods, so I'm going to spend a little more time considering how *DBS* can be used as a disciple-making practice, especially as our language listening skills grow.

DBS has been passed around quite a bit and I was most recently re-introduced to it through its use among refugees in a large Eurasian city by my friend, Joe. (So, Joe, you get the credit for this version of the model.)

By learning to ask a few simple questions when studying a Bible passage with groups of new believers and seekers, *DBS* is a great way to develop responsive listening skills. Joe usually starts by asking, "What does the passage say?" This helps people talk about the passage thoughtfully, in their own words. Then he may ask, "What do we learn about God?" This is usually followed by, "What do we learn about people?" To encourage and instruct people to apply the word of God in faith to their lives he may ask, "What do we need to obey?" This encourages accountability and setting goals. Finally, he may ask, "Now what do I need to teach others?" This encourages people to immediately reproduce what they are learning.

DBS is an elegant and reproducible model that plunges us into high-risk interpersonal communication situations. The questions are simple, but the responses will usually be complicated, because people are complicated. And we need to understand their responses. What I mean is, we as facilitators need to be able to understand more than just the questions we ask or the answers we anticipate. We need to understand the varied responses people give, responses we may not anticipate.

I asked Joe at what point he felt he could do this. Joe shared this endearing story with me. He was teaching some disciples in his new language to put on the character of Christ, and to love their wives. He could not understand why some of the married men still beat their wives after teaching them that this was sinful and not Christ-like. Their response helped him see that the problem was not in their disobedience to the teaching, rather in their inability to understand this teaching in their cultural context.

So when he gathered with them again, Joe circled back to the teaching and invited them to talk more about it. Once they were able to really address the issue from Scripture as a group, together with Joe, they began to really work through the importance of not beating one's wife in light of God's word. For many of these men this was a hard teaching to work through, but once they understood God's word they were able to begin to walk in obedience.

Our task is more complex than just telling people what the Bible says, or just telling them what to do based on our understanding of the Bible. There are so many layers we need to understand: the nuances, the culture, the worldview, the sin, the assumptions about acceptable behavior, beliefs about what is right and wrong. Perhaps a better way to approach the task would be to ask, "Do you understand what the Bible is telling you to do?" Or perhaps even, "How do you understand what the Bible is telling you to do?"

With these questions, we enter into discussions that lead us to better understand typical responses we are likely to encounter. We, as much as possible, need to understand the process of discovery our neighbors and disciples experience as they encounter God's word. This may differ from culture to culture and language to language. God is at work in their minds and hearts, as he as at work in ours. And he's using us to teach people in and through this process, as they hear the gospel, repent, obey, and develop Christian character. Joe described this as reaching a point where he understood and appreciated their cultural themes, what they thought about, what they felt. He began to understand DBS responses better as he was able to more and more engage them in heart-level conversations. Joe summed it up well, "I remember the first time I heard an Arab laugh and actually understood why he laughed."

DBS has been instrumental in helping Joe and many others facilitate discipleship and start churches all over the world. But it's endearing to hear Joe say that it also helped him get to know these guys at a deeper level, to understand them when they shared things beneath the surface of shallow conversation.

Inviting neighbors and disciples to respond to our questions, core to the DBS setting, means that we need to be fluent in our *responsive listening*. This is significantly more challenging than mastering our speaking ability. It requires an ability to make sense of and follow-up on what people are saying to us in the discussion about the gospel and how it applies to their lives. We can never assume that what we are saying and teaching is being understood the way we intend. And the only way to confirm this is to invite response, understand that response, and meaningfully attend to that response.

What a great opportunity for us to practice listening! The efficacy of the DBS approach largely depends upon our ability to understand what people are saying, and upon our ability to interact with them in meaningful, clear, and helpful ways to facilitate their understanding of the Bible. Whenever we engage our neighbors as seekers or new believers using DBS in our new language, we are stretched to understand their responses within their cultural contexts. In other words, as teachers or facilitators we need to understand how our neighbors and disciples respond to that which we investigate together from God's Word. The more we listen, understand, and meaningfully respond to our precious neighbors as we work through the DBS process together, the more they can begin to understand how the gospel applies to their lives, how to search it out, and how to pursue God in his word, every day.

Story Crafting and the Art of Listening

There was a definite process by which one made people into friends; it involved talking to them and listening to them for hours at a time. (Rebecca West)

In chapter 4, we discovered the value of asking ourselves the following questions when crafting gospel stories. We never just tell stories to ourselves. But we often need to practice telling them by ourselves. These questions help us consider our audience, anticipate their response, and practice as if we are really telling the story.

> What did you like about the story?
> What bothered or confused you about the story?
> What does this story show you about God/Jesus?
> What does this story show you about people?
> If this story is true, what should you do to obey God?
> How will you remember this story?
> Who will you tell this story to?
> What is the most important point of this story?

As it turns out, one of best ways to engage our neighbors with the gospel when we tell them simple stories from scripture is to actually ask them these same questions.[28] We can often discover whether people are truly hearing the gospel by the responses we receive to the questions we ask. If we ever wonder whether people hear and understand the gospel we share with them, all we have to do is ask. They'll tell us. So, what does this require of us? We need learn how to ask, how to listen, how to understand, and how to respond. This all takes time, practice, and intention. As we tell simple gospel stories, we need to embrace the perspective and posture of the listener, not just the teller. Sure, we are called to tell the Good News, but we are also called to listen and perceive how people *hear* the Good News.

Why is this so important? Any time we practice the art of listening as we pursue gospel fluency – whether we tell a Bible story, share truth from scripture, ask questions, practice Any 3, or use DBS – we are learning what it means to compassionately invite people to respond to the gospel. At the root of all interpersonal inquiry are the life stories to which people relate. We never ask questions in a vacuum. There are always stories behind them. As we share the gospel with our neighbors, we have great hope that God is already at work in their lives. God is also very much at work in our lives, helping us to tell, ask, and listen. As we share the gospel, we also prayerfully tap into power of spiritual inquiry and discernment as God indeed helps us learn what to ask and how to listen. God helps us to understand the stories of people's lives, and he helps us to understand their responses to the gospel.

Will we make mistakes? Probably. Will we always understand people in our new languages? Likely not. This is a learning process. We cannot become fluent in the gospel in our new language using these types of engaging approaches unless we practice using them. And in our practice, we will undoubtedly encounter struggles and misunderstandings. However, those we disciple will respect our struggle, if our intentions remain true. Joe testified how God used his faithful efforts, "When they see us making an effort to understand, they make an effort to be understood."

Whether we tell stories, use DBS, or practice Any 3, or enter just about any gospel conversation that involves questions, we're going to hit learning curves, face frustrations, and be forced to navigate ambiguities. Thankfully, God redeems our efforts, and brings people alongside us who can help us comprehend, disciple, and provide much-needed godly counsel from God's word. This is how the body of Christ works. And this is the active grace of God in our lives as we faithfully move forward in the language. We are bold, but we are feeble, and that combination represents our strong courage in the Lord. Through our example, people will be encouraged to grow in the Lord and to help others.

We make every effort to teach well, knowing that our friends, neighbors, national co-workers, and disciples will almost always have better language and cultural understanding than we do. This is a noble pursuit. We boldly enter into tough teaching contexts with the goals to teach well, listen hard, get input, and pass the baton, empowering those around us through godly wisdom, grace, and encouragement, rejoicing as they exceed us in their ability to disciple others. It is our faithful efforts, including our limitations, that will help us to do this. We will always face a certain amount of breakdown in nearly any robust language endeavor, probably most especially in the area of responsive listening. But this may be the most fruitful breakdown we can experience as we leverage it toward improvement. As we engage our neighbors, let's make the most of story crafting, DBS, Any 3, QAI and other effective, reproduceable gospel fluency methods that can help us learn to speak *and* listen well, so that we can share the gospel well.

Reflect and Respond

1. Consider one way you can more actively listen to people when you talk with them.

2. How do you respond and attend to your neighbors when you hear their difficult life stories?

3. Do people open up and engage more when you ask them questions? Describe how this has worked, or how it might work in your context.

4. Take a moment to pray for spiritual insight and fluency to more meaningfully listen and respond to your neighbors in the language.

7

LQ

The responsibility rests firmly on the learner's shoulders. A language is learned rather than taught.[29]

We may have strong intentions to learn a language, but many of us struggle with what that really means, or what it's going to take. We need to begin to understand that we are never truly "taught" a new language, rather we personally and actively *learn* it. And the responsibility for learning a new language is ours and ours alone. That's a pretty simple truth, but it's so easy to forget, especially in the middle of daily language learning challenges. Personal responsibility is also the most important component to intelligent and faithful language learning. We need to understand what it means to really practice intelligent language learning in order to learn the language well, in order to reach *gospel fluency*.

"LQ" stands for Language Intelligence. Our personal LQ has far less to do with cognitive aptitude and far more to do with our power to discover and harness language resources we all have within us and around us. Intelligent language learning is made up of a combination of mindset, desire, skills, knowledge, strategy, and appropriate action. What does it take to be an intelligent language learner?

One of our greatest assets that compels us to be intelligent language learners is our calling to share the gospel with all peoples. We have a strong desire to learn the language of our lost neighbors, for the purpose of sharing the gospel with them.

But intelligent language learning is more than desire. Intelligent language learning includes the knowledge and strategy to wield that desire into action. And, perhaps most important, it essentially includes the investment of actually doing it. We can have all the best vision, motivation, knowledge, and strategy in the world, but without actually putting it into practice, we might as well go home.

One of the most effective entry strategies I have found is one that pushes us to do what perhaps we didn't think possible – to learn enough of the language within a reasonably short period of time, whereby early on we are able to actually generate conversations in the language on a variety of predictable and familiar topics.

From Zero to Basic Conversational Fluency

I recently spoke with a group of newcomers entering new language settings. Each of them was a top-shelf candidate eager to learn. I asked them to articulate their goals, and they all responded by saying they wanted to learn as much as possible as quickly as possible. Several were parents with young children. At least one couple expected to manage a full-time business. I weighed their eagerness against the challenges. Young families? Starting a business?

I thought, what if they agreed to do whatever they could to fully invest in language for the first few months? Most people can make significant adjustments to family and business needs if they know there is a goal to reach and an end in sight. The bigger question was, how much could they actually learn in a defined amount of time? Would they be able to reach *basic conversational fluency* in, say, 90 days? 120 days? 180 days?

Reaching basic conversational fluency is without dispute the single most important first-step as we consider our language learning task toward reaching *gospel fluency* (see Appendix 4, *Twelve Weeks to Basic Conversational Fluency*).

What does basic conversational fluency mean and how do we get there? In other words, what does it mean to be able to carry on a basic conversation with reasonable fluency? More important, what does it look like to learn and practice language toward reaching this level? How do we stay on top of each activity and make the most out of our review so that we remain focused and confident in our progress?

It is essential that we have a clear understanding of each step along this path of fluency. Reaching *basic conversational fluency*, at least on a functional level, can be best understood as a step on the path toward more and more functional discourse in using the language.

Of even greater importance is recognizing the value of reaching a basic level of conversational fluency for the purpose of engaging in some entry-level cross-cultural ministry in the language. Essentially, our long-term aim is to reach basic *gospel fluency*. But this starts with reaching *basic conversational fluency*.

The following graph illustrates the generative effect of reaching a level of language in which creative expression yields basic conversational ability, which grows in discourse complexity as we continue learning the language and sharing the gospel with our lost neighbors through all areas of our common experience.

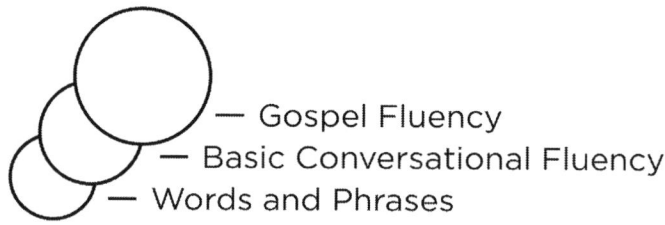
— Gospel Fluency
— Basic Conversational Fluency
— Words and Phrases

We need to start with the assumption that many of us, perhaps most of us, are naturally not very intelligent language learners. We do not have a strong understanding of what we need to do when we start learning a language. And even if we do, we generally don't know how to invest our time and energy well, with quick and lasting results.

I hated high school French. I always seemed to get stuck in the remedial classes with the worst teachers – poor me – and I ended up just as you would expect, a poor student. I learned very little language, and mostly just remember staring at incomplete exercise books that would eventually have to make their way to the blackboard. I listened to the upper level students actually carrying on conversations, and wondered, "How did they do that?" I had no idea how to get there.

I want to remind us all that we can do better than that. We can become intelligent learners. We can make life choices, develop patterns of thinking, and create pathways of learning that get us from zero to fluency. We need to be prepared to do things differently, in more innovative ways than many of us have ever done before. We can create a learning environment in our lives where we actually learn the language.

I want to take a serious look at the language learning plans we consider well before we actually engage the speech community, how we put those plans into practice beginning with day one, and how we keep moving forward each day after that for the first few months. We need specific plans that will quickly and efficiently help us reach *basic conversational fluency*.

Basic language skill development means we create and build onto meaningful communication foundations that are simple in structure, yet generative in nature. The natural process of learning a language begins with the use of simple words which form and grow into meaningful phrases, short and simple sentences which grow into complex sentences and structures, and simple familiar-themed paragraphs which grow into complete stories and discourses. Most significantly, it is the centrifugal force of regular and varied conversations we have with lots of people in the language that promotes this growth.

Soon after meeting with the group of new learners I mentioned at the beginning of this section, I wrote this note to them:

> The first few days, weeks, and months in the language are critical. Our incentive to learn is at an all-time high. We are ready and willing to invest. We're willing to push through barriers, try new things, and work hard. We want results. We want to get the language. But we need to remember that equally important are those days which come long before day one in our new language. It is that day when we capture a vision to learn the language. It's that day when we can see ourselves gaining the knowledge and skills, devising the strategy, and tackling the project. It is those days when we can begin to articulate why we really want to learn the language. Then we can begin to seriously consider how we plan to learn it. This is intelligent learning. And it all starts well before we learn our first word.

One of the realities we struggle with, especially among faith-based organizations, is somehow failing to seriously consider the actual capacity we have as learners to reach basic conversational fluency within truly foreseeable amounts of time – weeks and months, not years.

Recalibrating Progress

Intelligent language learners think of progress measured in weeks and months, not years. More specifically, for intelligent learners, time does not even necessarily mean progress. While it may sound nice, lots of time may actually be hurting us by fostering inefficiencies. "Work expands so as to fill the time available for its completion" (Parkinson's Law).

Don't let that happen to us. Wouldn't we like to get to a place of confidence and satisfaction in our language learning as soon as possible? Let's consider learning as much as we can, as rapidly as we can, and as efficiently as we can. Let's consider a 90-day challenge.

A quick internet search will bring up any number of language sites promising fluency in three months. While this sounds too good to be true, there is something to say about an initial push in language that enables us to quickly reach *basic conversational fluency* on predictable and common topics. Wouldn't that be great? There is something deeply satisfying when we reach a difficult yet attainable goal like this through a lot of hard work and sacrifice. Moreover, a basic level of fluency provides the foundation and traction we need to keep going. This would be a great investment of our first 90-days in our new language.

So, can we do this? I mean, is it really possible? I think it is. But it may mean looking at language learning in a more robust way. Some call this language hacking. Mark Zuckerberg, founder and CEO of Facebook, defines hacking this way: "The Hacker Way is an approach to building that involves continuous improvement and iteration. Hackers believe that something can always be better, and that nothing is ever complete."[30]

As intelligent language learners, iteration and continuous development become our primary path to rapid improvement, no matter how counter-intuitive they may seem. We become what I describe as *language minimalists*, suspending our needs for completeness, exactness, and perfection, and making the most of every resource right in front of us that we are able to utilize. We deliberately strive to get more from less, especially during that first 90-days of learning. Charles Kraft describes the very capacity of our inexperience as that which casts us into this role of learner: "We pretended no more. We expected to make mistakes, did, and received correction with a minimum of embarrassment. We were unashamed to be utterly dependent and often wrong."[31] Consider how the following description may help us understand how we can squeeze everything we can out of our initial learning endeavors:

> Intelligent language learners as "language minimalists" enter a speech community with the goal to reach "basic conversational fluency" as rapidly and efficiently as possible through focused relentless extended linguistic interaction. Never to be daunted by gaping errors in speech and comprehension, language minimalists quickly create spaces for controlled practice by hiring native speakers for real-time feedback, correction, and editing; and they make the most of powerful vocabulary practices including memory techniques and spaced learning. They ransack grammars for just-in-time lessons and leverage daily life experiences to create pungent content for here-and-now language learning charged with high-return, real-to-life high-participation language activities.

This makes me want to ask: What's keeping us from trying? Are we possibly victims of *Parkinson's Law*? What do we have to lose, to give it our best shot to make this work? To help us get out of the gate, I want to consider a few lessons and goals for our first 90 days that could help us to keep moving forward. The 90-day goal: *To reach basic conversational fluency.* The projected outcome: *To creatively tell a simple familiar story in our own words.* Consider the following from my own new language experience.

Going into my new language on day one, I wrote out my first 14-day goal: "I will meet people, get around, do basic tasks, and learn language while using the language to accomplish simple survival tasks."

I worked through some basic introductory survival lessons within the first two weeks. These mostly included survival expressions for everyday life, such as greetings ("Hello, how are you?"), introductions ("My name is..."), maintenance phrases ("Please repeat"), and simple questions, ("What is another word for...?")

I did these initial lessons with my language partner during a dedicated time and space using simple yet powerful communication methods including: *dynamic repetition; associations; Total Physical Response* (TPR) or listening while silently processing, and then physically and non-verbally responding; *roleplays; substitutions;* scene, event, and process *descriptions; procedures; interviews;* and *story-telling.* In-language *dialogue* with some sort of meaningful response (even non-verbal) was a necessary part of every lesson. (More complete definitions of these terms and samples of these lessons can be found in Appendix 4.)[32]

Is dialogue even possible on day one? You better believe it is! That was part of the problem with my French class. It wasn't conducted in French, to begin with, and I was never forced to be mentally and socially engaged in the language. Friends, if we're going to *learn* a language, we need to be *in* the language from day one!

In these language sessions with my partner, I received rapid exposure to new words and phrases through powerful methods of direct association using great memory techniques. I worked all of this into my *daily life situations* through comprehensible role plays and graphic descriptions of simple scenes and events, all by design, to flood my mind with readily-understandable input using here-and-now commands generating physical response ("stand up, walk to the door"), pictures, wordless books, stories, toys, videos; basically, anything that could help me associate the language I was learning with the life I was living.

After a few months, one of my 14-day goals was, "to understand and to simply describe basic familiar scenes and events from my life in the language." What this meant was that after several months of powerful exposure and language use, I was poised to reach a point where I could understand and describe basic familiar scenes and events from my life in simple, clear language. This laid the foundation for the creative expression I needed to reach *basic conversational fluency*.

My Son and the Big Boy at School

I practice journaling. Early on in my new language, just a few weeks into my learning, I was prompted to relate some of the events recorded in my daily journal to my language partner. He asked the simple question, "What did you do yesterday?" That's a powerful conversation starter. We sometimes just have to be forced to respond. I improvised. I simplified. I made mistakes. And that's just the point. This was a good place to generate, to create, and to work through what

I wanted to say with the simple language I had. My partner was there for me, to help me clean up my mistakes, and to help me work on my expression until it made sense, until I got it, one familiar description at a time. How can we envision this kind of practice in this kind of creative space with our language partners, working through simple descriptions and narrations of life events? Here's one from my journal:

> Yesterday when my son came home from school he told me what happened that day. There is a big boy at school who has no friends. This boy has no friends because he likes to hit and push other children. He is lonely. My son played with him today. While they were playing the other children laughed at them. But then other children started to play with them. The big boy had fun. He did not push or hit any of the children. They laughed and played together. They enjoyed playing together. I asked my son, "Why did you play with the big boy?" He said, "Because Jesus loves him and I want to be like Jesus." I was happy to hear this.

Mark 2:1-12: Jesus Heals a Paralytic

I wanted to be able to share the gospel from the Bible – simple familiar stories starting with those that have straightforward action, characters, and dialogue – stories that clearly communicate the gospel, that I could tell my neighbors right away. In Mark 2:1-12 (also found in Luke 5:17-26 and Matthew 9:1-8), Jesus forgives a paralytic his sins, and then he heals him. I live among people who believe Jesus was a miracle-performing prophet, but they do not believe he is God. They do not believe he can forgive sins. In this passage, Jesus confronts the disbelief of the religious leaders who watch him forgive and heal the paralytic. I wanted to be able to tell this story. I wanted my friends and neighbors to hear this story. I wanted them to understand that Jesus could forgive their sins and heal them.

I chose this passage primarily because it was simple and I was familiar with it. It has relatively few characters, a simple plot, and few complicated events.

I read the story first in English, and outlined it with notes, listing characters and events.

I then read the story in my new language. Pause for a second with me. This – reading the story in my new language – was nothing short of a huge victory, a breakthrough point for me. After months of slogging through new language – all these new words, phrases, sentences, and descriptions – I was finally at a point where I could actually understand a simple Bible story. I knew my calling, but now I was beginning to live it. I could take the training wheels off. My enthusiasm went through the roof when I was finally able to read a familiar story from the Bible in my new language, and actually understand most of it!

Just as I had done in English, though much more simply, I took notes, made an outline, and listed characters and events. My goal was to be able to re-tell the story in my own words to my language partner.

I kept the story simple as I told it. For example, instead of saying, "And Jesus, knowing their thoughts, said..." I worked on, "Jesus knew their thoughts. Jesus said..." This helped me learn new words and grammar, but it also allowed me to use simple grammar and vocabulary which I already knew, yet still tell the story in a meaningful and clear way.

The characters in the story were: Jesus, the Pharisees, other people in the house, friends of the paralytic, and the paralyzed man. The story breaks down into events which are active, and parenthetically reported, which illustrate a significant verb distinction in my new language:

Jesus was teaching – the people came – (the Pharisees and people were sitting) – (the power of God was present) – men came with a paralytic – they tried to enter the house – (they could not enter because it was crowded) – they went to the roof, dug a hole, and lowered their friend – Jesus said, "Your sins are forgiven" – the Pharisees thought, "No one can do this except God alone!" – Jesus knew their thoughts... Jesus said, "Which is easier to say – your sins are forgiven or get up?" – So, he said to the paralytic, "Get up..." – immediately, he stood, took his bed, and went home praising God – everyone was amazed and praised God.

This was one of many ways this story could be re-told. I presented this aloud to my language partner, using these notes as an outline to help me tell the story. My partner helped me say it better. I had him tell it back to me, and then recorded his voice so I could re-listen to the story in simple beautiful form. In this way, I worked with my language partner on this story, and other stories. I wanted to be able to tell these stories to my neighbors.

I am disheartened when I hear language learners describe unsuccessful attempts to use programs, try techniques, go through lessons, or check off goals, when they fail to realize that it is not the programs, lessons, techniques, goals, or strategies that yield success. Lessons like the one I just described above serve to help us improve, only to the extent that we are truly invested in the language we are learning, and in the people who speak it. Recall: all vision, plans, and strategies – everything we we've talked about here – including the lesson examples I provide above from the 90-day program, while significant as resources for intelligent language learning, still basically provide only the window dressing. Real change happens as we invest in learning new language, not through simply going to class or doing a program, but through the hard work of creative expression. We invest in reaching *basic conversational fluency* not through completing a series of lessons, but through immersing ourselves in the community of people who speak our new language, day in and day out. Measures of investment like these form the foundation of our language intelligence. These we need to thoughtfully pursue.

Creative Expression

I recall the first time I shared my testimony in another language. I was sitting in a taxi in Bangkok, Thailand with a sheet of notebook paper in my hand. On the sheet was scribbled about ten sentences that somebody had translated for me earlier that morning. I recited it over and over until I had memorized it. I tried to make it sound fluent. After some "taxi talk", I asked if I could tell a story. I held the paper in front of me and raced through all ten sentences, barely taking a breath. My taxi driver patiently asked me to say it again, only this time in my own words, so he could understand me. I learned a valuable lesson that day about the importance of presenting the gospel in a person's heart language, from the heart.

There is a big difference between saying something that we've memorized and putting together phrases and sentences in creative and meaningful ways with words we know. Both communicate a message, but one sounds rote – because it is – while the other is truly generated from our own thoughts. Language is not simply stacks of memorized phrases. It's not like we're building with Lego. Language is generative, interactive. One simple phrase, like a living cell, can reproduce into a thousand other expressions.

As we connect initial encounters with meaningful words, phrases, idioms, situations, and as we associate these experiences with our long-term memories, those mental, sensory, and emotional pathways that make up how we create vibrant memories with feelings and thoughts will be activated and used more and more. This takes practice and is like working a muscle. We need to develop our memory, and it will improve. Learning language is less about efficiency, and more about memorability.

Our minds are wonderfully able to remember things, to capture new data in a moment, and move it from the temporary storage of complex cognitive information – *working memory* – to the storage and retrieval of information beyond the initial few seconds – long-term associative memory. We do this all the time when we want to remember things – something someone said, a phone number, words to a song. And we do this deliberately and consistently when we review notes for a class or study for a test.

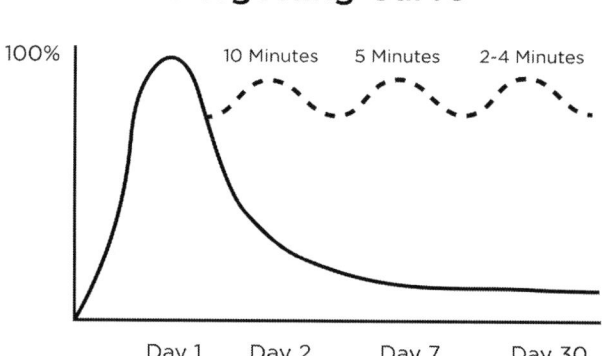

If we don't practice recall with regular review, we tend to forget. The dark line on the graph is the *Forgetting Curve* which represents what happens when we fail to exercise our ability to remember things. We forget almost everything we do not consciously try to remember.

The dashed line on the graph represents the application of *spaced learning*. Spaced learning is a method in which content is repeated or reviewed several times, deliberately interspersed with diversions and activities including rest and sleep. The practice of spaced learning helps us remember better and more easily.

Strategic-repetition practices like spaced learning are designed to get shorter and easier with each successive review. Consistent review minimizes the carnage of our poor memory practices by helping us practice associations and create better long-term memory storage. "Our memories are vast interlocking webs of data. They are like thick robust branches, and more and thicker branches means easier recall."[33]

Memories connect with our senses. We see them, hear them, feel, them, taste them, even smell them. Memories have meaning and personal relevance. We always have some sort of emotional attachment to our memories. We are able to, in a sense, relive our memories. We can, with practice, experience some memories as if we were in the moment. In other words, our minds actually have the capacity, at least to some extent, to re-activate our working memory by reliving long-term memories that just need more reinforcement. "Every time we recall information from long-term storage into working memory, we re-learn it."[34]

We can learn to apply this as we learn our new language, by attaching words and phrases to meaningful and sensory-driven experiences we re-live with our language partners. We may have shared stories that we tell again and again, stories that bring up sensory-driven memories and feelings.

This is especially helpful with familiar stories that have deep and personal meaning to us, such as gospel stories. We have so much texture with which to remember these in a new language when we listen to them and learn to re-tell them.

So how do we then move from memorized phrases to creative expression? As described, our brains are good at grouping things that seem to go together. We do this naturally by association, which is all a part of our memory process. We more easily remember groups of things, like kitchen utensils, or furniture items.

This is also helpful for combining words, phrases, and sentences into whole ideas. If we know the words, and meaningful combinations of them, our brains will prefer the meaning of entire topics, rarely focusing on the meaning of individual words.

We see this manifest in our selective attention when a few words or images are selectively removed from an entire scene or story. We don't even notice they are missing because we are not interested in the words themselves, rather in the entire meaning they convey. In normal life, we do this all the time. We filter out words we see and hear to get to the meaning behind what is being said. The following popular little puzzle illustrates this. Read the sentence below once through (without overthinking it) and then quickly count how many f's you see.

> Finished files are the result of years of scientific study combined with the experience of years.

How many did you see? Most people see three. Some see four. Only a few actually see six. Most of us filter out the "of" words. Words used to communicate an idea or topic are actually quite random, at least according to the way our brains work. Imagine looking through a windshield in a car. We see the road, not the windshield (unless we are intently looking at the bugs or cracks). This is because we focus on what is meaningful. If we focused on the windshield while driving we could cause an accident by not focusing on the road. When we drive, we don't even see the windshield, we see the road. Our brains do the same thing with ideas. We don't care about the words, we are more interested in the meaning of those words.

Words themselves are ultimately not our focus as we learn meaningful utterances in our new language. Instead, we are able – and actually prefer – to mentally process entire meanings of combinations of words and phrases.

This is true for how we learn to tell stories, provide explanations, or teach lessons. The orators and bards of old did not focus on the words, *ad verbatim*, when they prepared and presented orations. Public speakers today still focus on the *res*, the meaning behind the words, or the part that takes up meaningful residence in our brains, a specific *topos* ("place") from which we get the English word "topic." The best memory and speaking strategies used throughout the centuries thrived on *meaning-based extemporaneous speaking skills.* We need to practice these skills in our preparation and presentation of all discourse topics as our language improves.

What we're talking about here is the art and practice of creative expression. When we speak *extemporaneously*, we are allowing the topic or thought to reside in our brains as we try to communicate the ideas through the creative combination of words. We may even have notes, but our focus is on the meaning. The words are free-flowing, the discourse cohesive. It has the feel of being prepared, but not polished; vigorous, yet flexible, adaptable to the context.

Extemporaneous communication has a strong interest and confidence in the *res*, the topic of delivery. As we move from memorized phrases, to creative expression, the *res*, the meaning that is generated through our creative expression, becomes our focus. Our most significant improvement comes via frequent and regular self-analysis that rigorously addresses the question: Am I communicating what I intend to communicate?

We need to do our best to interpret our fluency of expression in light of the message we intend to communicate. Our goal is primarily not form or skill development, rather communicating our message clearly, accurately, and naturally. The practice of creative expression therefore takes our focus from the details and places it squarely on communicating the message, so that the details can take their place.

We can see the successful application of this in many forms of communication, whether language, music, public speaking, or other art forms. As his violin instructor, Joshua helps our son Will understand that music is primarily not a skill to develop, rather a message to communicate via the instrument. Every time Will plays a piece, or practices for a recital, the preparation and performance is far less about the measurement and analysis of skill development, and far more about simply addressing the question: Am I communicating what I intend to communicate? Skill certainly accompanies fluent expression, but our focus should always be on the message we want to communicate, whether through language, music, art, or whatever form we are working on. "The best preparation for a recital involves rigorous practice, recording, listening, and analyzing for improvement of expression, every day, for a month" (Joshua, violin teacher).

In many ways, the art and practice of creative expression described here is more rigorous and humbling than the practice of raw skill-set development, but arguably less tedious and ultimately more fulfilling. It helps us to see the bigger picture, the fluency in the overall message we are pursuing.

We need to remember that the story of the gospel, (that is, conversing the gospel), weaves naturally and often somewhat randomly within our daily dialogue, infused with (and therefore infusing) topics, questions, and our personal testimonies, all of which relate to our lives, our neighbors' lives, and the gospel message.

How we connect the dots between pursuing our goal to reach *basic conversational fluency* and finding those moments that draw us into gospel conversations with people, may be as unexpected as my taxi driver conversation. As illustrated, a memorized presentation with no true understanding will generally fall flat, yielding little true interpersonal communication. However, our simple personal stories, the questions we ask, and the conversations we get into are what really take us into people's lives.

Memorized phrases that punctuate a scripted attempt to say what we want to say, yet with no thought to engage any significant response, usually leave us little communication traction to pursue meaningful gospel encounters. In contrast, our simple creative personal stories that invite us into the lives of our neighbors – even taxi drivers – in meaningful and powerful ways, may just open doors to the gospel.

Immersion

Immersion is measured in nano-seconds. Immersion is a second-by-second decision to die to self and come alive to the new language and culture God has called us to. It is being with people, in the moment, not just passing time with people in a place.[35]

Immersion, measured in moments of relational and language focus, constitutes an inherent investment in the lives of people around us, as we learn their language. The single most important thing we can do to learn the language is spend deliberate time with people using the language. Immersion is the essential choice to engage.

Immersion takes tremendous focus and energy. I've heard it described as moments of intention and attention to the communication going on around us. We are brought into these moments because of our intentionality and our choice to attend to the people, to what is being said: the topic, the question, the moments in which we are invited to engage. When we immerse, we begin to attend to the scripts of life and to the communication flowing around us. These may be conversations between neighbors, and hopefully between us and these same neighbors, as we are invited to enter that flow. Immersion primarily involves listening to people and responding to them, in the fluency of the moment.

Immersion starts with listening to the language we comprehend. From the day we start learning a new language, we can begin to engage, respond, and experience what it means to immerse. Surrounding ourselves with language that we can understand, or getting abundant doses of *comprehensible input*, is one of the most powerful practices of immersion we can experience. On both a technical and relational level, immersion really does start with listening to what we understand.

But it doesn't stop there. One of the most powerful principles of comprehensible input is that our exposure to the language we understand actually creates a thirst for more, and we can build on this when we immerse ourselves in reasonably secure communication environments, such as our time spent with language partners. Immersive moments with the intention to learn create ideal settings for adding small amounts of new language input to large amounts of comprehensible input, thus expanding our comprehension, and therefore enhancing our immersion.

The practice of language immersion is less about mechanics and more about attitude. Immersion in a speech community, in a geographic sense, is a myth. Many of us can be literally surrounded by the language, yet never really immerse. We can remain disconnected, orbiting the culture, never fully engaging. The abundance of English, non-local communities, work responsibilities, or even just a part-time learner mindset can often set into motion an overwhelming tide that pushes us away from the language and culture.

I am inspired by learners who have the tenacity to zero-in on immersion opportunities even in the most unsuspecting places and settings. Just being in a place with people who speak a certain language does not necessarily mean we are immersed. Nor does having one-on-one conversations with Russian speakers in New York City mean we are not immersed.

> Immersion has never been less a matter of geography than it is today. Immersion is no longer measured in GPS coordinates. We cannot assume that our presence within a speech community naturally leads to language practice. Rather, immersion is defined by choices we make at any given moment to engage with people in their language, the language we are learning.[36]

There are very few spaces in our rapidly urbanizing world where the practice of immersion in specific speech communities remains a limited option. People are literally everywhere! One of the best ways learners can begin learning language before they even leave home, is to simply find these people, people who speak their new language, and get time with them.

How could this actually work? Church-based immigration or refugee programs, international student programs, and many other avenues provide ample means to find and engage communities of the people we seek. Language immersion programs throughout North America specifically designed to re-engineer our lives to get the most out of our specific early second-language experience provide basic knowledge, immersion skills, and, in many cases, immersion opportunities. Students who immerse themselves in the language for six months to a year can often reach conversational ability in their new language before they even leave home.

Imagine having the ability to converse on basic topics in the language upon arrival to a new location! Our entire entry experience at that point would springboard to a whole new level. I've heard this described as arriving to a new place with some friends: grammar friends, vocabulary friends, comprehension friends, and overall confidence-building friends. This is what we mean by putting strategy into practice, well before arrival. This is an example of intelligent language investment.

On one occasion Jesus sent his disciples on a journey instructing them, "Take nothing for the road," he told them, "no staff, no traveling bag, no bread, no money; and don't take an extra shirt" (Luke 9:3).

We need to shed false dependencies when we enter our new culture. By God's grace we should aim to use only our new language upon arrival and depend entirely on the help we receive in the language from sympathetic friends and new neighbors. "In our first 72 hours we should not be allowed to rely on anything in our own language."[37]

Does this sound crazy? It's not. It's actually one of the most powerful and intelligent things we can do as we enter a new language environment, setting into motion new ways of thinking, relating, and doing things. "After a week, as we learn to live in our city, our mindsets shift. We are no longer afraid to engage."[38] Fear is a powerful motivator. So is courage.

The insanity of the first 72 hours, even the first week, can push against our efforts to immerse. Immersion is a huge effort and there's a lot of resistance. Just setting it up can be challenging, and a "big sell" for people to get on board. We may be neither able to muster much sentiment within us nor around us to prioritize immersion plans over the logistics of life that seem so critical at the time. Sometimes the two just don't work well together.

If our focus remains only on getting ready to live, we will generally orient our lives toward the expediency of our life needs, overshadowing and sometimes entirely quenching the intentionality of our language needs, which are always less urgent, but arguably more important, for long-term cross-cultural fruitfulness. Some life choices may seem smart on the front end, but in the final analysis may actually hinder our reaching fluency in the language and culture. "Getting ready to live and getting ready to learn are two very different things."[39]

As we enter new language settings, we immediately enter the apprenticeship of one or another language orientation: either English, or our new language. For most of us, for myriad reasons, our default expression, our apprenticeship, will be toward English, unless we are very intentional in our daily orientation. "We don't need a blanket of English surrounding the new language we are trying to use."[40]

The global gravity of English is just that strong; it's like a global language tsunami. Imagine English is the ocean and "learning Dutch" is Amsterdam. We need to build a system of dikes to keep the floodwaters of English at bay. One dike may be a "No English" policy, mitigating the use of English for daily needs, conversation, and social media. Another dike may be the strategic location of our home, somewhere that limits our geographic access to English life, ministry, and media.

Our lifestyle choices may provide another purposeful dike to keep the flood of English at bay – what we choose to do in the language, every day. Our routines, choices of media, friends, and neighbors can all help us to create communities of practice in which we intentionally participate for greater exposure and immersion. Do we seek out people who can help us enter these spaces? Have we considered using our new language for tasks we would otherwise feel more comfortable accomplishing in English?

> I'm convinced that as newcomers [enter] a culture with the kind of orientation that puts a focus on relationships, [they] can get deeply involved in very, very meaningful relationships, and they not only can, but must do it from the very first day, right from the outset. If they don't, then they're just going to be tourists.[41]

The choice to immerse is not easy. It's intentional. It's hard. Many of us well-intentioned learners all too often find ourselves in the comfort zone of English when we should be in the immersive growth zone of our new language. This is because honestly there's not much that is immediately gratifying when we are constantly swimming underwater in the new expressions and cultural nuances, trying to catch a breath of sanity. There is truly a lot about language immersion that can just make us tired and frustrated. Therefore, it is always helpful when we can remind ourselves, or even better when someone else can remind us, that our choice to immerse in the language is not just an intelligent language choice, but it's also an obedient and ultimately, deeply fulfilling choice, one that resonates with our call, as we begin to experience the joy of sharing the gospel with our dear neighbors.

Reflect and Respond

1. Consider this: Our personal LQ or "language intelligence" has far less to do with cognitive aptitude and far more to do with our power to discover and harness language resources we all have within us and around us. What is one way you can improve your LQ?

2. Reaching basic conversational fluency is without dispute the single most important first-step as we consider our language learning task toward reaching gospel fluency. Describe how you reached, or how you hope to reach "basic conversational fluency" in your new language.

3. The single most important thing we can do in learning the language is to spend deliberate time with people, hearing the language, and using the language. Immersion is the essential choice to engage. What is one way you can adjust your life to better immerse yourselves in the language among those who speak it?

4. For those of you who live in diaspora or multilingual contexts, what is one way you can creatively immerse in the language among those who speak it?

5. Immersion starts with listening to the language we comprehend. How can you surround yourself more often with "comprehensible input"?

6. Our brains prefer to mentally process not just words, but entire meanings of combinations of words and phrases. What is something you can adjust in your learning strategies that would help you rapidly acquire phrases, descriptions, and even entire stories in your new language?

8

Deep and Wide

I will not be content until I can minister in [my new language] similar to how I would be able to in English. I know this is a lofty goal. But the gospel, as well as deep spiritual truths and doctrines, best communicates in the heart language of a people. I firmly believe this. This is what drives me. (Sam, second-year learner)

An international partner and I were talking with a national who used a phrase neither of us understood. We both caught the context and the conversation continued to flow but at one point my partner asked, "You know that phrase you used a minute ago to describe..." and we both were able to learn a new idiom. I was particularly impressed with the in-language tempo of his question and how it just seemed to fit within the conversation.

After another conversation I saw him pull out his dictionary and write in his notebook. The surprising thing about all of this is that this guy's language is great, well past the level where most of us would say we've learned "enough" to do our work. He has a fruitful ministry in the language and I sense that his lifelong learning posture contributes to this. I asked him about his language, why he keeps learning, and what it's done for him.

- He regularly prayed with local friends and ministered to them from God's word in the language.

- He did his personal devotions in the language.

- He digested books, articles, news, and other media to stay informed, improve expression, and develop precision.

- He took notes, kept a journal, prepared lessons, and taught in the language, regularly reviewing all of this with work and ministry partners.

- He described the joy of evangelizing the lost, discipling new believers, and training church leaders; and the practice of always improving his language to become better at doing these things.

I was inspired to hear my friend share both how and why he relentlessly pushed himself to continue learning. I was also humbled. We need to ask ourselves: are we inspired to continue learning, or are we content with mediocre language? Will we continue learning, or are we content to remain at a place where we are barely able to teach the gospel in our new language? Right now, I am going to assume that if you are still reading this, you are not content with mediocrity. Take courage, there are solutions.

There's a reason we talk about the need to go deep and wide in language. This is because there is a strong tendency for people to just remain shallow and narrow. Chances are, that's where we are, and we want to improve. I have good news! We can improve in our new language. We can dig deeper, and we can reach wider.

Deep and Wide

As we progress in the language, we need strategies that will help us speak and understand things at deeper and wider levels.
(Josiah Daniels)

As a corollary to the limitless radius of the gospel, we would do well to view our language progress from the perspective of breadth – how expansively do we understand and engage our neighbors, and our neighbor's neighbors, even reaching into the community and greater society? And from the perspective of depth – how deeply do we really understand and engage our neighbors' behavior, values, beliefs, and worldview?

Our understanding of these overarching social and spiritual dimensions in the scope and lives of our neighbors and their communities directly relates to our call to share the gospel with them. Indeed, this directly relates to our ability to understand our neighbors, and to communicate with them, in their language.

As we consider ways to measure progress in the language, I exhort us all to consider ongoing daily answers to these very real and relevant questions, as we practice *gospel fluency*:

> How wide is my language?
> How deep is my language?

We cannot always provide simple responses to these questions. But we can use them to gauge our presence and influence in the communities of our lost neighbors, based on our understanding and based on our level of language fluency. Perhaps a good place to start is by asking ourselves a few questions.

What can I do today to reach out just a little bit further, to understand my neighbors just a little bit better; their families, their communities, and how they do life? How can I reach in just a little bit more, to probe a little deeper, to understand what makes my neighbors afraid, or sad, or to find out what they dream of, or hope for?

If our initial goal is simply to go from being a "here I am" person in the language, limited in language, and therefore limited in our ability to reach out and engage, to becoming a "there you are" person, rich in language and relational outreach capacity, then we've made good progress. Consider the centrifugal effect of the gospel for all peoples beginning with me and radiating out to my neighbors and my neighbor's neighbors, as our social awareness and engagement expands.

Or consider our ability to only observe behavior at a surface level, due to basic language and culture awareness, limiting us to a bare understanding, perhaps even a misunderstanding, of the meaning behind why people do what they do, or say what they say. Then contrast this with the ability to perceive, to ask deeper questions, and to discover the *why* beneath a lot of the *what, when, where,* and *who* questions, that allows us to examine beliefs, values, and the meaning of life and reality.

We can generally sum up that the more language we know, the broader and deeper we can go. In other words, our limited ability in our new language may at first prevent us from understanding our neighbors and their communities to any broad level. We simply may not have the language or cultural awareness to know how to do this. But as we grow in breadth of cultural and social understanding, we begin to engage our lost neighbors in ever-broadening circles of cultural understanding and social influence.

Likewise, our limited language ability may at first prevent us from understanding what's underneath even the most simple and obvious behaviors. But as we grow in our language ability, and as we engage in ever-deeper conversations, we begin to perceive things beneath the surface, into the motives, values, beliefs, and bedrock reality of our neighbor's soul and spirit.

I am convinced that just as sure as we are called to share the gospel with our lost neighbors, and just as sure as the gospel of God is limitless in its power to change lives, God provides us with wisdom and insight into these two dimensions, as we learn their language.

Yet, as God surely does this, by his grace, we are called to learn, to rigorously learn, and keep on learning, with no end in sight, so that the radius of our understanding of the people to whom God has called us – both deep and wide – would never limit our call nor our ability to fluently share the gospel with them.

These circles are simple. We can draw them on a napkin. How broad is our language? What can we do today to reach out just a bit further, to understand our neighbors, their families, their communities, and how they do life?

Concentric Circles to Widen our Language

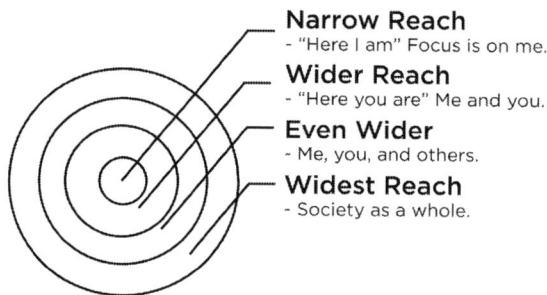

Language is the key which unlocks our awareness of the lost world around us. We want to have a growing "other awareness" that continues to reach out to all. We want to experience the gospel reaching our neighbor as a person, but also as a member of a family, neighborhood, and community.

How deep is our language? How can we learn today to reach in just a little bit more, to pull back the curtain, probe a little deeper, to understand what makes our neighbors afraid, or sad, or to find out what they dream of, or hope for?

How often in our cross-cultural evangelism and discipleship do we find ourselves engaging people at surface levels, teaching them only to change behavior, simply because we are unable to dig deeper into areas of character transformation that need to happen, because our communication is just that shallow?

The gospel reaches deep, into our innermost being. We can be sure that when we proclaim the gospel, it is able to communicate to the core of each person's life and bring about radical transformation at a level that we cannot fully comprehend.

Concentric Circles to Deepen our Language

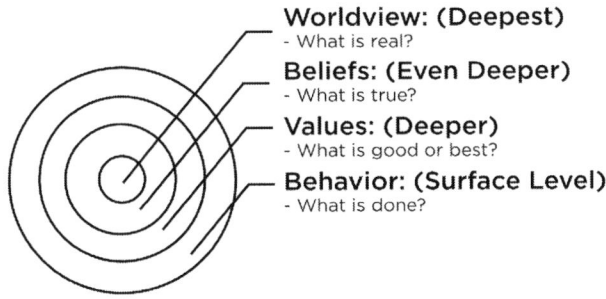

Imagine these circles like layers of an onion, as the gospel reaches deeper and deeper into our lives, transforming everything, from our surface-level behavior, our values, our beliefs, and even our worldview, reaching the very core of who we are.[42]

We have a great message to tell. It is a message of hope and salvation. As we faithfully learn the language to teach the gospel, we can rest in the assurance that God will use us in this transformational process, in our lives and in the lives of our neighbors. We can anticipate conversations that reach deep into their lives, giving us profound understanding and wisdom as we share the gospel and begin to see it bring about spiritual change. "Act wisely toward outsiders, making the most of the time. Let your speech always be gracious, seasoned with salt, so that you may know how you should answer each person" (Colossians 4:5-6).

I am convinced that as we prepare, practice, and engage in proclaiming the gospel to our lost neighbors on a daily basis we will begin to understand more and more just how deep and wide is the love of Christ for us, and for our lost neighbors. The gospel is powerful to reach into all areas of our hearts, our culture, our lives, our families and our communities.

We are stewards of the gospel of Jesus Christ. God calls us to the task of the Great Commission, commanding us to teach all that Christ has taught us, to all peoples. As we consider the practice of *gospel fluency*, I want to consider what it means to pursue gospel proclamation where we really see and experience something that is way beyond our personal ability.

The gospel – the message of the gospel – reaches deep and wide into the lives of people around us. It is the power of the living word of God that does this, not us. It is the power of the gospel that we depend on. So, what then does it mean for us to be stewards of the truth in another language? What does it mean for us to reach fluency, and therefore, to take the gospel to our neighbors, and to their community?

We pursue cross-cultural understanding through prayer, by God's spirit, and in faith, knowing that it is truly God who gives us understanding into people's lives. The gospel reaches into the recesses of people's lives that we could never reach, that we could never even understand in our own strength. "For the word of God is living and effective and sharper than any double-edged sword, penetrating as far as the separation of soul and spirit, joints and marrow. It is able to judge the thoughts and intentions of the heart" (Hebrews 4:12).

As we become fluent in the language, we become gospel carriers to our neighbors and to their families and communities that they represent, in all areas of life, in all society. When we consider our ever-widening and ever-deepening spheres of influence, we will then begin to realize more and more that this is not our work, rather it is our faith in the work of God.

The gospel reaches areas of our neighbors' lives that we cannot reach, that we cannot even begin to understand. Their lives are a labyrinth that we on our own cannot understand. The gospel has the power to wind its way into people's lives and hearts, radically penetrating lives, communities, and society.

This is what it means to be fluent in the language, and therefore, fluent in the gospel. It is our joy to see the living words of Christ reach our neighbors, to reach all areas of their lives, and the lives of their neighbors and communities.

We need to go deep and wide in our language learning in order to reach *gospel fluency*. We need to be aware that there are significant language and social barriers that will keep us from doing this if we are not careful. I've included a list of *top ten* barriers that commonly prevent learners from going deep and wide in the language.

Further, we need to apply healthy ongoing learning practices. These practices take deliberate effort and push us beyond our comfort zone, into a deeper and wider zone of learning that is sometimes not comfortable but is very rewarding when applied. I've included a list of *top ten* learning practices for healthy and deliberate ongoing learning. (This section may be a bit more technical than other sections of this book. Don't worry, it's not too long!)

Barrier #1: Lack of Vision

Fundamental to our success in language learning is the understanding that we are not called to learn the language, we are called to proclaim the gospel. We have no other reason to learn the language. At the same time, we have every reason to learn the language well, in order to be able to proclaim the gospel fluently. Language learning is relevant to in-language ministry. Always. And this perspective will help sustain our language progress, and our ministry practice. Sometimes, for any number of reasons, we can lose sight of the relevance of our language progress in ministry. When we cannot clearly see the direct ministry relevance of our language practice and progress, or even when the relevance clouds over for some reason, we can lose momentum in our learning.

Language learning is a long-term commitment that is often a challenge to sustain without a clear and long-term vision. Let's face it, learning a language requires patience, endurance, courage, a lot of hard work, and the payoffs are rarely immediate. It's hard to compete with so many things these days that bring us immediate reward and satisfaction. Learners who struggle deferring gratification may struggle with the discipline of learning language and may therefore confine themselves to a short-term view of cross-cultural ministry outcomes.

Barrier #2: Part-Time Learner Mindset

What is our mindset when we think about learning a language? What is our commitment? Our lifestyle? Language may not come easily or naturally to most of us. But we can cultivate and develop a healthy learning lifestyle. At least for an introductory season we need to consider full-time language learning – and a "no English" policy – until we reach basic conversational fluency. We may surprise ourselves, and discover that life in our new language has become our new normal. We should look for ways this is modeled by others around us well. If we don't see a good model, then let's create one! Our new language and culture is indeed completely new and different, and we may need to figure out how to work with these "new normal" lifestyle dynamics. This can be exhausting. But it's good for us to do this. We can still meet with that teammate for coffee, but we can do it in our new language. We can still read bedtime stories to our kids, but let's add stories in our new language. Let's put our English social media on hold, and open accounts with new friends in our new language.

Barrier #3: English-Dominant Identity

For many of us, our work identity or lifestyle practices pull us away from opportunities to learn and use the language. Time and energy are precious resources for part-time language learners who spend most of their days working in English. So we need to find creative ways to integrate language practice while sustaining productivity. Are there parts of our work or activities that can be done in the language? Our lives as foreigners, especially in urban areas, tend to involve things we do together, and we can end up spending a lot of our daily lives in English surrounded by each other. We as learners can be distracted by malls, English TV, English internet, and English social media, hindering our language progress. Meetings, travel, and electronic communication present huge challenges to those of us wanting to make progress. Smartphone apps have made it more complicated to isolate our attention to focus on language practice.

Barrier #4: Criticism or Ridicule from Co-workers

Criticism or ridicule from people who have high influence in our new language lives – colleagues and national partners – can literally shut us down, crushing our efforts to make progress. We need all the encouragement we can get, bucket loads in fact, and from the right people. Criticism or ridicule are a sure path to discouragement for those of us aspiring to learn the language and who simply want a word of encouragement that the rigorous and faithful language practices we are applying will yield the fruit of godly ministry.

Barrier #5: Lack of Team Support (or no place to share our cool stories)

Some of us may have mentors or supervisors who do not encourage us in language progress. This is especially true if they, too, are struggling in their language or culture acquisition. We may have people with whom we work who discourage us because of their lack of interest or progress. One of the most encouraging things learners can hear are testimonies from co-workers of fruitful in-language experiences. People around us are making progress and God is at work, and we need to hear about it. When we don't have opportunities to share or hear these great stories, we can lose momentum in our progress.

We need to have greater transparency on teams when it comes to learning and using our new language in life and ministry. In a recent conversation with language coaches, several talked about leaders and more experienced colleagues they knew and worked with who extended a sincere effort to sympathize with struggling language learners. In place of negative comparisons and shame, they chose to create healthy spaces for dialogue about language needs, and even sought to practice the language together.

Barrier #6: No Close Relationships with Nationals

Lack of exposure to the language is one thing, but the lack of affirming and supportive relationships with nationals is quite another and can seriously diminish our efforts to make progress. We make time for people who are important to us. Until our neighbors become important to us, we won't make time for them. We need to constantly evaluate our priorities as we relate to our neighbors. Learners who spend time with nationals generally make progress. Learners who don't, generally won't.

A related dynamic that can create barriers to ongoing learning is the tendency we have as international Christian workers to rely largely and sometimes only on paid relationships with nationals. If all of our language learning encounters depend on relating to those whom we pay for help, then our relationships and our language progress will likely suffer.

We will also likely experience truncated cultural acquisition and awareness if our relational network in the language remains so anemic. We need relationships with nationals, lots of them, and lots of time with them, to sustain healthy growth in our cultural understanding and awareness.

I recently heard of a learner preparing to bring flowers to a funeral in her new community in Central Asia. Prior to going she did the right thing and asked her neighbor who in shock told her that is never done and advised her to bring fruit instead.

Barrier #7: Excessive Social Media and Virtual Ghettos

Social media has created a global trend substituting virtual relationships over in-person relationships, which can have a strong negative effect on our language progress. Virtual communities tend to take on a life of their own and can distract us from daily face-to-face conversations that provide us the interaction so essential to sustain and improve our interpersonal language skills. The sheer volume of screen time we habitually engage in may actually rob us of the precious conversation time we need to have with neighbors. We may just need to turn off our phones.

Barrier #8: Intangible Destabilizers

Frustration, fatigue, embarrassment, stage fright, culture shock, and culture stress can all serve to weaken our resolve and throw us off balance in our learning progress. These toxic intangible destabilizers have the potential to really sabotage our learning.

We may find ourselves surrounded by social situations we struggle to understand, which make us feel negatively evaluated and perhaps misunderstood by those around us in our new lives. This kind of stress can literally rob us of our physical and emotional health.

When we face these kinds of stressful evaluative situations in our new language life, which for most of us is a daily challenge, we need to be aware of the dangers they pose, and find ways to overcome these extreme language barriers.

Barrier #9: Family Considerations and Challenges

Those of us who have experienced trying to balance learning the language while raising small children or negotiating schooling needs understand the true meaning of time and energy scarcity. We need all the help we can get to really make it work. Spouses may have different learning needs. Children have needs. Families need to work with these challenging dynamics to find ways to make progress.

As fathers, we need to watch our kids. As husbands, we need to help our wives get the time they need to learn the language. I've seen first-hand how easy it is for a mother to experience the crushing stress of daily trauma from when the doorbell rings, to when someone says something to her kids, or when someone just tries to talk with her on the street in passing, and she doesn't know the language.

I want to remind us that while we do need to find ways to manage language learning as families, we should never consider our family roles and identities as barriers to learning the language. In fact, we need to celebrate the huge blessing and value our family identities bring into our new language and culture setting.

God is intimately aware of our situations and needs and he is involved in caring for us and our families, whether through those in our new home (spouses and children), those back in our hometown (parents, siblings, and relatives), or those at our church, or on our teams. These special relationships are a vibrant part of our identity and testify to God's goodness and the gospel in our lives.

Barrier #10: Getting Stuck on the "Mediocre" Plateau

The "mediocre" mindset can be a dangerous barrier to fruitful ongoing language learning practices, corrosive to our souls and damaging to our calling as ministers of the gospel. Are we regularly tempted to think we have enough language to do what God has called us to do? Or, perhaps we don't think about it at all, and just become satisfied with mediocrity. I want to spend a little more time working through what some refer to as the *language plateau*.

The limited fluency we initially reach provides us just enough language to operate with mediocre or average proficiency, which then often leads to complacency, one of the main factors contributing to lack of growth. This is complicated by the way our brains work, prodding us to settle for mediocrity in just about any task, making it very hard to continue to improve without deliberate and conscious effort.

We may imagine that given enough time practicing any skill, including language, we will eventually master that skill, illustrated in the *Imagined Learning Curve* graph. This myth fails to take into account shifts in our cognitive development that actually deter us from mastery in just about any skill. What almost always happens with skill development, and language is no exception, is that when we reach "good enough" we hit a cognitive plateau in our learning, illustrated in the second graph, the *Language Plateau*. Whether it's typing, reading, playing an instrument, or learning a language, we are hard-wired to reach a level of basic autonomous proficiency that we often call *mediocrity*, just enough to do what we need to do to "get by" with ease in just about any skill, and then we simply stop improving.

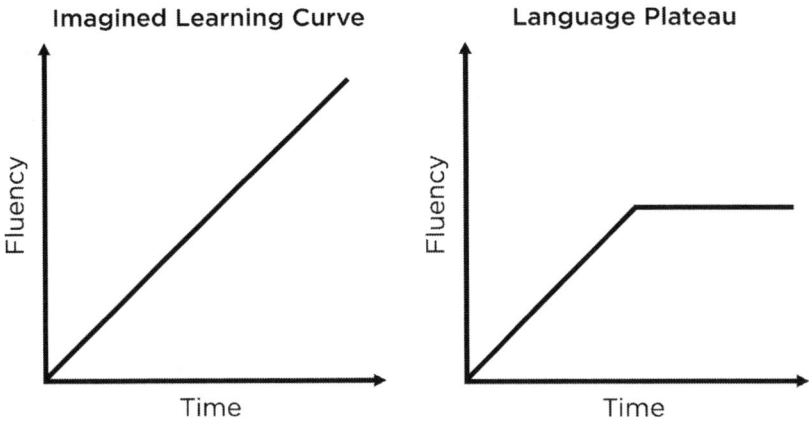

We may continue to use skills we learn for routine tasks or enjoyment – whether cooking, reading, or riding a bike – but as long as we don't have a need to continue improving our ability in that skill, we won't. In other words, we stop learning. Our brains are actually quite good at moving away from deliberate cognitive awareness we call *learning* once we reach a level of sustainable proficiency in almost any life task. We hardly ever learn any more than we need to learn. We may imagine that by repetitively doing something, we are somehow slowly improving, but we're really just doing the same thing, over and over again, without applying any further cognitive effort toward ongoing learning.

Mediocrity may be enough for many life skills, maybe even enough to "get by" in our new language, but it's not enough if we really want to share the gospel with our neighbors. We need to continue learning, and to find ways to work through this language plateau barrier.

How can we mitigate this? With hard, deliberate practice! Our learning paths may resemble the following two charts describing what often happens when we reach a *basic conversational fluency* (BCF) breakthrough point, the level of language most of us reach when we hit a plateau and risk failing to employ a conscious effort to continue making progress. It's at that point, therefore, we have two paths from which to choose: one of deliberate and ongoing progress (into our learning zone) or one of plateauing (remaining in our comfort zone), illustrated by the *Learning Zone vs Comfort Zone* chart.

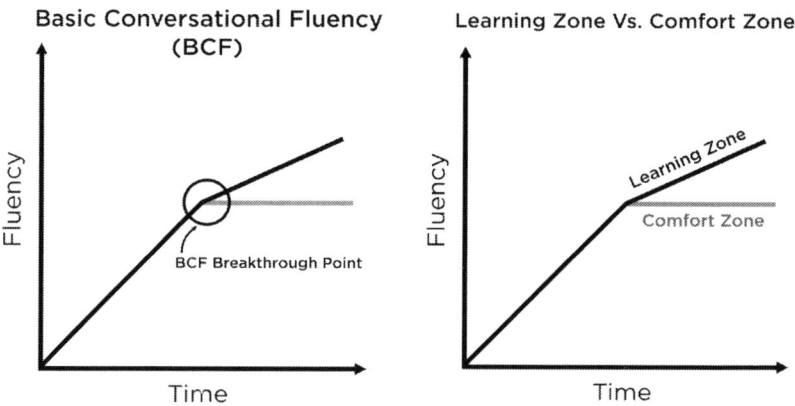

We need to understand that the path to mastery is very challenging. We will inevitably face increasing and very real obstacles of diminishing returns. High-frequency words that once came to us in easy-to-create sentences are now the less-frequent words, nuanced meanings, abstract concepts, technical terms, and challenging complex structures that take more time and energy to master with seemingly fewer and slower tangible results. We compromise by saying to ourselves that we've already reached *basic conversational fluency*, or enough to get by for most things we need in life. We may be tempted to stop growing, even somewhat subconsciously, and before we know it, we find ourselves just coasting for months, even years. What we need to realize is the road to continued language growth beyond the *breakthrough point* of *basic conversational fluency* is a deliberate choice, a conscious effort. We must *choose* to stay in the *language learning zone*.

We have to work hard to reach basic proficiency at any skill, but we have to work even harder to become really good at that skill. Language is no exception. Operating in the language learning zone means far more than simply autonomously using what we already know. Rather, it means cognitively pushing forward into learning what we do not yet know. This literally means we push ourselves to failure, the kind of failure that fuels a will to find a way to correct our mistakes and try again until we experience improvement. In this learning zone we need to view things and do things differently, perhaps like never before. And we also need endurance, perhaps like never before. But it's also where we experience tremendous joy, because this is where we begin to experience ministry opportunities in the language like never before.

When we are in the language learning zone, we find that we get to share the gospel with our neighbors more often, in more life contexts, and from more scriptures than ever before. This is that healthy and thriving path of ongoing learning where we can truly dive deep and wide into our language and ministry.

The way to get on this path, and stay in this zone, is by immediately beginning to apply healthy language *learning zone* practices. Here are ten practices that may help us get into the zone and stay there.

Learning Zone Practice #1: The Familiar Discomfort of Immersion

Breaking my normal routine and doing something out of the ordinary is at first discomforting. But then it becomes a "familiar discomfort" which is do-able. (Will, first-year learner)

The main reason we resist immersing into a new place and culture, with new people in a new language, is because it's uncomfortable. We don't ever naturally seek discomfort. We have to intentionally pursue it. We have to break old routines and create new ones.

So that's how it works for Will, who goes to the same place, to meet the same people, often at the same time, when he's practicing his language. This at least creates a familiarity that he can move toward as a "familiar discomfort." It's within these familiar zones, Will goes on to say, that other people then often come along and we get to talk with them. "It's refreshing to know I have a time and place I can anticipate, to be able to talk with people in my new language, within my new culture."

The connection is important. Will has made friends, so he doesn't feel alone in this immersion experience. "It's easier to do this with your friends. This makes the outside-of-my-comfort-zone experience more relaxing, enjoyable, and refreshing. I no longer focus on how nervous I am, and I can focus on what's going on" (Will).

Learning Zone Practice #2: Making Space for Creative Expression

When I work on my speech, I create a mental space that is separate from everything else. And when I practice it, I enter that mental space. This is my memory zone, my mental zone. (EWS)

Creating language requires mental space and this almost always requires a dedicated time with dedicated people. When we begin to create in the language by putting words together into hundreds and thousands of meaningful phrases and sentences, we need space for experimentation, trial and error, thinking about new words and combinations of words, remembering things we learn, mentally categorizing them, talking to ourselves; writing, talking, re-writing, and re-talking. We need a safe place where we can say things over and over again from our notes and from our memories, and where we can receive immediate, constructive, and positive feedback from native speakers so we can do it all over again, only better, the next time. Creative expression takes a tremendous amount of energy and we need the space and encouragement to allow this to happen.

Learning Zone Practice #3: The Art of Failing, and Getting Immediate Feedback

Regular practice simply isn't enough to improve; we must watch ourselves fail, practice failing, and get feedback on how to improve.

Doing something we've already learned simply isn't enough to help us improve; we must attempt things we cannot yet do with complete confidence, fail at them, and then get immediate feedback on how to improve and perfect them. Until we see the incredible value of failing – that is, pushing ourselves into areas of rapid growth, where failure leads to analysis, adjustment, and change – we will not improve. "Linguistic breakdown is the road to growth" (MT, co-worker).

We need to celebrate every small victory, and literally measure and celebrate even the most incremental points of success, especially those that emerge from failure. We must consider how failure truly is our path to improvement.

Masaaki Imai describes the benefits of incremental growth through the Japanese business and life practice of *kai* (change) and *zen* (for the better) or *kaizen* – small incremental deliberate continuous improvements over time that add up to a substantial competitive advantage.[43]

Success comes in waves. Ocean waves are interesting. Swell is created, in some measure, from the powerful back flow of the previous wave. Analogously, what may seem like failure or "going backwards" in our language journey may just be our best preparation to create the "swell" for us to ride the next wave, to practice the *kaizen* of language learning. The cycle may look something like this:

Test – fail – learn – improve – re-enter – test – fail – learn – improve – re-enter

Trial and error can often create the momentum we need to reach our next step or goal toward engaging people with the gospel. Through this process we can begin to connect the dots, to close the gaps, to really experience language progress. There is nothing inherently inspiring about failure, even when we know it's a pathway to growth. It's just hard. But there is everything inspiring – redeeming, actually – about the content, the story, that God is calling us to tell, and the anticipation we have in engaging people's response as they hear the gospel. This is inspiring. This makes us want to learn from our mistakes and improve.

Are we afraid to make mistakes? Do we hesitate when we speak because of an internal need for perfect delivery? Perfectionism may be the enemy of progress. The need to be perfect with our understanding and delivery affects our ability to effectively engage; hindering our ability to capture the gist of meanings, respond, and stay in conversations. Issues related to perfectionism can impede our confidence, and seriously stall any effective ongoing learning and practice. Until we see these as real issues, own them, and work through them with effective change or coping strategies, they will persist and probably worsen.

How can we distinguish a negative attitude of perfectionism from a positive attitude of high performance? Borne of an obsessive pursuit of flawless performance or behavior, perfectionism in language learning often creates a paralyzing fear of failure, and can lead to unhealthy comparisons and competition. In many ways, perfectionism has the opposite intended effect promoting only the illusion of progress while actually hindering it.

In contrast, high performing language learners simply have the will to continue improving past the point where most people plateau. They are not content with average ability, but identify specific points to address, work on them, and steadily improve. High performers tend to operate outside of their comfort zone and study themselves failing.

As we consider moving beyond mediocre ability, we need to be specific about understanding our language mistakes. We need to name them, and then work on them. *Specificity* isolates problems for more focused practice. Whether correcting a pattern of error, detecting the need to move from simple to more complete expression, fine-tuning pronunciation, or practicing a grammar point, we need to work on the problem, get feedback and correction, practice it again, then move on to the next one. Sometimes our learning programs need more diversity. But sometimes the problem is simply a lack of specific focus upon each task, and what we need to learn from that task.

High performers crave and thrive on immediate and critical feedback. We need to prepare for feedback. I mean that, literally. We need to prepare something to say, and then get feedback on how we said it, so we can improve. This is our primary goal with any controlled output session. We need to make the most of any time we have a sympathetic competent listener who can give us great feedback. For that reason, we must come prepared with something extensive to say, and get someone to help us work through it, to make it better.

Our focus should be on quality, not necessarily on quantity. Learners, especially those wanting to move beyond basic conversational fluency, need to work hard to continually improve expression: the greater need is not always new content; rather better, clearer expression.

Learning Zone Practice #4: Expanding the Language We Need

People will only learn the language they need.[44]

We may need to re-engineer our lives so that we put ourselves in situations where we need more language. We cannot measure what we learn by what we want to learn. We measure what we learn by what we need to learn. Sure, we may want to improve, but unless what we want becomes what we need, we won't learn what we want. If we want to improve, we must change the language we need and put ourselves into positions and situations where we need more than we have. "It's hard to continue to get the language you want, after you already have the language you need."[45]

Instead of relying on translators, consultants, guides, or assistants for in-language resources, let's start doing things ourselves, or at least engage our national partners to challenge us to take more active and complex in-language roles in our work. Speaking to groups usually requires more skill and effort than speaking one-on-one. We may be fluent in one-on-one conversations, but can we thrive in one-to-many situations (where we are the one)? When we put ourselves in situations where we have to lead a group on a topic, this will force us to learn more language. As we consider the language we have and don't yet have, let's change our lives so that we actually *need* to learn more language.

"What situations can we put ourselves into where we have a drowning sensation? We're not actually drowning, but we must learn to push ourselves to the point of need and growth."[46] Often the reason we feel like we plateau in our language progress is because we just don't need more language than we currently use. In other words, we have all the language we need. What is it going to take for us to realize that we need to learn more, consistently, constantly? We have a choice: we can make everything true about our lives so that we only need what we have, or know that we need more than we have, and reach out for help. "The first step toward getting what we need for what we want to do in the language, so we can do it, is knowing that we need it."[47]

Don is an excellent teacher of Old Testament. I love hearing him teach in the language. He has great language. I asked him what he did to reach this level. He arrived years ago as an English teacher and reached reasonable conversational fluency. Then he was invited to teach Old Testament and that was all it took for him to work hard to be able to teach it in the language. Don prepared lessons and then practiced them over and over again until he was able to teach them fluently.

Learning Zone Practice #5: Scaffolding

When we are in over-our-heads, we get the language we need.[48]

Watch one, do one, teach one.[49]

When my boys were kids, they practiced backflips as I spotted them with my hands. Soon, they were doing backflips on their own without my *scaffolding*. But they probably never would have attempted backflips without a little help.

We must find effective ways to move from un-deliberate usage to deliberate practice, from using language we are comfortable with, to using language just out of our range. This is a recipe for failure without some sort of scaffolding; someone there to help us work on new language, to help us understand it, and eventually master it. Scaffolding creates a space, a zone, for this kind of growth. We need to do whatever we can to create these spaces where we can freely and safely practice new content, forms, and usages with sympathetic language partners. This is a place for intense conversation, requiring attentive listening.

Scaffolded conversations are more intense than normal conversations with our neighbors. When we speak with our neighbors, in everyday conversations, our correct forms can easily slip away as we concentrate on meaning and message.

Our purpose during these special times is to attend to language "vitamins and minerals" that can help us grow in our language accuracy and complexity – cases, participles, endings, pronunciation – things that we often fail to attend to, and therefore are not able to fluently master in our normal conversations with people.

When we concentrate on communicating meanings and messages, we can really only concentrate on the nouns, verbs, adjectives, and basic word order. Unless we deliberately practice more complex forms, including pronunciation nuances, in some sort of controlled or scaffolded setting, we will continue to struggle to improve.

A more sure way to improve is to create dedicated spaces for deliberate practice, safe zones where we can try, fail, get immediate help, try again, and finally improve, until we master new accuracy measures which then become a part of our daily speech, allowing us to say what we really want to say. This process can help us learn to fluently communicate messages in more complex and correct ways. This is how we move from mediocre to great language ability.

How can we get the most out of our time with the key players we have in our lives as we practice language? Whether it's an hour of intense learning or just a few moments of dialogue, one of the best ways we can we maximize our language practice is to use *teach-backs*, which can provide outstanding scaffolding for our practice.

I recently experienced a teach-back at a sports medicine workshop I attended in my new language. For each set of instructions Denise taught us, she would stop and say, "Okay, now you do it," and we each would take our turn while she observed us and corrected us as needed. After a few false starts, we were usually all able to work through the instructions and activities with reasonable success. But, here was where the actual teach-back moment kicked in: Denise would divide us into small groups where each of us then would have to lead the same activities, going through them again, as if we were teaching and showing the activities to each other, just as Denise had originally demonstrated.

After first watching, and then practicing, we were confident and equipped to teach each other the intended outcomes, performing the desired tasks with reasonable success and confidence. We were actually able to teach them!

As Denise saw that we understood and performed one section of the first aid training with reasonable fluency, we would move on to the next section.

Denise could do all of her work fluently in the language. I asked her how she learned language so well. Not surprisingly, she said that her main method of learning language was using the teach-back method. This was a powerful "aha" moment for me. Here is how she did it, and how we can, too.

When Denise had something she needed to say, whether it was something in the field of medicine or sports, or something from the Bible, she would prepare it and present it, mistakes and all, to someone willing to listen to her and willing to provide helpful feedback in the form of a teach-back.

Denise now had a great example of what she really wanted to say from a key player who first heard her try to say it, and then gave her the gift of saying it back to her more beautifully. Denise's job, as is ours, was then to just close the distance between what she said, and what she heard back. She practiced and practiced, and then did her own teach-back again, to solidify the fluency, accuracy, and complexity of the content and task.

This was the main method Denise used to reach fluency in her new language. It was also her main method for coaching and teaching in her medical and sports work. It's simple, it's tough, but it works. I was inspired to see how this may work for me to improve my language.

When we have key players, such as language partners, teach us what we've taught them, we are getting beautiful examples of the language we are now highly motivated to practice. We really want to learn how to say this content, and how to perform these verbal tasks with greater fluency.

The learning we experience during these intense times of using gospel content with sympathetic native speakers may be the most powerful learning practices we engage in. This is also one of best opportunities we have to learn things about the culture, especially that which relates to the gospel, and how people hear and respond to the gospel. We need to learn as much as possible and get as much as we can out of this time.

Using teach-backs as a method of language learning and practice is one of the most powerful ways we can spend an hour with a native speaker. I will almost always ask my language partner or disciple to say back to me in beautiful language what I have prepared and said to them. Sometimes, I can respond immediately with improved speech. At other times, I just need to listen and learn, and work on expressing what I've learned from their teach-back before I attempt mine. As I work through this process, I become more aware of my optimal learning pace and style.

Don uses various forms of scaffolding including teach-backs for teaching the Bible. I've observed that he often prepares no more than 20 minutes of presentation, and then sets aside at least that much time for interactive dialogue and editing. He prepares for this time well, with questions and discussion points. He records responses on whatever he has available – a piece of paper, a whiteboard, a laptop, his phone. Don works toward making sense of these responses within the overall scope of the topic and uses what he can gain from this discussion as a springboard for related discussions and further presentation preparations.

What is right in front of us? How can we work with *that* pungent content and make it better? How can we build on our current expressive ability, getting just the right amount of help from the right people around us? How can we make a habit of always looking for that next faithful step toward reaching our next goal, our desired outcome, and put *that* into practice?

Learning Zone Practice #6: Dual Investment

It is very hard to be both accurate and fluent at the same time.[50]

Some of our most fruitful advanced language practices are those special times when we can work on fluency and accuracy together, at the same time.

Typically, in normal everyday speech, we use the same content with the same usages and though our language flows, it does not necessarily improve. We say what we want to say in ways we know, usually using language and forms we are comfortable using. This helps our overall fluency, but doesn't really help us improve our expression, grammatical accuracy, or complexity.

When we meet with a language partner, we often tend to receive an over-abundance of grammar or pronunciation help or instruction which may not be readily useful in our daily lives. At the very least, we may have a hard time immediately inserting the lesson into our daily speech.

We tend to oscillate between these two extremes from using what we know and not improving, to learning new things that we cannot readily apply. What we need is a healthy combination of both. This is best applied during our time with our language partner. We need to create a zone where we can feel confident with the content and meaning of personal stories – the words, phrases, and discourse – and at the same time, push ourselves to concentrate on the cognitive nutrition – the tough grammar, pronunciation difficulties, endings – which our brains tend to ignore when we focus on the message.

Dual investment is the practice of concentrating on the message – *what* is said – *and* the cognitive nutrition – *how* it is said (including complex grammar, syntax, and pronunciation) at the same time, with a dedicated language partner.

The practice of dual investment takes a lot of focus and energy. Often, the best place to start is by actively listening. For example, we may begin by listening to our language partner tell a simple life story. We may record the story, and then play it back, listening together. We may ask questions about the content, and also ask questions about the language. This is our time to push the edges for breadth and depth of meaning. This is also the time to discover and practice more natural, clear, and accurate expression.

Not long ago, I heard a friend ask his language partner, "What happens after you die?" What followed was an incredibly interesting discussion about the meaning and use of the word *disappear*, unlocking tremendous insights into beliefs about the afterlife, what is real, what is not, how we exist in this form, and how one day we will not, and how the use of the words – like *disappear* – can be so perplexing, yet so enlightening.

We can also practice speaking by switching roles. My friend's language partner could have asked him, "What happens after you die?" After a lively discussion, and a recording, we as learners could then ask, "What did I say correctly?" Or "What did I say incorrectly?" Or even, "How could I have said this better or differently?"

So, as we practice the discussion – for example, talking about what happens after we die – we are also learning the grammar and usages of words and phrases, such as *disappear*. As we talk about the content, we are also learning new endings, and new ways to say things better. The more we massage the words and texts, the richer our learning will be with each encounter.

Dual Investment allows us to focus on both accuracy and content. It gives us the mental space to think about what we want to say in the moment. We come prepared to talk, edit, stop, re-work, listen, talk, and do it all over again, all in real-time, aiming for both fluency and accuracy of expression in our words, phrases, and overall discourse. We are invested in the message, but we are also invested in the accurate expression of that message, all those great vitamins and minerals of correct syntax, pronunciation, grammar, and overall complexity of expression.

A language coach and I were recently discussing the value of real-time recordings of personal presentations and discussions. We need to get into the practice of hearing ourselves, immediately recognizing our mistakes, and then rigorously self-correcting. When we hear ourselves on a recording, we begin to self-correct, and this helps us get into the habit of doing it more and more.

The practice of self-correction in a safe place, either directly with a language partner or when listening to recordings of ourselves, can help us improve in both accuracy and fluency in real time. "Dual investment allows us to intentionally practice the usage of irregular verbs while thinking about engaging content. Most of us cannot do this in real time in real life. It takes a special setting. It takes a deep encounter."[51]

In this *transfer-of-learning process* our minds can hear the language and can take it in, into our mental lexicon, because it is present, salient, and meaningful. And because the language in this moment of *deep encounter* is so *transfer-appropriate*, our minds can also take it on and we can begin to use it in our daily lives. When we communicate the gospel with our neighbors, we don't want to be thinking about correct words or grammar. We want to be thinking about the message we are communicating. But we do want to communicate accurately. So, as we practice *dual investment*, we are able to think more and more about the message, and less and less about the form, because the word and grammar usages are now becoming hard wired, transferred, into our minds; the language is now ours, and we've moved from a focus on accuracy, to a focus on fluency.

Learning Zone Practice #7: Minimizing and Optimizing

Sometimes less is more.

How can we get the most out of our language learning? On a scale of 1-10, how can we stay in the 8-10 range in our strategies and practice? How can we detect and adjust what we are doing, for example, if we find ourselves in the 5-6 range? What does that even mean? Precisely this: We need to practice the right program or activity of learning at the right time, for the right amount of time, with the right people. In other words, we need to learn to be innovative and eclectic in our approaches to language learning so that we find what works for us when we need it, in exact measure and distribution. So how do we learn to do that?

Language Intelligence (LQ) principles of investment from the previous chapter may help answer these questions and guide us in the process toward getting the most out of our language learning experience. We must do everything we can to stay immersed, practice creative expression, and get structured input (grammar, etc.) when we need it.

The whole concept of immersion is based on our ability and choice to engage and invest with people in a social and language context. And we need to be intelligent and effective in our practice of immersion. We need to be consistently growing in the breadth and depth of things we can understand.

First, we need to surround ourselves with as much *comprehensible input* as possible, which will help us immerse in the language. This may mean different things for different people at different times. For more advanced learners, listening to the news and then discussing it may be immersive and engaging. But, for beginners, this content would be largely incomprehensible, and therefore completely unhelpful. We need input that we can understand, in which we can engage. Perhaps this would mean listening to a simple story with pictures or listening to a neighbor talk about her family.

Second, we need to ensure that we find ways to practice creative expression as much as possible whenever we use the language, consistently growing in our breadth and depth of language use in all topics of discussion and conversation.

Consider how we may use our time with our language partners. How can we be sure to enter our time together having personally prepared things to say that create opportunities to practice speaking with them in a safe place, where we can receive helpful feedback, and therefore maximize the value of our time together?

We need to bring our questions and thoughts: our stories of what happened yesterday, a simple Bible story, anything that can help us get the most out of our time together with our language partners. In this way, we will learn the art and practice of creative expression, how to avoid passive listening, and what it means to actively engage in conversations and discussions.

Third, we need to learn to capture those teachable moments when we need new grammar structures or vocabulary, so that we learn them effectively and use them immediately. In other words, we need to learn them when we need them. That may sound simple enough, but sadly, many of us are notoriously tempted to fill hours and notebooks with grammar rules and charts we cannot begin to effectively put into practice at that time. Instead, we just need clear, relevant instruction about how to use the language we need, when we need it.

For example, our first sentences in a new language are often about our immediate needs within our immediate environment. These may include descriptions, commands, or instructions that apply the use of very basic words and phrases, using simple grammar. Trying to learn more complex forms at this point would be premature and counterproductive if we cannot yet describe what is in front of us, engage in basic conversations, or talk about what we did yesterday. "There's a big difference between what we know and what we need at three months and six months of learning" (JH, co-worker)

When we find that we need to tell stories, describe what we did yesterday, or talk about events from our lives, then and only then are we really ready to learn the grammar we need for those specific language tasks.

Viewed another way, if we only go to class and do homework, we may not get the actual practice we need. Likewise, if we don't come prepared to meet with our language partners, we still may not get the practice we need. Many of us may just need to stop counting the hours we spend in language and evaluate the quality of the learning practices we spend filling up those hours.

> When you want to get good at something, how you spend your time practicing is far more important than the amount of time you spend. In fact, in every domain of expertise that's been rigorously examined, from chess to violin to basketball, studies have found that the number of years one has been doing something correlates only weakly with level of performance.[52]

Language learning *best practices* are those which fit well within our optimal learning zone for that season of learning, that day, that hour, and that moment. Our language learning zone is dynamic and can be best described as a measure of balance and rhythm, not necessarily intensity of learning. Intense activities are designed to push us hard, deliberately leading to healthy breakdown. That's how we learn. That's how we discover. That's how we perfect our language. But that also creates fatigue. Investment takes a lot of energy. We cannot sustain high levels of learning intensity for long periods of time. We may need to intersperse an hour of intense learning with two hours of conversational practice solidifying what we know. We need a balance of personal study, rest, followed by more intense practice. What is your language learning rhythm?

Not all language investment is created equal. It's easy to count hours, but it's much harder to measure the quality of those hours, what is actually learned and applied. What if we prepared, practiced, and presented a gospel passage to our language partner, and then created an audio that represented what we worked on? What if we submitted that audio as the significant substance of our work week? One person may get the same results in 10 hours which may take another person 15. Adding this dimension in an organized way as a part of our personal program design or curriculum may help shape the way we think about learning language toward more healthy and effective practices, that it's not just about "getting the hours" but much more about discourse ability and repertoire outcomes.

It's easy to fill our weeks up with language activities that don't get us very far. We can invest 10 minutes in a highly engaging activity and get a lot out of it. When asked how he learned Greek, Abraham Lincoln reputedly replied, "I used my 5 minutes wisely." We need to maximize time we have for peak performance. Language learning is often intense. If we spend too much time in intense learning activities, we will eventually lose concentration, wear ourselves out, or even get sick, potentially risking even more long-term effects of fatigue and frustration.

Learning efficiently is not about reducing the hours. That in itself is completely unhelpful. It's about maximizing the time we have with excellent practices and powerful learning rhythms.

We typically measure progress in language learning by the number of hours we spend in various activities. Perhaps it would be better for us to weigh the effectiveness of our language life through interpersonal encounters not measured by time, rather by what is done with people during that time. Learning better ways to get the most out of interpersonal encounters as we learn language and engage people around us – for example, preparing cultural questions, praying for people who we anticipate meeting, crafting gospel bridges and presentations, being ready with testimonies or personal life stories – can create powerful new spaces for language learning and meaningful interpersonal communication.

Learning Zone Practice #8: The Rhythm of Endurance

Run the mile you're in. (Ryan Hall, Olympic Marathoner)

Scott approached me to ask if I could help him arrange to do a language sprint. I'd never even heard of a language sprint! He described it as a burst of extreme language intensity for several weeks to hopefully jumpstart or infuse progress. He needed to do something and wanted to give this idea a try.

As a disciplined language learner and athlete, I had an idea that Scott was applying the basics of interval training he practiced with sports and fitness to language learning.[53] That made sense to me. Scott had spent years learning language for ministry in his community. He exemplified an effective ongoing learning rhythm he described as the "learner's posture" which he applied to his ministry practice. I love that concept. Scott never stopped learning, because the more language he learned, the better he could minister to his neighbors.

Scott had recently moved to a global city which took him out of his ministry language for a season. With a heavy travel and training schedule, and limited access to his ministry language and community, Scott could have taken a language break, but he didn't. As he prayed, the Lord led Scott to a community of unreached immigrants in the city from my part of the world who spoke the language I knew. I was thrilled as Scott began to learn their language and share the gospel with them. Scott was making progress and engaging in fruitful conversations, but it was definitely slow-going. With many other responsibilities, Scott had to make a strong effort to invest in the language and community with what little time he had.

After several months of limited progress, Scott and I began to put together his sprint, a four-week adventure that would include 60 weekly hours of intense, eclectic activities designed to push him to brink of his language input and output capacity, and then maybe a little bit more.[54]

We knew this would not be a sustainable pace but hoped he could manage it for a month. Scott's goals included: infusing his language with floods of fluency practice, nailing down some basic accuracy issues, overcoming some psychological plateaus brought on by the slow progress, and reorienting his learning posture so he could better engage his neighbors in his new language.

Scott spent the first three-weeks in my neighborhood. I barely saw him, but when I did, I could tell he was really pushing hard and making great progress. He was definitely getting tired but hanging in there. Scott arranged to spend his final week with his neighbor from his city who had returned to his hometown for a holiday. Honored to have Scott in his home, and proud of his improved language, Scott's neighbor did what most of my neighbors here do as he introduced him to everyone in the community as his guest which prompted many invitations to hours and hours of tea, conversation, and life in the neighborhood.

At the end of four weeks, Scott was tired, but fulfilled. He returned to his city having reached his goals. A week or two later I asked Scott if he had any surprising take-aways. He described that while the sprint had predictably helped him learn more language and engage at deeper and broader levels, it had unexpectedly helped him create a "new normal" for his learning and ministry practices in the language. The intensity of Scott's sprint seemed to ignite something in the normal day-in and day-out rhythm of learning and ministry that he practiced in the city. I guess interval training really does work for language learning! Basketball legend Steph Curry describes this interdisciplinary phenomenon, "When we overload ourselves in the workout with two basketballs and a tennis ball it makes the game seem a lot slower and you're able to process things a lot better."[55]

I was going to begin this section with something like, "language learning is a marathon, not a sprint." But it's really both, isn't it? As in any discipline – whether sports, academics, or language – when we aim for serious, ongoing improvement, we need to consider how to invest well in each section and season of our learning and practice healthy rhythms of endurance that push us to reach our full potential without suffering risks of burnout.[56]

I love the title of Ryan Hall's new book *Run the Mile You're In: Finding God in Every Step* (Zondervan, 2019). We can learn a lot from the guy who reached the pinnacle of elite distance running with God as his coach. As language learners, our greatest source of endurance, strength, growth, rest, and recovery is the joy of the Lord we find in our relationship with him. God cared for Elijah when he was facing life-threatening stress (1 Kings 19:1-9). God sustains, restores, and strengthens us to press on. He gives us the wisdom and courage we need to create healthy rhythms for each season of our learning. "The joy of the Lord is your strength" (Nehemiah 8:10).

Learning Zone Practice #9: Demystifying Progress

The benchmark for me is being able to communicate the gospel clearly in [my new language] in season and out and being able to effectively and intelligently disciple someone in [my new language]. (Sam, second-year learner)

What do I need to do to move forward? (Mel, first-year learner)

I want to help cast a vision and provide tools to reach discourse fluency so we can reach *gospel fluency*. We need to know when and how to create goals toward hearing and understanding simple scriptures that speak the gospel, how we can share our simple testimony in the daily conversations of life, and how to invite people to respond to the gospel in the daily context of our lives as we understand their world. We need to develop a new way of envisioning progress, where we are not thinking about levels, rather we are thinking about the repertoires of conversations we engage in, and portfolios of stories we practice.

We as learners have a stake in our language progress. Language policy for many sending organizations may articulate minimum level requirements as a starting point for effective ministry. Sadly, many of us often see this as a final level to reach, and nothing more. What prevents us from seeing the need to continue learning beyond minimum standards, to master fluency toward more fruitful ministry outcomes? How can we see beyond the enforcement of policy and begin to own the evaluation process of our personal language and ministry progress toward reaching *gospel fluency*?

Is it possible for us to reorient our perspective of language levels, viewing our proficiency not as a point or level, rather as the dynamic of what we can do, and what we cannot yet do, in both breadth and depth of expression, as well as pronunciation and listening nuances, so that we can find a path forward? Are we willing and able to take that next step, our next language assignment, whatever it may be, and begin to seriously align it with our overall calling and purpose?

> This week I was able to share the story in Mark 2:1-12 with my teacher. I shared with her three examples from the story, all relating to Jesus being God. Without preparing that passage I would not have been able to explain it so clearly. She asked some good questions. It was neat because God used an assignment to share gospel truths with my teacher. (Karen, first-year learner)

I love this perspective! This week Karen was able to make measurable progress in her language. This tells me Karen made it her goal to share this story from the Gospel of Mark. This was an assignment that she created for herself. No one else told her to do this. Karen made it her goal to share three examples all relating to Jesus as God. This defined her path of learning, guided her preparation, and helped her see truth in her new language in a new light which she was able to then share with her teacher.

I am a strong advocate for creating smart goals like these for every two weeks of our learning as we pursue *gospel fluency*. Creating smart goals is the best way to get feedback, as we saw Karen do with her teacher, and then monitor or track this feedback. This creates a personal history of progress and a veritable roadmap to fluency, providing a healthy and clear perspective for what we have done, what we are able to do, and informing us where and how we need to move forward with confidence and success.

When we, as learners, create our own personal progress history – that is, when we create regular and frequent goals, aspire and work hard to reach those goals, and create an environment where we can regularly present the outcomes of those goals for immediate feedback – we can then more readily see how our current daily language journey fits into the greater *gospel fluency* picture.

When we know where we are in our language ability, and when we have a pretty good idea of what we need to do to improve, at least for the next two weeks, and for the foreseeable future, we stop focusing on levels and tests and begin to enter into the practice and proficiency of our conversational and presentational fluency. The practice of using this kind of regular and frequent *documentation of progress* provides us the integrity we need to measure the dynamic development of our overall *discourse fluency*, which directly corresponds to our overall *gospel fluency* progress. (Appendix 3 describes *Language Portfolios* as a creative means to track personal language progress.)

Learning Zone Practice #10: Envisioning

I will not be content until I can minister in [my new language] similar to how I would be able to in English. I know this is a lofty goal. But the gospel, as well as deep spiritual truths and doctrines, best communicate in the heart language of a people. I firmly believe this. This is what drives me. (Sam)

Sam's perspective (which you may recall from the beginning of this chapter, reproduced above) represents vision. We always need to keep the vision of our language and calling before us. The best way I can explain or describe this is simply through the words of learners who relentlessly and faithfully practice this.

> I need to be grounded in the Word of God in their language. My language has to be at a place where I can take them to the Word of God, that my hunger for the Word is contagious, so they hunger and search for the things that deeply satisfy their souls, suffering, and pain. (Alice, diaspora worker)

Alice works with displaced peoples who have experienced great trauma and continue to suffer in ways we can hardly even imagine. She has entered into their lives, using their language, to listen, empathize, and share the eternal hope and great comfort of the gospel. She can only do this with great language.

> Language learning is one of the hardest things I've ever done. What was the game changer for me? I had "hard language" with no "ministry joy." It was torture. But when I found ministry joy in the hard language progress, it was no longer torture. It was rewarding. (Greg, first-year learner)

Greg began to experience the joy of language learning once he began to see the purpose in a new light, one that ushered him to enter into ministry while using the language. Even the simplest story or testimony we learn to tell can ignite a fire in our souls that continues to burn as we learn to share Christ in deeper and wider ways in our new language.

> I have a superior opportunity when I am able teach the word of God in my new language, and a superior need to engage people at a heart level. (Jenny, third-year learner)

Some see "superior" only as an ACTFL language level. I tend to agree with Jenny, that it's an opportunity and a need right in front of us, calling our names. Sometimes we just need to take the labels off our language levels and put them into the vision God has given us as we dive deep and wide into the ministry to which God has called us.

Reflect and Respond

1. How deep is your language? Describe a time when you conversed with your neighbor about heart issues.

2. How wide is your language? What is one way you can widen your language, cultural, and relational context, so you can more broadly relate to your neighbors on various topics of common interest?

3. Consider barrier 10, the *Mediocre Plateau*, and briefly describe where you see yourself on the *Learning Zone vs Comfort Zone* chart.

4. What have you been doing well? What is one barrier you have successfully avoided, and one learning zone practice you are currently doing?

5. What do you need to stop doing? What is at least one barrier you would like to avoid?

6. What do you need to begin doing? What is one learning zone practice you would like to start?

9

Language 180

God prepares our minds and hearts for each gospel encounter. The gospel is for us, every day. The gospel is also for our lost neighbor, every day.

Several months into our language experience in our new city we moved into a duplex with the local community mosque compound on one side and the community football pitch on the other. We began to meet our neighbors and soon our lives were full of invitations from tea with the women to football matches with the men.

Every day, conversations flowed from one topic to the next, and I did my best to share the gospel whenever I could. It was about that time that I began to have my quiet time in my new language, and I shared this with my language partner, Yohannes.

Yohannes, a new believer, began doing something with me which changed the course of my life. He heard me try to share the gospel and saw that I needed a lot of help. So, he told me to share with him whatever I had been reading from God's word that morning during my quiet time.

I truly believe God brought Yohannes into my life for this purpose. I would very simply re-tell whatever I had read that morning, in my own words. Yohannes would patiently listen to me. Then he would ask a question. Maybe another. Or offer a thought. The more we did this, the richer our discussions became. We went through many Bible passages and talked about many things that helped me better understand how Yohannes, and therefore how my neighbors, heard the gospel. You see, Yohannes was not only my language partner, he was also my neighbor, and theirs.

As I prepared and practiced working through the gospel by myself, and then with Yohannes, I found myself, in my mind and heart, more ready, confident, and eager to share the gospel in my new language with my lost neighbors.

I would return home and sit with the guys at the mosque after prayers, or on the soccer pitch after practice. We would talk and through our conversation I would share Christ with them, every day, more and more, from God's word. I was becoming fluent in the gospel in the language of my neighbors. And God was using Yohannes in this process.

Language 180

Toward a sustained lifestyle of evangelism and discipleship in the language, we practice learning the language to communicate the gospel 3 hours per day, 60 minutes in each of three activities, for a total of 180 minutes.

I have experienced the desperation of not feeling fluent enough to share Christ with my lost neighbors. Often distracted by grueling seasons of travel, meetings, other work, or for some other reason or excuse, I just needed to re-engage. Distractions abound in our hectic lives. I needed something to keep me alive in the language and ministry God had called me to. And I wasn't alone.

I talked with some other guys who were feeling the same way. We challenged each other to read the Bible and pray in the language for our personal devotional time. For many of us, this was an uphill climb, but well worth it and deeply enriching to our souls.

We practiced going through what we learned from God's word, every day, first by ourselves alone with God, then with a trusted friend, and then again with a lost neighbor. Our aim was to log three hours per day, one hour in each activity, for a total of 180 minutes per day. We started calling this *Language 180*.

Language 180 gave me the drive to share my faith and disciple people as I became more fluent in the gospel in my new language. *Language 180* represents the heart and soul of *gospel fluency* as an on-going fruitful practice in cross-cultural ministry. *Language 180* raises my level of communication ability and gives me the fluency I need to regularly and confidently proclaim the gospel and disciple believers.

Summary of Language 180

Language 180 is a solid basic-conversational-fluency-and-beyond strategy designed to get us on the path toward *gospel fluency*. In hour one, we work through many simple familiar gospel passages, learning what it means to *ruminate* on Scripture in our new language, to personally identify with the message of the gospel.

In hour two, we practice sharing the gospel with a trusted friend, neighbor, ministry partner, language partner, or teammate. We practice telling them what we have worked through that morning alone with the Lord and engage in conversations about the topic. We invite their thoughts and questions so that we can learn, discover, disciple, and be discipled. We literally model what it means to share the gospel with our lost neighbors.

In hour three, very likely broken down into the accumulation of many conversations in the chai house, on the soccer pitch, in homes, at work, and with all fluency, we get to share the gospel with our neighbors, that very gospel we have been so diligently preparing and practicing throughout the day. This is Language 180. This is *gospel fluency*.

Gospel Fluency Preparation: The First Hour

Think about language learning as a part of your worship to the Lord. God can meet you in your second language. God can speak to you from his word in your second language. (Josiah Daniels)

You can't give what you don't have. (MM, co-worker)

Our preparation in the word of God, in our new language, is not a time just to gather information and prepare a speech; it is a pursuit of our holy God who loves us dearly. From the intimacy we have with God, our communion with him is also very much how we live in the expectation to testify of his goodness, his very real goodness, to those around us. When we realize how desperate we are to encounter God even when our neighbors may not even know his name, we step into our calling to close that gap. We – rather God in us and through us, and through his word as we proclaim it – invite them to come to him and to encounter him, and we can live and walk in that expectation.

> This week I grew in my understanding of God's word. After spending so much time looking at Mark 2, I realized that when I studied it in my new language, I noticed things that I hadn't seen before. I'm thankful that God allowed me to understand more about Him through studying the Scriptures in [my new language]. (Karen, second-year learner)

I simply want to remind us of the importance of filling our hearts and minds with the word of God. What God does in us he will do through us. Everything emerges from our personal relationship with Jesus. We need to be in God's word, sharing his word with those around us; this is who we are, this is our life, he is our life.

My neighbor Levent drank too much and beat his wife. We actually lived close enough to hear them fight and see a lot of the fallout from this on a daily basis. One evening over tea in our home with him and his wife Berrin, I asked Levent about his past. He had grown to hate his job as a government employee and so retired early. He was tired of the corruption, and wanted to start over, but he still just wasn't able to shake off some of his bad habits.

I had been reading through the book of Mark. That week I had read the story of Jesus calling Matthew out of a life of sin and corruption, and how this had changed his life. Jesus said, "It is not those who are well who need a doctor, but those who are sick. I didn't come to call the righteous, but sinners" (Mark 2:17). I thought about how God had rescued me from my life of sin and had so supernaturally changed my life.

I shared the gospel from this Bible passage and encouraged Levent and Berrin to consider Jesus' offer of new life. Levent listened hard. We prayed together. I asked God to convict them of sin, free them from addiction and abuse, and save them through faith in Christ. I sensed new hope and an open door to the gospel where there had been none. I live for these kinds of gospel conversations with my neighbors.

I have found that on days when I tarry in his word, and wait, and listen, in prayer, I find food for my soul. I dare not rise from my knees until I am satisfied from his holy word. We can step back and see the tapestry that God is weaving in our lives and testify of the gospel to our lost neighbors, and we continue to abide in him in this process.

I have found that on days when I am rushed, or lazy, and I am not nourished from his word, the gospel is not so near to my heart. While God by his grace may use me on those days, I still run the risk of personal self-doubt and defeat.

We need to pursue and encounter God's word every day. God's word is a personal reminder to each of us of the gospel in our lives. How do we prepare to share the gospel with our neighbors? We begin by reminding ourselves of the gospel from God's word. How is the gospel, the leaven of the gospel, changing us, working through the whole dough of our lives, today? This is our daily walk, and our daily witness. "When we get a good glimpse of God and his gospel, we are strongly encouraged to live boldly and proclaim boldly" (David Platt).

Meditating on Scripture

I have a personal practice of writing down or printing off 8-10 verses in my language every morning for reading and meditation as I pray. Rick Warren talks about how important it is to meditate or ruminate on Scripture:

> Rumination is what a cow does when she chews her cud. She rolls her cud over and over in her mouth. That's similar to how you meditate on Scripture. Cows eat the grass, chew it up, and send it to their stomachs pretty quickly. There it lies in the stomach, soaking up all of those acids and chemicals. Then, after a while, the cow burps it back up with a new and renewed flavor, chews on that grass and some other grass, and does the whole process over again. Cows repeat this several times. They get every ounce of nutrition out of the grass. Biblical meditation is kind of like that; it's thought digestion. God wants us to get every ounce of spiritual nutrition out of his Word. He wants us to chew on it, digest it, and then chew on it some more.[57]

I try to ruminate as I read Scripture in my host language. We should never stop learning, in our minds, and in our hearts. Let's use whatever we can do to help us learn the language to reach gospel fluency. These are great practices for getting God's word in the language into our souls and into our daily conversations.

As we practice ruminating on God's word in our new language, at first in very simple ways, we learn what God is saying to us through his word, in the language. This is indeed a cognitive challenge for us and can be a slow process. We desperately need traction and patience. In God's word, and by his strength, we find hope in this process.

God renews our minds as we read and pray through Scripture. This process continues and will continue for as long as we learn the language, and as we read the Bible in the language.

We honor God as we learn to read his word in our new language. He enables us to understand his word, and to begin to teach it with greater fluency and confidence as we make progress.

This is an important part of our testimony. We testify of the gospel in our lives as we learn to proclaim with greater fluency in the language. We testify of God's strength in our weakness as we learn to communicate the gospel fluently in our new language, a task which at times may seem impossible. This really is God at work in our lives. He is the one who empowers us to teach the gospel to our neighbors in their language.

This whole practice needs to be a part of our hour of preparation. This is a time of reading, but is also a time of meditation, and a time to ascend to God's presence in prayer. There is spiritual benefit to praying and meditating on scriptures in another language. God ministers to our hearts as we abide in his presence.

> Take time. Give God time to reveal Himself to you. Give yourself time to be silent and quiet before Him, waiting to receive, through the Spirit, the assurance of His presence with you, His power working in you. Take time to read His Word as in His presence, that from it you make known what He asks of you and what He promises you. Let the Word create around you, create within you a holy atmosphere, a holy heavenly light, in which your soul will be refreshed and strengthened for the work of daily life.[58]

David Matthis, Executive Editor of desiringGod.org, provides twelve carefully selected "gospel passages" that get at the very heart of the biblical good news in just two to four verses. He exhorts us, "These short sections are ripe for memorization, and at least warrant some extended time of reflection. Build your life on them and around them and let them shape and flavor everything. Soak in them – and soak them in."[59]

What a great concept – *to soak in them and soak them in*. Gospel preparation in our new language is a time to meditate on God's word and abide in his presence, and to contend for the hope we have in God, in our hour of need.

My goal is to work through Scriptures in my new language with spiritual integrity, as well as doing everything I can to maintain the integrity of the text, while expressing the discourse in a way that communicates the intended message.

Gospel Fluency Practice: The Second Hour

Go alongside someone, a national brother or sister, helping them in tough training or discipleship situations. Sweat through it,

bear through the embarrassment. Their response will be one of honor and encouragement. And they, the nationals, will do likewise.
(Carlton Vandagriff)

I love to hear Yuri talk about the gospel. I try to get as much time with him as I can. He appreciates my efforts when I come prepared to share the gospel from God's word in his language, my new language. He's a willing and patient partner in this process.

Yuri shares with me what God has said to him through his word. And I try to do the same with him. This practice has been good for both of us. I get to listen to how Yuri shares his faith, what he says, how he listens, and how he responds. This is great practice for me. But it's far more than practice. It's testimony. It's an act of brotherly love and encouragement. We sharpen each other.

We meet as often as we can. I consider my personal time with Yuri a gift. I know I am learning so much. But I also know that Yuri is growing as a disciple through our relationship and through the time we have together. We have both grown in our faith, and in our faithfulness to share the gospel.

Yuri now regularly shares his faith with his lost neighbors from a fresh and daily understanding of the gospel in his life. This is because he spends time, as he describes it, bowing before the Lord, in God's word, and in prayer. I love that image. And he doesn't get up until he hears the gospel, once again, loud and clear; as the Lord calls him, once again, to share the gospel with his lost neighbors. This is a great practice of discipleship and evangelism.

If I can learn this from Yuri, and if I can in any way encourage Yuri in this practice, then this is how I want to spend my life.

Key Players: Ministry Partners

We bear the burden of reaching all peoples, though we also bear the burden of equipping the saints to reach all peoples.
(Mark, co-worker)

I will most gladly spend and be spent for you
(2 Corinthians 12: 15).

Yuri is a key player in my ministry, and in my language learning. As we have described the synchrony between language learning and *gospel fluency*, there is also certainly a strong relationship between the fruitful practice of *gospel fluency*, and our spiritual investment in the lives of national partners and team members.

As we progress in language and ministry, our national partners become some of our most important key players in our pursuit of *gospel fluency*. Our language practice should demonstrate to them our desire to proclaim the gospel to our neighbors, who are also their neighbors. This means learning to pray in the language with them. This means learning to teach the Bible in the language from them.

Drawing on the influence and help of national partners, Will sent me this note of exhortation:

> I had a long talk with our national ministry partner about what it means to be a good worker. His two exhortations were to: 1) Know the culture better than you know the language and as good as you know the Bible and 2) Make the local church feel responsibility for itself. He also gave several examples from his years of ministry partnership with foreigners and it has helped give me a goal to shoot for.

These are pearls of wisdom. What an honor to learn from guys like Will's national ministry partner. When they can see the value in our language and culture development for the purpose of more effective ministry, ministry that actually empowers the local church, they can become key advocates and players in helping us improve our language and ministry practices.

Key Players: Language Partners

I am more convinced than ever that we need to bathe all of our "language partner" relationships in prayer, seeking the Lord's favor and wisdom as we invest time, energy, and money into these key players in our work.

Language tutors, helpers, and conversation partners, usually hired, hold a huge stake in our learning. They are the ones who generally provide the intermediary controlled input and output we need to stay within our language learning zone.

Language partners who have this disproportionate role and impact on the language learning transfer process so critical toward creating an environment for our progress represent our *single most influential* resource to ensure the best results. In other words, language partners are usually our best resource for the controlled and powerful input and output practice we need to effectively learn language and can yield our best practice toward sustained fluency. That means we need to carefully consider what we need from our language partners, and how to best work with them. We must draw from our language partners the critical and helpful feedback only they can provide, in the high-investment environment we create with them.

The best way to do this is to prepare well, and to present and dialogue on many topics of great interest every day. We need to be surrounded by language partners who are invested in our progress, who take interest in helping us, who truly partner with us in the process.

We need to pray for our language partners. As significant as their roles are in our lives, so our roles are in their lives, particularly in our gospel witness. God will work in and through these relationships for his glory as we pursue fruitful language and ministry.

Key Players: Peers

Our peers are most often our co-workers and teammates who are also learning and using the language right along with us. They are key players in our language learning endeavors precisely because they, too, are on the journey. We may be a step or two ahead in language, or a step or two behind, but we can always benefit by learning from each other. How can we best do this?

We need to know how to cultivate the value of peer practice and peer review on our teams. We as learners need to be grateful for any help our teammates can provide. What a privilege to have co-workers help us as we help them in the language learning process, as we help each other become more fluent in sharing the gospel. It's amazing how an environment and attitude of humble cooperation on a team cultivates such a positive collective language experience.

Many learners are hesitant to practice their new language with non-native speakers, including teammates, fearing that this will promote bad listening and speaking habits. In fact, the opposite is true. Practicing with non-natives does not hurt our language progress, and can actually enhance our language practice and progress, as long as we include diverse practice with native speakers. We should never be shy to use our language, mistakes and all, with any and all native and non-native speakers – teammates, peers, national partners – everyone!

Jenn and Lauren have coffee together each week for accountability and prayer. Every other week they enjoy using only their new language as they converse and pray together. Jenn is more fluent, but is patient with Lauren, who is an eager and able learner.

Scott and Rick meet with a national disciple. Scott starts off reading and talking through a few verses. Rick, more experienced in the language, picks up from where Scott leaves off. Each week, Scott gets better and contributes more.

A couple of singles at the end of their first year on the field meet for lunch with their team leader to talk about how things are going. They decide to have the whole conversation in Russian.

No-Shame Policy

We need to shed the shame on our teams. Every team should work toward some sort of peer-to-peer language practice as a part of their team culture. I'm not talking about formal lessons, scripts, and certainly nothing evaluative. I'm talking about a common practice that praises and encourages a pursuit of *gospel fluency* for all – through furious resolve, and profound humility. I don't know how else to say it: We just need the attitude of Christ to permeate our teams (Philippians 2:5).

As language learners we can so easily experience inferiority, inadequacy, insufficiency, and insecurity due to the psychological challenges of learning a new language. Add to that the spiritual darkness most of us live around that can exacerbate these feelings as we try to put the language into practice.

We need opportunities in team gatherings to share really cool stories about what God is doing through our pursuit of *gospel fluency*. This infuses an atmosphere of encouragement, characterized by Christ-like humility. The shared exhortation to pursue *gospel fluency* is a good example of how teams can really practice loving one another by sharing joys, burdens, and meeting needs.

So, let us encourage one another. We need to embrace no-shame policies so that less experienced learners can freely and enthusiastically practice and learn the language from their more-experienced peers, or vice versa.

Let us not be deterred or inhibited to use our new language with other learners, teammates, and even international partners. Remember, speaking the language with non-native speakers does not in inherently yield poor language habits, and can be a great practice. Do we know of international teams who already practice speaking the language with each other as the common language of the team? If we don't, we need to get ready for it. This is the future of our work.

Fluent Gospel Proclamation: The Third Hour

If I were to do it over, I would want my neighbors to know that they too can really dialogue with God all the time, even before they come to Christ; and I would pray with them, all the time.
(David S, veteran co-worker)

Tell them why it's real! Just tell people what God has done for you! (Timur)

Sometimes real-life gospel conversations with neighbors in a new language are just hard. It's especially difficult to share the gospel with non-believers who have such a very different view of the world and of the truth. We need help. We need encouragement. And we need practice. How can we take the engaging content of the gospel that we have prepared and used in a safe environment with encouraging partners, and share it fluently through our daily conversations with our lost neighbors?

> I am realizing that once my language increases, I had the mentality that spiritual conversations would be easy. However, I am quickly learning that every person in our city believes different things about their own religion and have been taught different things about Christianity. My challenge is knowing when to be direct, because they aren't afraid to be. (Abby, third-year learner)

Fluent gospel proclamation is the culmination of hours of deliberate preparation and practice. As we prepare and practice, we become fluent in the language of our neighbors, able to proclaim the gospel to them, through all walks of life. This is our hope. And this is our prayer. As we prepare and practice understanding and speaking the message of the gospel from the Bible in our new language, we become fluent – both mentally and spiritually – to share Christ with our lost neighbors. Each new day in God's word in our new language brings a fresh awareness of the gospel to our minds and hearts, and a renewed desire to communicate the gospel to all those around us, at all times, in their language.

Our commitment to prepare and practice *gospel fluency* on a daily basis sustains and develops our fluency in the language and in the gospel through an expanding and deepening repertoire of gospel passages from the Bible. Our pursuit of this level of fluency – both in the language, and in the gospel –

is something we all can do. We can practice this pursuit. We can become fluent.

I rejoice in the opportunities I have had to minister to Elias, my artist friend; to my military-background neighbor; to Levent, who struggles with alcohol, and his wife Berrin, who suffers abuse; and to so many others whom God continues to bring into my life. It is these gospel encounters that I long for. I have Christ's commission to follow. We all do. God prepares our minds and hearts for each gospel encounter. The gospel is for us, every day. The gospel is also for lost our neighbors, every day.

As I consider our call to proclaim the gospel in our new languages, to reach *gospel fluency*, and to practice *Language 180* or something like it, I am deeply aware how fully and wholly I must depend on God's grace and on his strength in all of this; and I am reminded of Nelli, who hosts our house church in her home, along with her husband, Yuri. With no use of her arms and legs, restricted to her bed and wheelchair, physically unable to do anything for herself, she is fully dependent on her husband as her caregiver. In a more real sense, she has placed her dependence, her faith, fully in God. How do I know this? Because every time I see her lying in her bed, she peppers our conversation – as she does with neighbors she encounters everyday – with Scriptures she has read through and through, meditated on, believes in, and testifies…and she exhorts me to do the same.

Recently, my youngest son and I were visiting Nelli with a few of his friends. In true form, she exhorted these boys to read Philippians 4:12-13 from God's word with these instructions:

> First, have your dad read the passage aloud, slowly, and twice through. Listen hard, listen to God.

Then wait, in silent prayer, for five minutes, and think about what you just heard.

Then take five minutes to write down what you just thought about.

Then, as a group, talk about what you wrote down, one by one.

Simple, profound teaching. I was not at all surprised to hear as these boys shared – each with tears in his eyes – what the Lord had so powerfully taught them from his word through this dear sister's exhortation:

> I know both how to make do with little, and I know how to make do with a lot. In any and all circumstances I have learned the secret of being content – whether well fed or hungry, whether in abundance or in need. I am able to do all things through him who strengthens me (Philippians 4:12-13).

Daily Readings

I choose short vibrant readings from the Bible to guide my daily preparation, practice, and proclamation of the gospel. The gospel of Jesus Christ which I read in the Bible every day is what I practice with my language partner and with those whom I am discipling.

This is what I read, pray through, think on, and talk about with people. It's on my mind and heart. This is how the gospel enters into conversations I have with neighbors throughout the day.

I began doing *Language 180* as a daily practice working through the book of Mark. I then read through several other books, including some selected scriptures. Here are two of the reading plans I have followed. These are just examples. I encourage you to use whatever God puts on your heart. Just proclaim the gospel to yourselves and to your neighbors, every day.

MARK

WEEK	DAY 1	DAY 2	DAY 3	DAY 4	DAY 5
1	MARK 1:1-11	MARK 1:12-20	MARK 1:21-28	MARK 1:29-39	MARK 1:40-45
2	MARK 2:1-12	MARK 2:13-17	MARK 2:18-22	MARK 2:23-27	MARK 3:1-6
3	MARK 3:7-19	MARK 3:20-30	MARK 3:21-4:20	MARK 4:21-34	MARK 4:35-41
4	MARK 5:1-20	MARK 5:21-43	MARK 6:1-6	MARK 6:7-13	MARK 6:14-29
5	MARK 6:30-44	MARK 6:45-56	MARK 7:1-23	MARK 7:24-30	MARK 7:31-37
6	MARK 8:1-13	MARK 8:14-21	MARK 8:22-30	MARK 8:31-9:1	MARK 9:2-13
7	MARK 9:14-32	MARK 9:33-50	MARK 10:1-16	MARK 10:17-31	MARK 10:32-45
8	MARK 10:45-52	MARK 11:1-11	MARK 11:12-26	MARK 12:1-12	MARK 12:13-17
9	MARK 12:18-27	MARK 12:28-34	MARK 12:35-40	MARK 12:41-44	MARK 13:1-14
10	MARK 13:15-31	MARK 13:32-37	MARK 14:1-11	MARK 14:12-26	MARK 14:27-31
11	MARK 14:32-42	MARK 14:43-52	MARK 14:53-65	MARK 15:1-15	MARK 15:15-20
12	MARK 15:16-32	MARK 15:33-41	MARK 15:42-47	MARK 16:1-8	MARK 16:9-20

SELECTED TEXTS

WEEK	DAY 1	DAY 2	DAY 3	DAY 4	DAY 5
1	GEN. 1:1-2:2	PSALM 148	GEN. 2:2-25	PSALM 8	GEN. 3
2	ROM. 3:9-20	GEN. 6-9	GEN. 11:1-8	ROM. 3:21-26	ROM. 5:12-21
3	GEN. 12:1-9	ROM. 4:1-12	ROM. 4:13-25	GEN. 15:1-21	GEN. 22:1-18
4	IS. 52:13-53:12	JOHN 1:1-9	ACTS 8:26-40	GAL. 3:6-18	HEB. 11:1-19
5	EX. 31:18-32:14	EX. 32:15-33:6	EX. 33:7-23	EX. 34:1-14	LUKE 18:18-27
6	MATT. 5:1-10	MARK 5:17-24	MATT. 5:27-30	MATT. 5:38-48	ROM. 10:5-15
7	JOHN 1:10-18	JOHN 1:19-28	JOHN 1:29-34	JOHN 3:1-21	JOHN 4:1-26
8	JOHN 11:1-44	LUKE 15:11-32	LUKE 19:1-9	MATT. 27:32-56	LUKE 23:26-43
9	LUKE 23:44-55	LUKE 24:1-12	LUKE 24:36-49	ACTS 2:1-21	ACTS 2:22-47

The Gospel Diagram

Our goal is biblical fluency.

Brett had been sharing the gospel with Mahmut, but some things were still a little unclear. Brett then called Brock who came and spent an hour or so sharing a simple *Gospel Diagram* from selected Scriptures with Mahmut. This clarified the gospel for Mahmut and he placed his faith in Christ.

Brock's *Gospel Diagram* comes from years of experience simply sharing the gospel with his neighbors in their language from many Biblical texts throughout Scripture – stories, prophecies and other key passages – to provide a grand narrative of the gospel using the following diagram.

I love how Brock keeps it simple. I annotate Brock's description using Scripture texts that he often uses, while keeping the graph itself Scripture-free. In doing so, I want us to consider how we could abundantly and effectively apply various Scripture passages using this diagram or something like it to help us better proclaim the gospel while practicing *Language 180*. Brock begins with two horizontal lines that stretch to infinity:

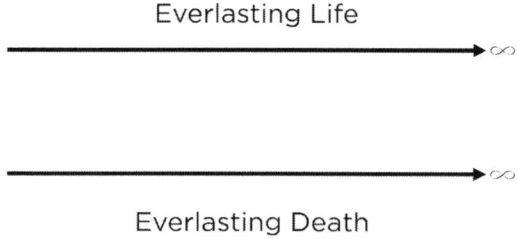

These are our only two options from now until eternity – everlasting life, or everlasting death. There are no other options. And we need to understand what they mean. We were created for eternal life with God, illustrated by the top line. The Bible explains it this way.

In the beginning, there was eternal God (Genesis 1:1-3). God created everything (1:1-26). God created man in his own image (1:27) for one purpose: to inherit everlasting life with God (1:27).

Everything was good (Genesis 1:31). God created woman to be with man and they lived perfectly in God's garden with neither shame nor sin (2:25), though God warned them not to sin (2:15-17).

Then the man and woman sinned (Genesis 3:1-7) and immediately sin and shame entered the world and came into their hearts. They were cast out of the garden. Their destination now was eternal death (illustrated by the downward "Fall" arrow.) This, too, is our destiny because of our sin. We lost everything, and fell to eternal death, forever.

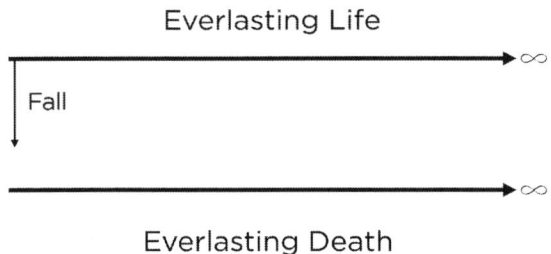

The man and woman tried to solve their shame by covering themselves with leaves (Genesis 3:7), but God provided the skin of an animal (3:21) to cover their shame. Though their relationship with God was now broken (3:23-4), God promised a descendant who would come as a savior (3:15).

Men continued to sin. Brother killed brother. All hated God. God destroyed the world with a flood. Because of his faith, God saved only Noah and his family in the ark (Genesis

6-9). Men at Babel then tried to build a tower to reach the heavens, and to make a name for themselves (Genesis 11:1-8), illustrated by the "Babel" tower image and upward arrows leading to infinite futility. It is only through our faith in Christ – not through religion, philosophy, or good works – that we can be reconciled to God.

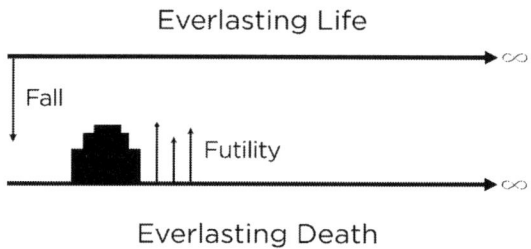

2000 years before Christ, God called Abraham out of his home to go to a land that he would show him. Abraham believed God and followed him (Genesis 12:1-3). God blessed Abraham with a son in his old age. Then God told Abraham to sacrifice his son, Isaac (22:1-14). Abraham obeyed God, and because of Abraham's wholehearted faith, God provided a ram for Abraham to sacrifice in place of his son. By faith, Abraham pointed to Jesus, God's only son, who would be sacrificed for our sins (illustrated by the "Prophecy" arrows pointing to our future hope in Christ.)

Moses (1400 BC) led the descendants of Abraham out of slavery in Egypt by the power of God through signs and wonders. The last sign was the death of each firstborn in all of Egypt. The angel of death 'passed over' the homes of the people of God, who had marked their doors with lamb's blood (Exodus 12:1-14, 21-32), and were therefore saved. By faith, Moses also pointed to Jesus (see "Prophecy" arrows) who saves us by his blood.

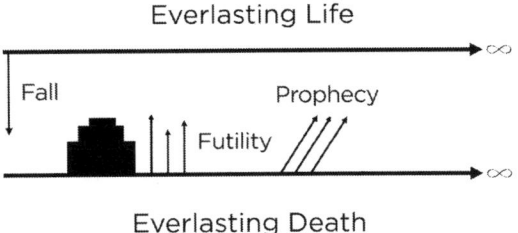

Isaiah (700 BC) prophesied about the eternal Lamb of God who takes away our sins (Isaiah 52:13 – 53:12) pointing to Christ's sacrificial death. John 1:1-18 says that Jesus Christ was the Word of God, God himself who had come to live among us. John the Baptist said of Jesus Christ who came to earth as a baby and died on the cross for our sins, "Behold the Lamb of God who takes away the sin of the world!" (John 1:29) illustrated by the cross of Christ. Jesus died on the cross to take away our sins. Only when we put our faith in Jesus can we be cleansed from sin, reconciled to God, and inherit eternal life.

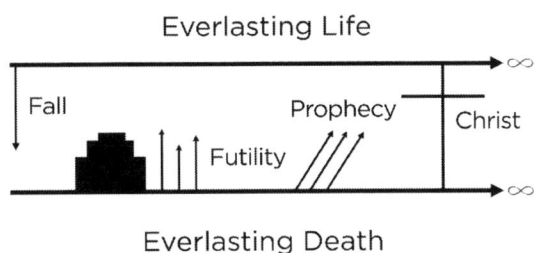

Jesus testified of himself as the fulfillment of all law and prophecy (Matthew 5:17). He prophesied of his death and resurrection (Luke 18:31-33), and actually died on the cross for our sins, and rose again from the grave (Luke 23-24). Jesus is God's only son (John 3:16), and those who believe in him are saved from eternal death to inherit eternal life (John 20:24-31).

We have all sinned and fall short of God's glory (Romans 3:23). But God showed his love for us in that while we were sinners Christ died for us (Romans 5:8). We deserve eternal death, but God's gift to us is eternal life through faith in Christ Jesus our Lord (Romans 6:23).

Jesus is the Passover Lamb (1 Cor 5:7), the last and only sacrifice (Hebrews 10:12), the final word of God to us, the heir of all things, through whom all things were created, the radiance of God's glory, the exact imprint of his nature, who upholds the universe by the word of his power, who made purification for our sins by his death on the cross, and is now seated at the right hand of the Majesty on high (Hebrews 1:1-3). "For you are saved by grace through faith, and this is not from yourselves; it is God's gift – not from works, so that no one can boast (Ephesians 2:8-9).

This is the faith that transforms our lives. This is the gospel message we are called to know, live, preach, and teach. As we follow Christ's commission to make disciples of all peoples let us never pursue anything less than a full-on commitment toward total fluency in our gospel message, encompassing the entire breadth and depth of all biblical truth in the languages and cultures God calls us to learn.

We cannot transmit the faith we do not know.
(Jen Wilkin, from The Future of Missions)

Reflect and Respond

1. Describe your personal Bible study and prayer life in your new language. If you currently do not practice having your quiet time in the language, how can you envision doing this? Do you read a short passage, write in your journal, or take audio notes? Be specific.

2. Envision talking about what you've learned with a key person in your life – a language partner, ministry partner, someone else. How can that person help you improve your ability to share the gospel as you together practice what you've prepared? Take a moment to pray for that person, even if you don't yet know him or her.

3. Reflect on this statement: When we intentionally prepare and practice "gospel fluency" each day, we are prompted to share the gospel with our lost neighbors each day.

4. Imagine doing *Language 180* every day, or as often as you can. Describe the challenges; the benefits.

10

1000 Cups of Tea

Recovering the lost art of neighboring across cultures.

My pastor Mike and I would meet for coffee every week when we were in the US for a season. It was a highlight. I just enjoyed the time together. We talked about a lot of things. Common interests. What happened over the past week, joys, needs; always food for my soul. "How are the kids?...How was your week?...How's work?...Did you guys have a good time at the picnic last Thursday?...How's was your wife's visit with her sister?" Whatever we talked about just added great mortar to our friendship.

I don't remember a lot of the specifics we talked about. I *do* remember the care, the friendship, the love; that I mattered to Mike; that he was my pastor and friend, and that our time together was important to him. It was time together that I loved. And I think what I loved most about this time was that it was never rushed, and somehow conversation would wind its way into our hearts. Mike would share what was going on in his life, and ask me how I was doing, at a heart level.

We had long finished our coffee, and Mike just knew when and how to drill down, inviting me to explore our hearts together. Those were some of my best times with my pastor. Encouraging, God-honoring, sometimes a little messy, but I always came away from those times spiritually uplifted.

"People may not remember what I preach, but they remember how I pastor" (Mike Fritcher).

I realized there is a certain understanding, in a *discourse* sense – if we were to call this kind of conversation "discourse" – and even in a *spiritual* sense – if we were to pull back the curtain to see the inner workings of the Spirit of God throughout the conversation – to how topics of conversation and discussion tend to oscillate from more surface levels of mutual interest, to deeper levels of heart interest. Mike knew how to do this. He was wise. He was discerning. He was a pastor. He did this with such authenticity, such genuine affection and care. I felt loved and trusted. I felt pastored.

I think of the many times Jesus dined with sinners, tax collectors, his disciples, Pharisees, good friends such as Mary, Martha, and Lazarus. He must have spent hours and hours with people in their homes, "reclining at the table" (Luke 11:37, Mark 2:15, John 12:2, etc.). These verses do far more than just create context and setting. They demonstrate the abundance of time and attention Jesus must have intentionally invested with people to reach them where they were, as he ministered to them. It was through hours and hours with neighbors in their homes, over meals, just being together, that we see the path to the gospel Jesus trod with them.

In Luke 19, when Jesus first met Zacchaeus, he told him to climb down from the tree because he was going with him to his home to be his guest. Zacchaeus came down and welcomed him gladly. Jesus honored Zacchaeus by entering his home, at risk of his reputation. Zacchaeus was the chief tax collector, and people grumbled that Jesus went to dine with him in his home.

Something happened to Zacchaeus' heart during this encounter that brought him to repentance. We can infer that Jesus honored Zacchaeus by entering his home, and probably showed him great affection as a good doctor would his sick patient. Whatever they talked about at the dinner table must have led to a level of trust and openness that brought Zacchaeus' heart to a steeping point of hearing and receiving the gospel Jesus shared with him.

In John 21, the disciples had been fishing all night and had caught nothing. Jesus told them where to cast their net and in one attempt they caught 153 fish. Peter dragged the net ashore and John, the writer, emphasizes that even with that many fish, the net was not torn. Jesus invited them to breakfast. These fishermen must have had a lot to talk about as they ate. The Bible then says that, "when they had finished breakfast, Jesus said to Simon Peter, 'Simon, son of John, do you love me more than these?'" (John 21:15).

I don't want to miss the effect of this transition. It does not say that Jesus asked Simon Peter this question *during* breakfast, rather very specifically tells us that he asked him when they *had finished eating*. There is something very special and powerful about their dining together, on the beach, right then at that time, that communicated mutual affection, trust, and created an environment of grace. Jesus knew the rhythm, and John, Peter, and the others got it. They had just dined together. They knew Jesus loved them. This was an incredibly important part of the whole dynamic of Jesus reinstating Peter. He didn't bark the order. We need to remember that when Jesus pulled Peter aside to talk with him, his fingers were probably still greasy from the fish they shared together, and his clothes smelled like the smoke of the fire they were sitting around.

> The single desire of our hearts can be expressed in a thousand ways, through the loss, beliefs, pain, shame, hopes, dreams, failures, fears, through a thousand scripts of life, over a thousand cups of tea.

I live in a tea culture. There is a certain art to brewing tea correctly. It has to steep. You have to know how to boil the water, when to add the leaves, and how long you need to wait until it's ready to serve. I remember hearing a colleague laugh about the first time he was called upon to serve tea. It turned out to be hot water and leaves – tasteless! His guests applauded his efforts, and then proceeded to show him how to really make tea.

Conversations, like tea, need to steep. They take time with people face to face. Our hearts are warmed by the friendship, the honor, the affection. Sometimes we just need to watch and learn from our neighbors how to do this.

My German friend Marcus told me about a conversation he recently had in his new language here in this city with two local friends who were both followers of Christ. One of them asked, "Why are we Christians so anti-social?" He said it shocked and confused him, so he asked him what he meant by that.

Marcus' local friends described recently attending a neighborhood meeting at their former place of worship, and then getting calls from at least five people the next week, just asking to hang out, have tea, or go to a movie – no other agenda. Anyone who did not show up got called. "Hey, what's wrong? Why aren't you here? Are you okay?" And this happened all the time, every week. They always called each other up, and they always went out for tea.

At first, Marcus protested, "It's unbiblical to not love each other." But after hearing several more examples of the same kind of experience, he began to wonder, "Do you think this is because local Christians have learned how to socialize with each other from us foreigners?"

Marcus explained to them that we in the West often feel that to call and invite someone right away seems like pressuring someone. To call every two or three days is against our Western culture. To invite someone without a reason seems awkward for us. To just knock at the door and visit someone without planning it a week in advance feels rude.

Sadly, Marcus' local friends understood all too well what he meant. One of them confessed that when his American believing friend recently invited him for a meal, he sensed an agenda. Sure enough, he had one. Yes, he sighed, he is now well adjusted to the way Christian foreigners behave. When Marcus asked him if he would just show up at a Christian friend's doorstep uninvited, he said no – but he does it all the time with his local non-believing friends.

I was convicted when I heard this story from Marcus. Together we agreed to make a habit of calling for no other reason than to ask friends and neighbors how they are. "Let's show them that we care, that we think about them, that time with them is important just because we are with them. Let's drink more unscheduled tea!"

I shared this story with Mateo, a Latino friend living in our city. Mateo has led many people to Christ. He spends lots of time with people. He disciples people. I treasure his advice: "Let's do less meetings and drink more tea together. What we do in our culture is not important, if people here think different. The way local people do things must be more effective, in order to achieve God's Kingdom purpose here. Love needs to be lived in a practical way."

Considering our value for community, we need to put this into practice in our lifestyle with our neighbors. If our neighbors practice community with each other better than we do with each other, let alone with them, then we are not practicing who we say we are. We are a community of faith. We are also a faith of community.

What does it mean for us to honor our neighbors enough to give ourselves to the time and space needed to have tea together, regularly, with no agenda? We must love the person in front of us enough to put down our phones and attend to them.

Tom Brewster described a conversation over tea in his home with an African neighbor who confessed how so often he was received by foreign believers at the door post of their homes as if to say (as often they did), "What do you want?"

About two and a half hours into the conversation it became apparent why Tom's guest had come when he reached into his jacket and pulled out a gift wrapped in newspaper. Do we ever wonder, as Tom did, "How many gifts have never been given?"

How many times have we found ourselves just trying to get something done with a neighbor, a disciple, or a national co-worker, without inviting them into our lives for conversation and tea? "Some things just can't be done leaning against a door post."[60]

When we come into our conversations and relationships with an agenda, people sense it and will not robotically respond to what we're driving at. We don't drive people to the cross, we lead them. It's these hours and hours of "steeping" our relationships in genuine affection and trust that lead people to respond in repentance and faith as Peter did, as Zacchaeus did.

One of the special advantages we have as guests and language learners is the opportunity to come into a conversation over tea, coffee, or cool water, with a certain amount of preparation that adds to the sense of strong interest we bring into the topics of mutual interest, hence, the relationship.

I spoke with a learner who had done some research on his neighbor's home village in central Anatolia before meeting with him for tea one day. This preparation he had done provided great context for their conversation. My friend's neighbor was so honored that my friend showed such a genuine interest in his village. This led to multiple future conversations about childhood, family, and the differences between life there and life in the city, and even opened up an invitation to the village, to meet his neighbor's relatives and neighbors. Every conversation brought new opportunities to learn and prepare a little bit more for the next conversation through thoughtful questions and discussions on related topics.

One of the things we try to help learners practice is the art of transitioning from one topic to another. When we, as learners, engage in conversations with our neighbors, we commonly enter these conversations unprepared and, therefore, to some extent, unengaged. As much as possible, let us aspire to enter into conversations with neighbors in their language with this mindset: "I am interested in being here with you. I want to engage in topics of common interest. I have been thinking about this. You are important to me."

This means we need to take extra time and energy to invest, to prepare our thoughts on these topics. We're not trying to drive an agenda. We're not trying to manipulate or steer conversations toward certain topics. We're just trying to learn how to engage in the flow of conversations better, to take a more active role, to engage. We need to learn to prepare the tea and serve it well, with the true humility of genuine love and interest.

When we get this, when we learn to humbly and genuinely honor our neighbors in ways that speak to their hearts, we begin to see the joy of the Lord percolating through the conversation, working as leaven through the relationship. This can make all the difference when we learn to do this well.

Conversing the Gospel

The Essential Dialogue

We all want to live this way. We all want to be like Mike, don't we? We've all got a ton of stuff going on, and lots of reasons that may keep us from doing this, but at the end of the day, this is the how we see ourselves learning language and engaging in interpersonal discipleship. What are some of the reasons that keep us from doing this?

Maybe we're just too busy, period. When we are too busy for people, genuinely too busy, we need to seriously reevaluate things. There's very little we can move forward with if we just don't have time to learn the language and sit down and talk with people.

Maybe we just don't know how to engage our neighbors in a rhythm of life that allows us to get time with them, on their terms and, to some extent, on ours. We as learners habitually end up speaking only with our language partners and possibly a few others, and we stop reaching out, or we don't know how to reach out to our neighbors beyond the comfortable small circle of those we currently know.

While our small circle of friends may adjust their listening and speech when talking with us, we easily get lost trying to understand and follow along when others speak at normal speed, and they may have a hard time understanding us or conversing with us. We need to reach out and take the first step with prayerful courage, humility, compassion, and faith. Sometimes we need to just walk across the street.

We may hesitate reaching out and getting time with our neighbors simply because our language feels weak and we just don't know how to get out of the gate when it comes to using the language as we would like to. We try to talk with people and can barely stay in the conversation. People get bored and distracted when we try to talk about things in our lives.

Without doubt the most important thing we as language learners can do to improve our weak language is simply to use the language with people. And the best way to do this with confidence is to ensure we have healthy amounts of controlled input and output practice with dedicated language partners, giving us the foundational practice we need as we venture into normal daily conversations. We need to regularly practice what we learn, and use what we practice, and get to know our friends and neighbors as we converse. In this way, our speaking and listening begin to weave into those essential dialogues and discussions we long to have with them.

My friend Jim in his *Pathfinder's Guide to Language Learning* talks about different strands of learning we all need, including the rules of the language, input, output, and fluency practice.[61] Many learners place the emphasis in that order: working on the rules, and then getting input from class and tutors, with little investment in creative output, and especially in the abundance of spontaneous dialogue so crucial to improving daily conversations with native speakers so that we can actually become fluent in the language. Jim emphasizes, we should always do our best to maximize our conversation time with nationals. "Conversing with nationals is the best thing you can do for your language learning" (Jim).

This can be very challenging at first, because of the limitations of what we are able to understand and say. It also takes courage and humility to get out and use what we are learning, especially with all the mistakes. But as we learn, practice, and then get out and use the language in daily conversation, we can improve our fluency in the language.

Our oldest son, who had grown up in Central Asia, began learning German while attending boarding school for his last year of high school. While shopping in town one day, he dropped a ring and it rolled under the aisle rack. He couldn't get it out and tried to ask the attendant for help. This required a level of German, or visual description, that apparently the attendant didn't have much time for, so Jake did the next best thing. Several young men who looked Central Asian were walking by and Jake, who looks German, asked them for help, quickly explaining the situation, only not in German.

These guys had probably grown up in an immigrant community in Germany, so Jake wagered he'd be able to make himself understood, and he was right. What he did not count on was how shocked they would be when they heard Jake speak their mother tongue, and not German. At first they just stood there, then cautiously responded to him, first in German, while Jake politely tried to explain, "No, I'm not German and don't speak German very well." As they finally caught on, each approached Jake, eager to help him find the lost ring, even teaching him how to say, "I dropped a ring" in German.

When we cross cultural barriers of any kind, whether it's meeting someone from another school or another country, it seems there is always a moment of pause. "Wait," we wonder, "should I be doing this? They don't know me, and I'm going to need their help. And I'm not sure how they're going to respond. This is a little risky." And it's easy for us to take the path of least resistance and not get out and practice. Through transactions like these we learn to embrace the risks knowing that most of the time the relational and language dividends are well worth the price. "I can risk 10 minutes of awkwardness for a potential lifetime of friendship" (Jake).

What about our fears in speaking with neighbors? I want to address some of the very real and powerful emotions we often face when we think of spending time with neighbors, in their language. These can range from irrational thoughts, to stress; from anxiety, to hesitations; from insecurity, to feelings of inferiority. Those of us who have experienced these negative emotions do our best to avoid them. Sometimes, however, they are just there, staring us in the face. Often meeting new neighbors for the first time, or even spending a second, third, or fourth time with them, can evoke uncontrollable, unexpected, and even weird emotions of fear and anxiety within us.

None of us is immune to the emotional irrationality of the fear of failure when it comes to sharing the gospel as a "performance." I recall the first time I tried to bring a short simple familiar gospel story I had prepared into a conversation with a group of neighbors in my new language. I had told it once or twice already, to myself, and to a few others for practice, but here I was, with my neighbors, suddenly very nervous. My mind went blank. I knew what I wanted to say, but for some reason I could not say it. This was not a cognitive issue. I knew the story. I just couldn't tell it. Everything went foggy. This was something about my emotions taking over my mind. I began to sweat.

Though I had prepared and practiced, in that moment the fear that my neighbors would criticize my poor expression made me feel ashamed. This was no longer just my language lesson, this was real life and my perceived need to perform overwhelmed me. The stress of that moment sadly created the opposite effect I had desired. I really wasn't able to tell the story very well, and we went on to talk about other things.

This happened more than once in similar situations. This need to perform well was a distracting burden and started to become a barrier to my fluency practice. Sometimes I no longer even wanted to meet with my neighbors.

I resolved to give this to the Lord by bathing the issue in prayer, and then faithfully practiced the story again and again with language partners. Only now, I would not just practice the story in isolation, rather I would practice telling it while also talking about other life topics. I learned how to weave the story in and out of natural conversation. I learned how to take turns in the conversation even while telling a story. I learned how to *converse* the gospel.

Monumental as this was, a true language and gospel fluency breakthrough, I am absolutely convinced that what really helped me overcome emotional stopping points in conversing the gospel was the peace of God that filled my soul as I prayed. I prayed daily, but I also prayed in the moment when I began to feel stress rise. The Lord gave me strength to press on and overcome my fears. And he continues to do so.

Learning to converse the gospel in our new languages is some of the hardest work we will ever learn to do. We long to learn the language, to really share the gospel with our neighbors. It's hard work. It's a labor of love.

> People often ask me what it takes to become fluent in a new language. I tell them it takes a thousand cups of tea. We have to reframe our understanding of the boundlessness of gospel fluency. Ultimately, our investment is not in the hours and tasks. It's in the relationships.

There is no way around it. We need to learn to converse well, and to do that we need to rigorously practice conversations in our new language. That may sound silly to those of us who just like to get out and use the language in conversation, but it's not that simple for the rest of us. I've talked with many learners who struggle with things like appropriately taking turns or transitioning to other topics while conversing in their new language, or just not knowing how to introduce the gospel into conversation in a natural way. These things take time and a lot of practice.

Our gospel is not something we are selling, and we don't want to make it sound like a sales pitch or something worse. We want to communicate meaningfully from our hearts, and we grieve when our language skills prevent us from doing this well.

It is as important for us to know *how* to communicate the gospel as it is for us to know *what* to communicate. In other words, we may wonder why we should go to all the trouble to learn how to have conversations with our neighbors on lots of topics of mutual interest. Why not just skip all that and get to the gospel? Chances are, if we leapfrog over those seemingly unimportant conversations and topics, we will be neglecting the leaven that actually leads us into fruitful gospel conversations with our neighbors. I discovered how valuable this was as I practiced doing both together. We all should be eager to share the gospel. But we need to be wise that what we share really is communicating the gospel in such a way that our neighbors will hear it, which usually happens through conversational circumstances that take a lot of work for us to learn and work through, but actually make the gospel meaningful and accessible, as we sincerely intend. "I can spend an hour talking with a guy and come away with 5 minutes of incredibly fruitful gospel conversation" (Scott, co-worker).

When we bring the gospel into our conversations, we need to learn to communicate it with clarity, accuracy, and natural fluency. We learn to do this through rigorous and deliberate conversation and presentation practice. This sustains the integrity of meaning-based gospel communication. It also helps us learn the language well.

Conversation Portfolios

I encourage learners to enter into a process of bi-weekly progress assessment in these two areas of practice – conversation and presentation – from the moment they are able to tell a simple familiar story. The process begins with setting a two-week goal to tell and explain stories or topics. Our first two-week goal may be, *I will fully narrate and explain a simple gospel story.*

Then, we practice telling and explaining stories every day for the next two weeks with dedicated language partners. We tell a story, they listen. They give feedback. Then they tell it. We listen. We retell it. And that's the improvement cycle.

Then, at the end of two weeks, to demonstrate progress toward our goal, we narrate and explain a simple gospel story. We get immediate feedback. Even better, we record it for feedback from other key players in our learning process – perhaps another language partner or a coach. They all can help us determine whether we reached our goal, and what to do next. With each new goal we should simply aim to communicate what we intend to communicate.

What if we could hear ourselves speak? How would we make sure we are saying what we want to say? Listening to or watching ourselves communicate through audio or video recordings can be incredibly helpful, but also incredibly tough. Not many of us like to hear ourselves speak, especially in another language. And that's the whole point: we must be willingly listen to ourselves make mistakes so that we can begin to close the gap between what we *are* communicating, and what we *intend* to communicate. This takes courage and humility.

And *that's* the main purpose of recordings. Only from this posture of self-awareness and self-correction can we then heartily and maturely welcome outside feedback. We need to view any feedback we receive from others who listen to us speak – perhaps live, perhaps via recordings we submit – as a gift, and leverage this feedback with joy.

Personal recordings have the capacity to bring out the best in our language introspection, self-evaluation, and self-direction, laying essential groundwork for us to enthusiastically receive and specifically respond to input and feedback from coaches and other key players in our language life. Feedback from others may not always be what we want to hear, or what we feel like we need to hear, but it can always be helpful in some way, adding dimension to the essential question: Am I communicating what I intend to communicate?

Feedback criticizing errors in our form or skill development can be particularly difficult to receive, though it can be helpful, if we are humble and practical enough to receive it, and interpret it in light of the message we want to communicate. In other words, in the same way that regular and frequent recordings of our language can provide opportunities for us to listen to ourselves, for self-analysis, we need to endeavor in our purpose and self-awareness to understand how generous feedback from others, no matter how picky it may seem, can help us communicate what we intend to communicate. This is the purpose of regular recordings, and complements the goal of pursuing *gospel fluency*.

This process follows a simple logic model addressing the question: what is my next 14-day goal, and what do I need to do today, tomorrow, and the next day in order to reach it? For our next two weeks of learning, we set another goal, one that is slightly more challenging than the current one. We follow the same learning process, or *change management process*, via the documentation of progress. Every two weeks we set another goal, demonstrate progress at the end of 14 days, get feedback, check improvement, determine next steps, and create another goal for the next two weeks. We need to learn to break it down this way, removing all barriers that get in the way of our goals, and adding practices that will help us to reach them.

A certain *dialogue readiness* is significant for any given conversation. Without it we may enter conversations with only a passive awareness of topics of common interest, thereby forcing us to take a backseat in the communication process. Effective dialogue practice takes considerable time and effort to develop, so that we will be more ready and poised to engage our neighbors on many topics with deep interest.

We can practice moving toward this more mature dialogue ability with our language partner by finding ways to engage, appropriately interject, ask questions, and respond. We learn to take turns, and how to transition to other topics. We simply practice talking about lots of things. We work from topic-lists that we share, and we create our own lists to ensure we are conversing deep and wide in every area of life.

Finally, we put it all together. We practice telling our prepared stories within the flow of dialogue. This takes a lot of work to prepare and a lot of practice. We do this in controlled settings. In time, our two-week goals may include *telling and explaining a story in the flow of dialogue*, as various topics are introduced and discussed. "Your end-in-mind is the story that you have in your head, that you communicate to those you work with and who partner with you" (AO, co-worker).

Language learning is a lot more like art or writing than it is like science or math. Perhaps that's why one of the best ways to measure personal progress is through the creation of an audio portfolio chronicling our growing ability to express ourselves in the language on many life topics. Creating audio samples of our language as often as every two weeks to add to our portfolio becomes a veritable roadmap, guiding us to greater fluency in the language.

Our *conversation portfolio*, therefore, may be viewed as the culmination of this process, a portfolio made up of presentations and dialogues showcasing our ability to prepare topics, present them, and fluently talk about them in normal conversations with our neighbors (see Appendix 3, *Language Portfolios*). Portfolios help us develop and sustain the ability and confidence to successfully manage sharing the gospel through just about any conversational topic of strong mutual interest that we may find in real-life ministry situations with our lost neighbors.

Conversation portfolios can help us winsomely, clearly, and naturally share the gospel with our neighbors as we learn their language and culture. Portfolios do not represent an endpoint, rather a launchpad for developing and using gospel fluency practices in real-life settings. The more we practice them, the more we see and experience how the gospel can enter into our conversations through many topics of vibrant mutual interest. As we learn to talk with our lost neighbors on daily life topics in our new languages, we also learn to bring the gospel into those conversations.

Breadcrumbs

Conversations are never memorized.

One of my neighbors recently compared conversations we often have in our language to that of following breadcrumbs on a trail. (I was actually surprised when he asked if I knew the story of *Hansel and Gretel*.) We never map out entire conversations in our heads as we enter into them. If so, then they are not really conversations. Rather, we get to pursue them with wonder and interest as one conversational morsel leads to another.

I was talking with Ron and Gina about gospel conversations during their recent visit to our city from their place of ministry. I mentioned what my neighbor had said about breadcrumbs. Ron later shared this beautiful testimony.

> As I was thinking more about the breadcrumbs idea and just how relational people are in our part of the world, I thought about a dinner we recently had with our neighbors. We were there for several hours, and conversation was mostly small talk or random things, bits of truth shared that fit the moment, but not big chunks. Then around midnight the guys asked me to compare Christianity and their religion. It was a super sweet conversation. But I don't think I would have been heard if it didn't slowly lead to that point where they wanted to know.
>
> About a month later, the brother-in-law from that family grabbed me as we left their house and said, "I want to know more about these things. I'll invite you to my house soon where I'm not a guest, too. We can speak freely." He invited us to come when we get back. Praying it happens.

I love hearing about gospel moments like these. I pray along with Ron that more of these will happen, like the conversation he anticipates with his neighbor's brother-in-law. It is conversations *just like these* that God is inviting us into with our neighbors.

> I also thought about Sam and his questions as we've studied gospel truth. They seem random sometimes, but they're not random to him. He asked me one day as we were studying how we can be saved, "Do you shave

your armpits?" I was super confused but answered. And for once, I asked why. He said, "In my religion if I don't trim or shave every 40 days, then I will be unholy and unclean. In Christianity do you have this rule? Or are you really saved by someone else's actions?" Breadcrumbs... (Ron, co-worker).

What an interesting conversation...and, how beautiful for Ron to tune-in and respond to what Sam was really saying, and seeking! We may wonder in amazement how through seemingly random "breadcrumb" conversations like these we actually get to meet our neighbors right where they are. And that as we understand and share thoughts, beliefs, desires, concerns, and hopes, we get to introduce them to Christ in incredibly meaningful ways. But are we willing to invest the time, listen well, attend to the relationships, and pursue these essential conversations for the sake of the gospel among them?

When it comes to the gospel, even if we think we have communicated all the right words, content, or information, chances are that without a rigorous and regular investment into the daily lives and conversations of our lost neighbors, our gospel may risk sounding like a lot of noise they just tune out, especially if they feel treated as evangelism projects, simply because we were too lazy or selfish to really get to know them and honor them as our neighbors. The hard work of the gospel is in a life lived through humble interest and enduring love. The intangible work of God in people's hearts is far richer than we can imagine, encompassing the texture of life that God uses to bring them into the centrifugal pull of the gospel.

In other words, God's love is caught as often as it is taught. People will usually see the gospel more clearly when it's lived out in our lives, up close and personal. As we share our lives with our neighbors, they begin to hear it for themselves. This means our spending time with people and relishing those unexpected simple meaningful moments that we capture together: the question asked, the thoughtful comment, the response to a text, the smile. These will lead to those deeper and richer conversations as we grow in the language, but it happens through relationships of trust. Sometimes it takes a thousand cups of tea. This is, as Paul well said, the more excellent way.

1 Corinthians 13

If I speak human or angelic languages but do not have love, I am a noisy gong or a clanging cymbal. (1 Corinthians 13:1)

The gospel message, however eloquent, is empty without love (vv. 1-3). There is a spiritual dimension to our teaching that is more powerful than words, which needs to infuse our words. It involves words, but more significantly, it involves God-led sympathetic listening, and God-led opportunities to respond and invite people to respond in spiritually meaningful ways through all aspects and topics of life involving our interpersonal interaction with our neighbors. Essentially, this is the language of love (vv. 4-8), the very heartbeat of the gospel.

There should never be an incongruence between communicating the gospel in our new language in truth from our minds, and in love from our hearts. Communicating the gospel fluently in another language requires skill. But this skill does not sustain the message of the gospel. Only our ever-growing love relationship with the Lord, and our love for our neighbor, buoys our message as we speak it and as we live it in everyday ways and in everyday conversations. These holy passions – love for God and love for our neighbor – represent all obedience to God and faithfulness to the gospel message; they alone will sustain our cross-cultural ministry in the church and in our community. "No one has ever seen God. If we love one another, God remains in us and his love is made complete in us" (1 John 4:12).

The Bible says that people reject the gospel because they do not know the love of God (1 John 4:7-8). I want to make sure that no one rejects the gospel because of the words I say or the way I live. Let's be careful that people don't reject the gospel because they sense it is not real in our lives or words.

As we learn to connect gospel conversations with the stuff of daily life that we share with our neighbors, they will begin to see the reality of the gospel in our lives. The gospel should rarely be an isolated presentation that doesn't in any way connect with our lives.

There is a strategic place and role for the abundant distribution of evangelistic presentations and materials. But let's never forget that we are living, breathing, walking stories of the gospel. We need to honor our neighbors, for them to personally see the gospel in our lives, in all areas of our lives, for this glorifies the Lord (1 John 4:9-21).

Midnight Football

I recently played a midnight (soccer) football match with some believing friends and a group of guys who I later discovered hail from what some refer to as the "mixed-martial-arts capital of the world." I had no idea what I was getting into! A few of us foreigners were the weak links on the teams, so I just followed Jack's advice to "run fast and try to stay out of the way." It felt great to be alive after the match!

The next evening, we had tea with one of their leaders. Ali is well respected in his community, as well as in his village, hundreds of miles away. He talked about his childhood and the languages and cultures found deep in the mountains of his mysterious homeland. Ali asked my colleagues to join him on a trip home, quite a unique invitation to this part of the country, and one that came from someone with enough social capital to actual back it up. I am convinced the hours spent playing football and having tea with Ali and his friends are what built the trust required to extend this kind of an offer to enter the homeland of some of the most unengaged and unreached people on earth.

As we sat and drank tea with Ali, I thought about how much these friends of mine have lovingly given up for a greater gain. Some things were obvious – moving their families, setting up business, developing ministry partners. But it's probably more often in the unsuspecting ways – getting laughed at when we speak funny, kicking a ball around in the middle of the night (when we'd rather be at home with our families, or in bed), and just getting time with these guys on their turf; playing their games, and speaking their language, made all the difference. This is the stuff of life that seems to lead to invitations into homes, and to the gospel in conversations.

Kofta

I recently went with my college-age son to get some kofta at a new buffet in our neighborhood. It was pouring rain as our kofta friend welcomed us, his only customers, into his tiny place. We sat on barstools, drinking the tea he offered, with only the counter separating us from his workstation. As he kneaded the ingredients, Adam asked (as he always does) where he was from. He told us stories of the Black Sea where he had worked as a chef, offering specific and downright fascinating details about breakfast preparation in various locations.

More interesting to me though was watching my son honor this big brother throughout our conversation. That's how Adam viewed him. Through his mannerisms and responses, sharing about what he was studying in school and his future plans, Adam showed true interest and respect as our new friend offered advice on life, work, honesty, and obedience.

When the wraps were done, I gave our kofta friend a 20 in the local currency, more than enough for our food, and waited for change as other customers arrived. He suddenly hesitated – a simple miscalculation, but he wrote it down again just to make sure. Adam caught the glimmer of shame because of our friend's poor math skills and responded immediately, "Thank you, big brother. You just instructed me in honesty, and now you have shown me by example."

Virtues of the Christian life are more often caught, viewed, and demonstrated, than they are taught, and this can happen in such unsuspecting moments. Our unexpected exchange as we left the shop seemed trivial, but it really was a big deal, once I opened my eyes. And it has opened the door to many future conversations over tea, kofta, honor, the topic of honesty, and the gospel. (I try to go when it rains.)

I don't think it ever crossed Adam's mind not to respect this poor man's honorable work, and the good food he prepared for us, as his big brother. I asked Adam about this as we walked home. "Simple," he said, "honesty is a far more important life virtue than math skills." I agreed. I thought of a question a neighbor once asked a colleague, "Do you love me because you want me to become a Christian, or do you want me to become a Christian because you love me?"

We may need to ask ourselves this as we consider how and why we spend time with our neighbors, and as we share the gospel with them; toward loving them, honoring them, and considering the integrity of our intentions as we share Christ with them. We love our neighbors out of our obedience to God, and because God loves us, and this is why and how we demonstrate God's love to them. We know God's love because we are redeemed, and the love of God constrains us as we live out our lives before our neighbors in our new communities.

The invitation to the gospel is supremely enriched by our genuine expressions of love. This may indeed happen over a single brief encounter, where we may never see each other again, but it more often happens in those regular, repeated, and unhurried, "steeping" encounters that happen over the span of a thousand cups of tea.

Reflect and Respond

1. Who do you spend time with every day? How can you spend more time with your lost neighbors?

2. When you spend time with your neighbors, what do you talk about? What are their common interests, deeper concerns? How do you relate to them?

3. *Conversations, like tea, need to steep. They take time, with people, face to face. Our hearts are warmed by the friendship, the honor, the affection. We need to watch and learn how to do this from our neighbors.* Think of a way you could honor your neighbors by spending time with them without an agenda [example: unscheduled tea]?

4. *We need to learn to converse the gospel, where our speaking and listening weave into the essential dialogue and discussion.* What is one way you can learn to "converse the gospel"?

11

God Speaks My Language

The power of testimony

Six months after arriving to our new city we had reached a breaking point. As with most journeys, it started out with a lot of enthusiasm. We began learning language and getting to know our neighbors. We almost immediately faced unexpected personal challenges. Pregnant with our first child, Jenn was regularly harassed by men, even afraid at times to leave the protection of our home. Our front door then became the neighborhood garbage dump. With a growing sewage pile-up and a rat infestation we felt more and more unwelcomed. Complications in the birth of our son left us hanging by a thread, uncertain about our future. Hurting and confused, we desperately needed God's comfort.

As we cried out to our Heavenly Father, he indeed met with us and comforted us. God's comfort and presence, more than anything else that first year, was the message of the gospel to us as a young family. From that overflow, this became our testimony of the gospel to our neighbors.

We learned to pray from Psalm 61, what it meant to lift our hearts up to God, "Hear my cry, O God, listen to my prayer, from the end of the earth I call out to you." We sensed God's hand lifting us out of the pit – Psalm 40 – as we waited on him. Praying through Psalm 23, we sensed God's presence with us even as we went through this dark valley. We found God's deep compassion for us as he spoke tenderly from Isaiah 40, "Comfort, comfort my people." And as the chapter concludes, we too began to learn what it means to wait on the Lord, to put our hope in the Lord, for he would renew our strength.

> Now may the God of hope fill you with all joy and peace as you believe [for the impossible, for the unseen, for his supernatural intervention, those things that are yet to be] so that you may overflow with [be overwhelmed by, and abound in] HOPE by the power of the Holy Spirit (Romans 15:13).

Jenn asked me to include our parenthetical notes (and the capital letters) along with this scripture (above) because that's how we remember it spilling out in our prayers and journals.

It was during times like these we were deeply comforted by Paul's open-hearted testimony throughout 2 Corinthians. He introduces his letter with these amazing words of comfort and hope in the midst of severe difficulties and suffering. In just the first paragraph (1:3-7), Paul uses the word "comfort" an astounding nine times. Count them.

Parakaleo ("comfort") literally means "to call alongside," abiding comfort, resident comfort. God knows our affliction, and his compassion and mercy toward us are deeply personal as he comes alongside us with his abiding presence. He is our hope and strength. And as we experience once again the incredible joy and hope of life in Christ, we come into a deeper understanding of what it means to host Christ's presence in our lives, and we regain the joy of stewarding the gospel as our supreme identity in Christ. "We need the gospel as much as those we are teaching" (Richard).

The reason I share this story is because chances are it's your story, too. Anyone who has lived in a totally new culture and learned a new language has some sort of identification with what I just shared. The details may look a little different, but each one of us has gone through, or is going through experiences where we come to the end of ourselves, and in desperation we cry out to our God who saves.

And that's the point. Our story is that Jesus saves us. This is good news. And this is the good news that we tell others who desperately need to hear it.

Jesus calls us to the nations, but he first calls us to himself. Just as we received the gospel when we first came to Christ, the gospel comes alive again right before our eyes as we receive God's goodness, his comfort, his salvation in our times of need. We live full circle. Ours is a living witness to the good news of Jesus Christ. Our supreme task – our delight – is to remind ourselves of the gospel each day. As we speak the gospel to our hearts, then in the overflow we speak it from our hearts. This is the daily testimony – our testimony – that we bear to our lost neighbors.

God Speaks My Language

Whenever I talked with them, all I could ever think about was "Jesus."[62]

Back home over coffee one day with our pastor, Mike, and his wife, JonAnne, we were talking about the challenges of cross-cultural ministry. How can we be more aware of God at work in conversations and situations? How we can be more spiritually attentive to what we are hearing in those encounters? JonAnne summed it up well, "When I'm in those conversations, I really feel God speaks my language. He shows me who I am in him, and what he's given me, and how I can share it with my neighbors both here and around the world."

JonAnne spoke of finding her space in ministry and reaching out to people around her in need of the gospel. She described "hearing God speak her language" as the message of the gospel from God's word spoken to her heart through quiet moments in his presence, empowering her to sow into the lives of those around her. She talked of walking in faith and taking risks in sharing Christ with people. JonAnne shared with us that through this walk of faith and obedience she has been able to witness God change lives.

We need to be fluent in sharing the gospel with our lost neighbors, in listening and attending to their response. But, more than anything, we need to be fluent in hearing Jesus. We need to hear him speak our language, as he reminds us of the gospel from his word and by his Spirit, as he guides us to our lost neighbors and gives us wisdom, insight, words to say, and ears to hear.

The letter of 1 John is a testimony of the gospel. John wrote about what he had seen and heard. He starts off the introduction to his letter,

> What was from the beginning, what we have heard, what we have seen with our eyes, what we have observed and have touched with our hands, concerning the word of life – that life was revealed, and we have seen it and we testify and declare to you the eternal life that was with the Father and was revealed to us – what we have seen and heard we also declare to you, so that you may have fellowship along with us; and indeed our fellowship is with the Father and with his Son Jesus Christ. We are writing these things so that our joy may be complete (1 John 1:1-4).

And near the end of the letter he closes with this reminder,

> And this is the testimony: God has given us eternal life, and this life is in his Son. The one who has the Son has life. The one who doesn't have the Son of God does not have life. I have written these things to you who believe in the name of the Son of God, so that you may know that you have eternal life (1 John 5:11-12).

We need to become fluent in sharing our testimonies with our lost neighbors. Not just one testimony. And not just one memorized version of our testimony. Rather, our daily testimonies, vibrant and fresh, borne out of the overflow of God's transforming work in our own lives. Just as God speaks to us from his word and by his Spirit every day, we have a message to tell our neighbors. Our God saves! He saved us yesterday, he saves us today, and he will save us tomorrow. This is our testimony.

I once visited a house church deep in the heart of Central Asia where a regular part of Sunday worship was having everyone practice sharing their three-minute testimonies. It was amazing to see young people, new believers, elderly, all gathering in pairs to practice their testimonies with each other. I did it right along with them. In the first minute we said what our life was like before Christ, in the second minute how we came to Christ, and in the third minute how our life was changed since coming to Christ. The cool thing was, they did this just about every week. And each week, things were added and adapted to their testimonies as God continually demonstrated his miraculous gospel in each of their lives.

Let's never hesitate to update our 3-minute testimonies or any testimony, each day, as God reminds us of the gospel and as we see him at work in our lives in so many ways, redeeming, rescuing, healing, comforting, leading, and demonstrating his love.

Perhaps our testimony today for our neighbor is about something God did in our lives years ago, or maybe something he showed us in his word just yesterday. It may be a simple gospel story we told our kids or our roommate last week. As our neighbors hear these stories, they may at first only indirectly relate to them, yet this may very well be the intended posture and understanding from which God woos their hearts. God delights in the word of our testimony, for this is our personal expression of the gospel at work in our lives. "...our inner person is being renewed day by day" (2 Corinthians 4:16).

If we truly believe in the transforming work of God in our lives, then our testimony of salvation should be fresher today than it was yesterday. And we carry this testimony in our minds and hearts, the gospel, to hungry souls, hungry to hear these words of life.

The gospel fills our hearts, restores our souls, and transforms our minds. It defines our lives, captivates our hearts, and renews our testimony. When we share the gospel from God's word, it is borne from our hearts and fills the atmosphere with the presence of Jesus. We bear the aroma of Christ. We speak words of great hope. We have confidence not in ourselves, but in the message of the gospel. What does it mean for us to have a posture to really engage? It means we have something to say, a story to tell. It means we anticipate hearing something from the Lord from his word, and therefore we indeed have something to say. In other words, we anticipate that God is wanting to communicate the gospel through our testimony to our neighbors.

How does this practically work out? Whether we use hand-written verses and thoughts, show a short video clip, read directly from our Bible, or do all of the above, the important thing is we need to be vitally aware of the extent of our investment, in the moment, with people, as we communicate the message of the gospel and engage in their response.

As believers, we are called to communicate the gospel, and we are also compelled to understand and respond to the hunger that people have for the gospel. This is the compassion of Christ. As we share, we also meditate on the gospel, on the very words of our Lord, and God will prompt us during our conversations with people as we remain in quiet dialogue with him.

Excavating Our Hearts

The testimony of a language learner

It's amazing how something as simple as learning to tell a story in the context of a real-life conversation in our new languages can be so emotionally destabilizing. Remember how I struggled the first time I tried to tell my neighbors a short gospel story in my new language? I was able to speak with confidence as I told it to my language partner but had no such confidence in speaking with my neighbors. I came away from that experience feeling pretty miserable.

The pain of failure in our language learning pursuits can be very real and pervasive. I've personally grieved for myself and for others who struggle with this. The fear of failure is a common struggle among language learners who regularly put themselves into situations like this, again and again, using new language, risking mistakes at every turn. Sometimes all we can pray is, "Lord, give me the heart to fight and lose."

I'm not that confident learner who has never felt the excruciating pain of trying hard, yet failing. Sometimes we just feel spent, with nothing left in our emotional tank but shame, fear, defeat, and humiliation. So where do we go from there?

There is really only one place to go. We go to God. We realize our complete dependence on him, give him our humiliation, and take one step after another on the path of courageous humility.

This path and posture of humility in our language learning needs to be prayed, voiced, shared, received, and celebrated as we discover our second language identities the Lord forms in us, in the midst of transitions that are often excruciatingly painful. It is in death to self that we find greater hope in Christ, and we learn to embrace the noble irony of this calling. We are called to reach the end of ourselves, so that we can begin anew, to depend on Christ as he introduces us to our gospel calling in a fresh way in our new language and community.

This is deeply personal, profoundly redemptive, and immensely powerful as we testify of the glory of the gospel in our lives, and through our lives, to our lost neighbors. This is the glorious paradox, that as we struggle to tell them the good news in our new language, they somehow will hear it loud and clear, not despite the testimony of our struggle, but through it, and because of it.

So where does this leave us? It leaves us identifying with the Lord, with our lost neighbors, and with a hope and a joy that is magnified in our personal understanding, and expression, as we walk through the pain and despair of deep personal failure, into the reality of the gospel that permeates and lifts us from our very real struggles.

In reality, our gospel fluency comes alive when we proclaim it from this posture of victory in Christ, even as we struggle in our language. This is our testimony; as we share Scriptures from our minds and hearts – from our rumination, recitation, reading, and meditation – with words that communicate the gospel in and through our lives, as we engage our neighbors.

It is only by God's marvelous grace that we overcome the crushing weight and defeat of cross-cultural failure. This is an astonishing crucible of identity in which we personally engage as we discover what it means to be people of the gospel called to the nations and to our lost neighbors.

Prayer – The Buoyancy of the Gospel

Do we pray until our hearts break for the lost? (Sean, co-worker)

I plead my case to you and watch expectantly (Psalm 5:3).

I don't understand it, but God answers prayer. Sean spoke of God giving him a renewed burden and greater passion to share the gospel with his lost neighbors as he labored for hours and days interceding for them. That in itself is an amazing answer to prayer which inspires me to pray more! I am convinced that as we pray more for our lost neighbors, we can expect in faith that God is already at work in us, in them, and in the future gospel encounters we will have with them. Prayer really is the buoyancy of the gospel.

As we pray for our lost neighbors in our new community, God gives us insights that only come through that time we spend in prayer. As we pray, God will speak to our minds and hearts, giving us greater compassionate awareness and sensitivity to his interests in those for whom we intercede, our relationships with them, possibly even concerning the next conversation we may have with them. God will direct us in these encounters, for his glory.

Prayer gives us confidence and hope in God's purposes for our lost neighbors, strengthening our faith as we rise to engage them with the gospel. Prayer and intercession should be our daily practice, an anticipation of gospel proclamation opportunities that emerge from our daily mental and spiritual posture. We should be in constant conversation with God as we meditate on his word. "Devote yourselves to prayer; stay alert in it with thanksgiving" (Colossians 4:2).

We enter with confidence and authority through prayer into the word of God. As we intercede for our lost neighbors, we begin to anticipate God-directed gospel encounters with them. This is how we begin to live, looking for "miracle moments" with people all around us.

Do we wonder why we don't have more opportunities to share the gospel with our lost neighbors? The better question may be, do we wonder why we miss so many opportunities because we fail to pray, and therefore we aren't looking for these moments with spiritual readiness? "Let our prayer and praise be not the flashes of a hot and hasty brain, but the steady burning of a well-kindled fire."[63]

Intercessory prayer of this nature is the steady burning of a well-kindled fire. I join my colleagues in regularly praying for those around me by name. Five-by-five-by-five, or 5x5x5 is one of the most fruitful ways I've learned to pray for the people God brings into my life. This reminds me to pray regularly for 5 lost people I know, 5 new believers I know, and 5 unreached people groups, every day. I'm always sharpened to share those for whom I am praying with co-workers, and to hear theirs, including the really cool stories of what God is doing in people's lives through those prayers.

God has a direct interest in every conversation. When we pray for people even as we have conversations with them, we become more aware of God's purposes for the relationship, more aware of his activity in the relationship, and more aware of his direction in the conversation.

Some gospel conversations may even surprise us. As we pray, God may even give us supernatural wisdom for transformational encounters that may go against cultural norms. Think of Jesus sitting by a well asking a Samaritan woman for a drink or responding to a Pharisee who came to him at night. Somewhat surprising and confusing for Nicodemus, "you must be born again" was exactly the gospel message he needed to hear, right then and there.

What may appear to be counter-cultural may be exactly the message or invitation God is prompting us to extend. While we do want to be appropriate in our communication, God calls us to be transformational in the encounter.

> What do I lose when I have a praying life? Control. Independence. What do I gain? Friendship with God. A quiet heart. The living work of God in the hearts of those I love. The ability to roll back the tide of evil. Essentially, I lose my kingdom and get his. I move from being an independent player to a dependent lover. I move from being an orphan to a child of God.[64]

Through prayer we begin to understand again who we are in Christ, our sonship, our place in his kingdom, even when everything in the world around us – new cultures, languages, peoples – seems to be spinning out of control. As we pray, we enter into a deeper awareness of our purpose for that day, our assignment as God leads us. We become more spiritually aware, and as we pray for people, whether in our closet each morning, or in the moment as we are talking with them, we can expect God to be at work in the situation. We become more sensitive to what he is doing, and how he wants us to respond.

Right-Here, Right-Now

Steward the seed, steward the moment.

My pastor Mike lives in the moment well. When he's with you, he is really with you. In any given conversation he'll get to "How's your heart?" before you can count to ten. And he really means what he's asking. Somehow Mike has cultivated this ability to get to the heart of any conversation from just about any topic. And everyone he knows seems to wait for it, expect it, and look for it. "Thanks for asking, Mike. This happened to me yesterday. I'm having hard time with this or that."

And then Mike steps into what I like to think of as *right-here, right-now* moments. Believing God is at work in the moment, as we speak, Mike addresses the response with godly and grace-filled authority, an awareness of what I understand to be the dynamic testimony of God in our lives. As God brings us into relationship, into conversation with people, we may have a *right-here, right-now* testimony to bring into the conversation. It may be something that he is doing in our lives, or is telling us from his word, but it will always address whatever God is doing to immediately bring godly encouragement, salvation, hope, admonition, or some other beautiful facet of the gospel into the conversation.

Just as we are renewed day by day in the presence of Christ through his word and by his Spirit, we have the joy and opportunity to bear the testimony of what God is doing right here and right now as we engage our neighbors with the gospel. We need practice cultivating a heart of expectation, a will to obey, and a practice of responding immediately.

The ancient Greeks had two words for time. *Chronos* refers to chronological or sequential time. *Kairos* means the right, critical, or opportune moment. It signifies a time lapse, a moment of indeterminate time in which everything happens.

Kairos moments represent the vibrant, pungent, present activity of God in our lives and the lives of those around us. We can anticipate these moments every day as we read his word, hear his Spirit, and follow his call. Are we ready, waiting? Are we ready to share the gospel from what God is saying to us *right here, right now*?

Our testimony is as vibrant as our daily walk. We need to anticipate that God will speak to us from his word in our neighbors' language – which we are learning – by his Spirit, for that person, at that moment. "Right now matters" (Tim, co-worker).

Does this sound beyond our ability? It is. But God empowers us. Through his strength, God speaks to us from his word. And he does so in the language of our neighbor, for his glory, his good pleasure, our edification, and their salvation. This is the reality of the Kingdom, and we can live in this greater reality with enthusiasm and excitement. "The gospel is good news for me as much as it is for you" (Richard).

As I write this I am looking at a still-life picture on our wall that my wife painted in our neighborhood women's art class. I call it her "Van Gogh." It's splotchy, but it's beautiful. Lots of great color, almost 3D in effect. It's a painting of a grape vine with branches full of ripe grapes, like you would find anywhere here in Anatolia. It is surrounded by the words of Jesus from John 15:5.

> I am the vine; you are the branches. The one who remains in me and I in him produces much fruit, because you can do nothing without me.

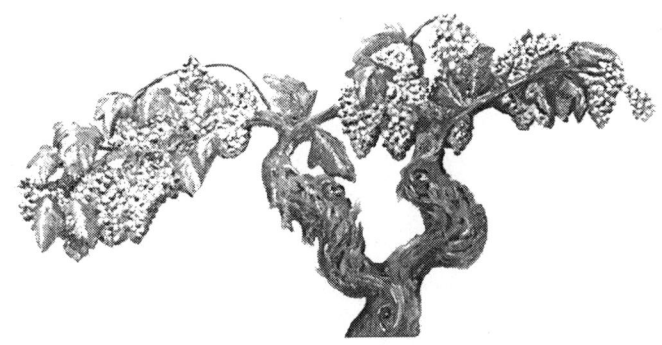

Jenn and I pray for these art-class ladies. Many of them are religious. Most are skeptical. It would seem they are impossible to reach for the gospel. But we pray for these ladies. We ask the Lord for divine curiosity to fill the art room, that these ladies would wonder just what this spiritual grape vine is all about.

Several of the ladies began to approach Jenn, asking her about her painting and why she was stenciling verses from our New Testament around the grape vine. Jenn explained that we, as followers of Jesus, are like branches, drawing nourishment from Jesus, our vine, to produce life-giving fruit. She shared the gospel from John 15.

The ladies were intrigued. They understood the beauty of this spiritual illustration about life and about God. They knew the cultivation of grapes like the backs of their hands, but they had never seen it in this light. As she finished her painting, Jenn continued the conversation day after day, sharing the gospel. Several of the ladies have asked for a copy of the New Testament. As for the painting, it's hanging on our wall, ready as a gift for a neighbor the next time she comes over to have tea with Jenn.

"We must do the works of him who sent me while it is day. Night is coming when no one can work" (John 9:4). This was a daily theme in the ministry of Jesus. We see him responding to people in moments of divine outreach that can only be explained by his deeper awareness to the here-and-now prompting of the Spirit of God in his life. He had the bigger picture. Whether he healed a blind man (John 9), or raised a dead man (John 11), Jesus captured every moment. "'Aren't there twelve hours in a day?' Jesus answered. 'If anyone walks during the day, he doesn't stumble, because he sees the light of this world'" (John 11:9).

We need to start with what we have. If all we have is five minutes of time, language, or relationship, let's start with that. Five minutes in a seemingly pointless conversation can open up amazing doors to a whole community of language practice and gospel ministry. As we pray with anticipation, and as we keep our eyes and hearts open to all opportunities, we'll begin to discover that God gives us *right-here, right-now* moments with people all the time.

Not long ago I was listening to 1 John in the language while I was running. As I was listening and meditating on the Scripture, I came to the beginning of chapter 3 and suddenly remembered that these were the verses my mom shared with me when I gave my life to Christ as a child. I had read this passage many times. "Why remember this now?" I wondered. Right then I came to the corner of the road where an older lady was standing. I'd seen her before, getting on a minibus to head to work. She was alone this day and the bus was still down the road. I knew why the Spirit had prompted that memory. I had just a couple minutes before her bus came. I stopped and shared this one verse with her. "See what great love the Father has given us that we should be called God's children – and we are!" (1 John 3:1).

I told her how God had led my mother to share this verse with me, that I was God's child by his great love and mercy, through faith in Jesus, and that is the reason I wanted to share it with her that she would know God's love for her. She let me pray for her and I gave her the audio scriptures just as her bus pulled up. As she got on the bus, she smiled and put her hand to her heart in thanks. I never saw her again.

I've heard these referred to as "miracle moments." Jesus lived in the moment well. He responded to what seemed to be moments of spiritual opportunity. I think they happen all the time all around us. We're just not very aware of them. Jesus was.

In John 5, Jesus asks a lame man at a pool, "Do you want to get well?" (v. 6). We are not told specifically why he zeroed in on this man, and then asked him this question. But we do know that he did it in that moment with the intention to heal him. So right then and there, the lame man told Jesus his life story of 38 years of disappointment in about 15 seconds. Amazing. Jesus opened the door with his question, "Do you want to get well?" and the man walked right to the gospel. Jesus knew this man in a moment. How do we know our neighbors? It may take longer than a moment, but God is at work in every encounter. We live in similar moments of decision. Many of these are moments to immerse, or disconnect; to engage, or to walk on.

In-the-Moment Prayer

Pray constantly (1 Thessalonians 5:17).

A lifestyle of prayer is one of the best ways for us to live well in the moment – to own the moment, by praying, always, and responding, immediately. How well do we spend time with people? It may be normal just to spend time with them, and complete our business, and then we're done...but what if there was more? A bigger assignment? Did we pray for that person, perhaps silently, or perhaps aloud by invitation, as we were with them? Do we pray for them by name before we meet them? Do we ask and anticipate God to enter into the conversation, a conversation that is not just about God, rather of God actively giving us insight and softening their hearts right there before our eyes as we engage?

Do stories our neighbors tell us, and questions they ask us, in conversations with them, influence our prayers for them? What do we really know about their lives? Their stories? Interests? Families? Maybe not much...yet. Maybe we just need more time. Or maybe we just haven't asked because we haven't thought about it, or prayed about it. People want to tell us their stories. Will they at first be difficult to understand? Probably. Therefore, we need to all the more pray, listen, and engage as we enter into these conversations.

Do we pray, with anticipation, for encounters with people who need Jesus, in the sense that God delights to bring us into these miracle moments of spiritual engagement? Are we responsive? Do we live with confidence in the authority of Christ, that he is guiding us to these encounters, and in these conversations? Things may look different than we had originally planned. They almost always do. These are teachable moments, gospel moments.

Practically, this may mean learning and regularly using words of blessing whenever we can. Jon does this in my new language every time I'm with him, with everyone. I've heard Jon say many times, "God gives us the gift of communication to bless" and he lives by this motto. He engages in conversation using whatever he knows and has learned through the people he's met. He shares what he can. And opportunities to share the gospel open up when I am with him. That's always encouraging.

Several months ago, on one of Jon's visits to our city, an elderly gentleman greeted us as we were walking through his neighborhood. As is his practice, Jon reached out with gospel words and verses of blessing using what language he could. Hamdi responded with gratitude and I missed an opportunity right then and there. That night, Hamdi was on my heart. I prayed for Hamdi. The next day Jon and I went back and by God's grace we found him in the same neighborhood and we did what I believe we were supposed to do the day before. We spent an hour sharing the gospel with Hamdi.

Forgiveness and Reconciliation

The testimony of the gospel through the church

"I just want to kill him!" Yes, these were indeed the words that came out of her mouth as we were having a meal in our home. Fatma was clearly angry with her brother. We knew there was strife in her family, between Fatma and her parents and with her two brothers, we just didn't know how deep it was. After talking with her about the situation, there seemed to be layer upon layer of hurt and unforgiveness.

Fatma was the only believer in her home. Her family were kind gracious hosts when we first met them for a meal in their home. What a contrast to their hurtful words and deeds Fatma suffered through every day.

This situation represents what we so often experience with broken relationships around us. We grieve over the toxic effects of unforgiveness in the lives of new believers and neighbors like Fatma and her family.

It's amazing how the Lord begins to peel back the layers that cover the veneer of people's lives, to expose their hearts and their desperate need for forgiveness.

Where I live, lack of forgiveness is probably the most deeply-rooted corporate and cultural sin that holds people in darkness and bondage, veiled from the gospel. Bitterness crouches underneath a veneer of familial love, spreading anger, expectations, lies, jealousy, gossip, feuds, and rifts. People talk about love, but it's not love. Only God is love. Only God saves.

Our local church had been praying for Fatma. What I have learned over the years from Mike, my pastor back home, is that as we have been forgiven, we need to likewise walk in forgiveness. "Our first act of obedience as followers of Jesus is to forgive: Lord, by the act of my will and the power of your Spirit, as you have forgiven me, I forgive the offender."

I try to live that way, and I shared this with our local house-church. At dinner one day in the home of a neighbor, Jesus told a tale of two debtors, one who owed much, the other little, and both were forgiven. He then asked his host the question, "Which of them loved more?" Simon responded, "I suppose the one who had the bigger debt forgiven" (Luke 7:43).

You see, unforgiveness may run deep in our culture, but forgiveness can run deeper. Jesus told this tale to Simon because a sinful woman had come into Simon's house to anoint Jesus. "She came there with an alabaster jar of perfume. As she stood behind him at his feet weeping, she began to wet his feet with her tears. Then she wiped them with her hair, kissed them and poured perfume on them" (Luke 7:37-8).

Simon, a Pharisee, was offended. He even doubted Jesus as a prophet for letting this happen. Then Jesus told his parable. Upon Simon's response, Jesus reflected back on what had just happened. The woman showed lavish love upon Jesus, because she was forgiven much. But as for Simon, his love was meager, because he saw no need for forgiveness.

We read through this passage together, and that evening, Jenn along with all the women of our church stayed with Fatma through the night, ministering to her until morning.

They loved her, prayed for her, and continued to wash the wounds of her heart with the water of God's word.

Fatma received God's forgiveness, recognizing her deep need and desire for it. She also forgave her family, and began to show love for them as only Christ can do. You see, her love became lavish for Jesus. And this is the love that she poured out upon her family.

Fatma's life as a dedicated follower of Christ began that morning. She began to walk in a deeper practice of forgiveness and love, understanding more and more how much God had forgiven her, and loved her. The women of the church continued to support Fatma with prayer, words of encouragement, and love. This was their ministry. And that's how we see the ministry of the Spirit flowing in the lives of believers, reaching into the lives of their lost family members and neighbors.

As a result of Fatma's forgiveness, two of her neighbors came to Christ, as did her younger brother, Doruk. I am convinced that as she and others shared Christ with these neighbors and with Doruk, they were able to understand the message of the gospel better because of the change they saw in Fatma's life, from unforgiving to forgiving, from unloving to loving. The gospel Doruk heard was also the gospel he saw in his sister's witness. And the gospel Fatma's neighbors heard was also the gospel they saw in her life. In our part of the world, that is a testimony to the supernatural power and grace of God within us, and among us.

The forgiveness and unity we experience as church is hugely attractive to new believers, and to their onlooking families and neighbors who have never before experienced the love of God expressed in the fellowship of the redeemed. Our testimony is a living testimony, by definition. Life is breathed into the words of witness of those who are in Christ.

Fatma's testimony and the testimonies of others like her, who have received salvation, healing, forgiveness, and freedom, have given new believers in our church a renewed hope in the active work of God within the community of faith. God heals, unifies, restores, forgives, and saves. He changes our hearts as we experience his forgiveness, salvation, and healing. This is the reason people gather as the church in my part of the world, in homes, in neighborhoods.

My local brothers and sisters in Christ risk much to gather as a church. They are often confronted by neighbors or authorities, and there are usually negative consequences. Where I live, there is a price to pay to be church, but believers here have counted the cost. There is something powerful and purposeful when we gather in excited testimony of Christ's uniqueness, displaying his goodness in our lives as living testimonies of the gospel. We gather for the supreme purpose to worship Jesus and testify of the sanctifying work of the Spirit of God in our lives, the work of the gospel.

Reflect and Respond

1. How have you recently shared your testimony with lost neighbors or new believers? If you haven't, how do you envision doing this?

2. Describe how and when you pray for lost neighbors or new believers God may be calling you to evangelize and disciple.

3. Do you anticipate gospel encounters with your neighbors? What is one way you can be more attentive to God's work in their lives and in your relationships with them?

4. *Ours is a living witness to the good news of Jesus Christ, a daily testimony that we bear before our neighbors.* Think about one thing that God has done in the past or is doing right now in your life that you can share with them as a testimony of the gospel in your life.

12

Pilgrims

The greater journey is that he pursues us.[65]

I am honored to participate in house church in our new city with a group of young families and singles who week after week share from their hearts updates on life, language, culture, and gospel ministry. They all came to live in this big city following Jesus' gospel commission. Sometimes I get this mental picture of us all camping, only not in the woods, but in a big, stress-filled, Central Asian city, and it's not just for the weekend, it's for life. And that's often how I see these precious brothers and sisters. They've made some radical choices to do some crazy things with their lives and families (Luke 9:61-2). I'm reminded of Christian in Bunyan's *Pilgrim's Progress*, "To go back is nothing but death; to go forward is fear of death, and life everlasting beyond it. I will yet go forward."[66]

Everything is new when we come to a place like this. Not shiny-new, either. Difficult-new, rough, hard, bewildering, challenging, tiring, unfamiliar, often unwelcoming-new. Home is far away, and there's a lot about life as we once we knew it, or as we possibly remember it, that feels farther and farther away with each passing day. We can no longer answer the question "Where is home?" I spend a lot of time thinking about these things. "There's a bit of placelessness in all of us" (Ben, house church member).

I grew up in a place between worlds. My passport country and where I consider home – two very different places – have never truly reconciled, but that's OK. I've learned to live with the tension of being a *third culture kid* even as an adult. That's probably why I love interacting with other TCKs, especially young people who are in the middle of thinking about what this all means for their lives. I recall one young man recently telling some of his younger TCK friends about his experience returning to his passport country. He described it as just another trip to another country. Final destination – unknown.

The great hope about our life journey as followers of Christ is this: we really *do* have a final destination. Sometimes when we take ourselves out of our familiar sense of home, whether San Francisco or North Carolina, and enter that place of other, whether New York or Istanbul, somehow we jolt awake to the greater journey, that pilgrim-journey that clears our minds and hearts and allows us to see the Kingdom in a new and fresh way.

We are called to proclaim the gospel to our neighbors, at home, or around the world, and this is our gospel pilgrimage. But we need to remember that the greater pilgrimage is about our identity in Christ, that every day God pursues us, and every day he forms us more and more into the image of his son. This is really all the same journey, just seen on two levels. As God transforms our lives with the gospel, every day, everywhere, he calls us to testify of this good news. This is the greater story. This is why we go and share the gospel.

Traveling Light

Take nothing for the road (Luke 9:3).

When I think about traveling light, I think about the Central Asian nomads who traditionally lived in yurts. Yurts are portable, circular, felt-covered tents made from wood, and decorated with embroidered felt rugs. They are held together with camel skin strings and take about an hour to assemble, and can be transported by a team of horses or camels.

When I think about the families I church with here in this city, and the constant state of flux so many of us seem to endure in order to sustain life here, it's like we are modern-day nomads in our modern-day yurts. We move to unknown places, living in faith, learning to be nimble as we adjust to life as we now know it, trying to learn some language and culture, and somehow finding spaces where we can begin to thrive in life and ministry. Nothing is easy. We give up a lot.

I think about the disciples who left everything to follow Jesus. I think of Jesus. Jesus personified the ultimate expression of giving up everything for the sake of ultimate love (John 3:16) by leaving heaven and "emptying himself" (Phil 2:7) and coming to be with us. He calls us to do the same. He called fishermen to give up their nets and follow him (Mark 1:18).

In Luke 9, when people said they would follow him, he reminded them "that foxes have dens, and birds of the air have nests, but the Son of Man has no place to lay His head" (v. 58). When one asked to bury his father, he told them to let the dead bury their dead (vv. 59-60). Another wanted to say good-bye but Jesus told him not to look back (vv. 61-62).

Jesus, "who for the joy that lay before him endured the cross, despising the shame" (Hebrews 12:2) calls us to radically give up everything to follow him (Luke 9:23-5), and he knows exactly what that feels like.

Jesus equips us for ministry in ways that seem counter-intuitive, minimal. Even when it seems impossible, Jesus gives us everything we need, somehow, including the language. But we need to depend on him completely. He equips, he empowers, he commissions, but it often does not feel that way.

In the beginning of Luke 9, Jesus called the twelve together and gave them power and authority (v. 1) and then he sent them to proclaim the gospel, the kingdom of God, and to heal (v. 2). He told them to take nothing for the journey "no staff, no bag, no bread, no money; and don't take an extra shirt" (v. 3). The instructions were specific, the equipment, minimal. The Bible says they preached the gospel and healed everywhere (v. 6).

Immediately after the apostles returned and told Jesus everything they had done, they withdrew to Bethsaida, presumably to be alone (v. 10). However, the crowds learned of this and followed them. Jesus spent the entire day teaching the people and ministering to them. The day wore on, so the twelve came to Jesus and told him to send the crowd away to find lodging and provisions in the nearby villages and countryside, for they were in a desolate place (v. 12). But Jesus said to them, "You give them something to eat" (v. 13).

Isn't that interesting? Jesus had just taken the disciples through an amazing lesson in complete and total dependence on the power and provision of God when he had commissioned them to preach the kingdom of God and heal throughout the villages. Immediately upon returning and reporting to Jesus everything that God had done through them, they once again were faced with the dilemma of trying to figure out how to respond to Jesus' command in obedience and faith.

The best they could come up with was, "We have no more than five loaves and two fish – unless we are to go and buy food for all these people" (v. 14). That's probably the best I could have come up with. Jesus then tells the disciples to feed 5000 men, plus women and children, with this handful of loaves and fishes. In the same way, Jesus puts us in situations where we must depend on him completely. Communicating the gospel in another language can sometimes feel this way. And it sometimes feels just as risky. We're asked to give up a lot, enter into high-risk situations, and do things we could never, ever do on our own.

What have we got to lose?

The farther you go with God, the more you have to give up.[67]

The pilgrim identity comes to us on several levels. When we journey into new cultures and languages, our identities completely shift. Everything we are experiencing is new on the outside, and it feels like everything is changing on the inside.

God is well aware of these changes, and, in fact, is intimately involved with all that is going on within us, and he uses these changes in our lives – those happening on the outside and on the inside – to reshape us and bring us into alignment with who we are in Christ. He radically forms us into the kingdom people he wants us to be – vibrant, nimble, and ready to bear his glory, and to be his ambassadors among the lost.

God shapes us into his image for his purposes as we enter other cultures and learn other languages. This is perhaps the greatest journey of all for us – the inward and downward journey – as we become kingdom-pilgrims of the gospel.

"Then Peter responded to Him, 'See, we have left everything and followed you. So what will there be for us?'" (Matt 19:27). What actually do we risk losing when we choose to share the gospel in another language that we don't know well – but are learning – among people who may view us with suspicion, where we indeed risk being misunderstood on several levels?

We are called to the journey of the Great Commission. Our journey, our pilgrimage, has everything to do with how we host the presence of Christ in and through our lives among our lost neighbors in places where Christ is not known.

And that's what I think keeps the people in my church learning language, sharing Christ, praying for their neighbors, loving their families well, and living this crazy Central Asian nomadic life, in concrete yurts, in the big bustling city, day after day, year after year. Their fervency, their joy – it defies reason. "He is no fool who gives what he cannot keep to gain what he cannot lose" (Jim Elliot).

We Come from a Long Line of Nomads

I guess we can blame Abraham for starting us out on this nomadic journey of faith. God called Abraham to leave his home, and to go to a place he would show him. Abraham obeyed God, and literally lived for the rest of his life in tents, on the move, watching his son's generation, and his grandson's generation grow up around him, living in tents, on the move, wandering through the land that God had promised them, living as foreigners in that land, and holding onto the future promise of inheritance.

> By faith Abraham, when he was called, obeyed and set out for a place that he was going to receive as an inheritance. He went out, even though he did not know where he was going. By faith he stayed as a foreigner in the land of promise, living in tents as did Isaac and Jacob, coheirs of the same promise. For he was looking forward to the city that has foundations, whose architect and builder is God (Hebrews 11:8-10).

And that kind of perspective – one that envisions the future promise of God and lives in expectation of its fulfillment, in full-throttle faith – just doesn't make sense until we begin to understand that God's kingdom is our final destination. And this journey to his kingdom may take us to the unfamiliar new language or new culture, compelling us to live with great faith and share the hope we have in Christ with all those whom we encounter on this pilgrim path.

One of the most vibrant images of our kingdom pilgrimage is prophesied by Zechariah about the exiles returning from captivity. This is a word of great hope to those returning to Jerusalem, the city of their ancestors, which they had never seen. But it is also a word of great hope for all of us traveling to the city of God, his dwelling place.

> The Lord of Armies says this: "Peoples will yet come, the residents of many cities; the residents of one city will go to another, saying: Let's go at once to plead for the Lord's favor and to seek the Lord of Armies. I am also going. Many peoples and strong nations will come to seek the Lord of Armies in Jerusalem and to plead for the Lord's favor." The Lord of Armies says this: "In those days, ten men from nations of every language will grab the robe of a Jewish man tightly, urging: Let us go with you, for we have heard that God is with you" (Zechariah 8:20-23).

These exiles, these pilgrims, were on a journey of hope, of vision, and of invitation. Their hope was in a promise to return to the city of God, the same city Abraham hoped for, whose architect and builder is God. Their vision was a city filled with the peace and very presence of God. We catch a glimpse into this vision, a city filled with laughter, joy, and deep contentment.

> The Lord of Armies says this: "Old men and women will again sit along the streets of Jerusalem, each with a staff in hand because of advanced age. The streets of the

city will be filled with boys and girls playing in them" (Zechariah 8:4-5).

This was their invitation, as it is ours. There is something magnetically compelling about this whole scene which our souls long for – the palpable peace of God, his dwelling place, his Kingdom. We each have inklings of Eden. We yearn to be invited.

Consider the immensity of this prophetic word – not just for the exiles returning to the land of their fathers, but also for us, as we envision a journey toward our destination during which ten men from the nations of every language grab our robe, shirt, or jacket, and beg us to take them with us (8:23). Can we put ourselves into this kingdom dynamic? Isn't this what drives us to the nations, to live as neighbors among them, and to share the gospel with them? It is this vision that motivates us to plant our lives into a 21st Century Great Commission location among neighbors whose languages we learn so we can share with them the good news of the Kingdom. Our God reigns. Our God saves.

Identity Shift

Thinking back, when I consider the precious people in my church, what is really happening to us when we actually move to new places, enter other cultures, and learn different languages? Research indicates that we certainly change when we do this. Our identities necessarily change as we adapt to other cultures and learn new languages. This is a normal part of the interpersonal cross-cultural engagement process. It's also a major contributor to the stress we endure as we encounter and invest in new cultures and languages. In our city, often even answering the simplest questions in our new language – questions about who we are and what we do – can be surprisingly disorienting. We find ourselves having to manage a growing sense of uprootedness, placelessness and restlessness as we try to orient our lives within this completely new culture and language. We do our best to create simple truthful responses to the most basic questions like these, though they tend to roll around in our minds and hearts as we continue to ask ourselves: "Who are we here and now, in this place? And just what have we gotten ourselves into?"

So, the real question is not whether we change, rather how we manage to invest in this change when we are faced with the challenges of learning another language and entering a new culture. This represents a huge shift in the way others may view us and the way we view ourselves as our personal life settings become increasingly complex: how we communicate, how we see the world, how we respond to others who see the world differently from us, and so on.

Ultimately, entering into a new language and cultural setting represents a fundamental shift in our identity. The more we engage and immerse, and the more language we learn, the more we change.

We really cannot stop this process, and there's a danger in trying. We can hide out in same-culture enclaves, isolating ourselves from the people around us. Or we can drown ourselves in work, meetings, or travel. Whatever the reason or excuse, our lives can quickly reduce to a shadow of who we are called to be if we stop growing in the language of our neighbor. Only when our second language identity ossifies does our language cease to grow.

Some of the most compelling and inspiring research into the dynamic of second language identity introduces the concept of a *second-language vision*, or envisioning the personal changes we anticipate as we learn a new language. Essential to any new language task, we need to envision our second-language-selves, and what it may take for us to move toward this vision.

How do we see ourselves right now in our native language? How do we see ourselves in our second language – perhaps at present? In the future? Are our second-language-future-self visions plausible? Are they within reach? Are we afraid about anything related to who we see ourselves becoming in our new language? Perhaps we have a fear of failing, or a fear of the unknown, or just a fear of our new language? Are we in touch with our here-and-now selves enough to know how they affect our *future selves*, or our visions for the future?

Zoltán Dörnyei has done what frankly I consider to be breathtaking research on this subject of second language (L2) motivation, conclusively testifying to a superior identity for people who are motivated by a vision preceding even a second-language vision; that is, a divine vision, and a divine text driving that vision.

> We have found that when the three key components examined in this study – divine call/vision, L2 learning vision, and a sacred text – are pooled, synchronized, and channeled meaningfully, they appear to generate an unusually high "jet stream" of motivation for language learning. Learners are caught in a powerful inner current that propels them to acquire language with exceptional intensity, persistence, and longevity.[68]

Pause to consider what this actually means for our identities as we enter new languages and cultures. As followers of Christ and as people of the gospel, we indeed have a sacred vision, a sacred text, and a holy and great commission which defines our call and shapes who we are to the very core. When Jesus commissioned us to take the gospel to all peoples, he promised to empower us and to be with us. That means that as we are called, we are empowered to teach the gospel to all nations. By faith, our effort is to learn the language, and adapt to the culture, for the sake of the gospel. But, it is this very effort, fueled by our sacred vision and calling, that draws us into this jet-stream of learning, defined by a deep, Spirit-filled, abiding motivation to live and share the gospel with every breath we take.

As Jesus calls us, he empowers us to live the impossible task of taking the gospel to the "nations of every language" (Zechariah 8:23). Indeed, we may find our personal identities shaken to the core. We may struggle to muster courage and resilience to press on. We may even come to the brink of giving up. I know I have. I'm pretty sure many from my church have. I'm pretty sure we all have.

Humility

The downward journey is a gospel story.
(Paul Miller)

So, what gives us the courage and tenacity to press on and learn language well as we take on a second language identity? Core to our identity is our relationship with Christ. And yet, in the process of learning a language and going across cultures, there is a certain attitude that necessarily accompanies our identity in Christ that allows this shift, this incarnation, to happen with grace.

> This appreciation of learning others' culture, language, etc., takes time to develop, time to listen, time to sit and bond. I don't mean just head knowledge, but one needs to live among the people and make their culture his culture, their language [her] language, etc. Isn't that

just what it means when the Bible says, The Word became flesh and dwelt among us (John 1:14)?[69]

This attitude is found in one word: humility. There is a strong connection between humility and the transformation of our identities. When we are called to teach the gospel to all peoples, we are called to an intentional shift in our identity, a process requiring humility and patience, as well as courage and endurance.

What we need to remember is that our identity shift is already happening in our spirits (2 Corinthians 5:17), and therefore we must press in to believe that God is shaping us into who we are in him, to display the gospel in word and deed, in signs and wonders, to our lost neighbors. People will see and know the salvation of God when they see it displayed in our lives.

Our identity in our new culture is a display of the attitude that was in Christ Jesus (Philippians 2:5-8). And this is simply confirmation that God is already transforming our lives, and we are therefore on display for the lost to see and hear the gospel (2 Corinthians 2:14). Andrew Murray says it best:

> Believer! Study the humility of Jesus. This is the secret, the hidden root of your redemption. Sink down into it deeper day by day. Believe with your whole heart that this Christ, whom God has given you, even as His divine humility wrought the work for you, will enter in to dwell and work within you too, and make you what the Father would have you be.[70]

God takes us on the same downward journey that he took his son. The incarnation of Jesus is our supreme example of humility. Paul invited the Philippian church to join Jesus on this journey. "The downward journey is a gospel story."[71] God invites us on this journey also.

We must take on the posture of humility, compassion, and love, as well as a willingness to suffer personal loss for the glory of Christ among the unreached. This includes an enthusiasm to embrace the challenge of a new language and a new language-related self, to "become all things to all people" (1 Corinthians 9:22) as we consider the gospel for the unreached in "regions beyond" (2 Corinthians 10:16).

Our lost neighbors will vividly see the gospel in our witness; our verbal witness to the gospel of Christ, as well as the testimony of the redemptive work of God in our lives, as we enter into their lives and learn to communicate the gospel to them with understanding. This is a walk of faith that we experience, and that they will see.

Paul (2 Corinthians)

One of the most compelling life stories of the gospel across cultures is found in the testimony of the apostle Paul. God called Paul to take the gospel to the Gentiles (Ephesians 3:1-8, Acts 9:15, Romans 1:14), to "regions beyond" (2 Corinthians 10:16), "where Christ had not been named" (Romans 15:18-20). Paul understood this to include people who were completely unknown to him, wholly unreached, "excluded from the citizenship of Israel, and foreigners to the covenants of the promise, without hope and without God in the world" (Ephesians 2:12).

Paul "became all things to all people", in order that some might be saved (1 Corinthians 9:22). In other words, the further and deeper Paul ventured into the world of his Gentile neighbors to preach and display the gospel of Jesus Christ, the more God formed Paul into the image of his Son, to be his witness.

Paul departed from all he had known as a Jew and entered into the world of the Gentiles – barbaric, polytheistic, animistic, atheistic, unwelcoming, dangerous, unfriendly. In many ways, he was signing his own death warrant. Live or die, he was never the same person again.

Arguably the most personal and autobiographical of his letters, 2 Corinthians vividly captures Paul's life among the Gentiles transformed by the power of the gospel. Paul opens his heart to this church through this letter in ways that allow us in a sense to join him on the journey, to see how he actually lived the gospel he preached. Maybe we're in a small house in Achaia with a group of believers listening as the apostle shares from his life over lamplight. Or perhaps we're walking the lonely Roman road bound for the next Asian village, listening to Paul talk about the gospel. We are taken down paths of painful risk, radical joy, deep humility, and profound boldness as Paul gives his life away for the gospel among all peoples.

"We don't want you to be unaware, brothers and sisters, of our affliction that took place in Asia" (2 Corinthians 1:8). I don't think we can overstate the intensity of Paul's life, in the sense that he and his companions felt completely overwhelmed, beyond strength, despairing even of life. Near death, they put their hope in God, and God delivered them; God, who raises the dead. And they trusted that God would rescue them again (1:8-10). They fully expected to face death, and fully put their hope in God. This was just life as they knew it. It doesn't get any more real than this.

Persecuted by his own people, Paul gave up a lot to take the gospel to the Gentiles. Rejected and ridiculed, Paul worked with all of his energy to make the message of the gospel clear and accessible to those who were wholly unlike him. He willingly departed from his identity as a prominent Jew, soberly aware of the suffering and rejection he would endure for the sake of God's glory among the Gentiles. This is how he chose to live. This is how he counted the cost.

Through all of this it was God – the "God of all comfort" – who comforted Paul and his companions in their affliction, so that they would be able to comfort those who were experiencing affliction, with the comfort with which they themselves were comforted by God (1:3-4). Paul knew affliction, and he knew the supernatural abiding comfort of God. Paul knew weakness and peril, and he intimately knew the daily deliverance and salvation of God (1:5-6).

Paul gave about as much attention to his suffering in this letter as he did to the deliverance and salvation he found in Christ. These two dynamics were inseparable in his mind. Core to his identity, Paul's affliction was a distinct and sure pathway to God's glory through the entire span of his life and ministry, which Paul described throughout the letter (7:5-7; 6:4-10; 11:21-33). Paul's testimony was one of both suffering and victory; one did not come without the other. Paul's identity in Christ was completely consumed by the gospel – displaying it and proclaiming it. Paul gave up everything for the sake of the gospel, and in return he gained everything for the sake of Christ.

Paul identifies less as a Jew, and more as simply a follower of Christ. Finding common ground where he not only could honestly identify with his Gentile neighbors, he was able to bring them great hope.

Though Paul was clearly seen as a foreigner in places of ministry among the Gentiles, he most supremely identified himself as a follower of Christ (2:14). Everything about Paul's life – his words, his deeds, his very identity – was consumed by the gospel and the glory of Christ through all of life's experiences, the aroma of life to those being saved, and the aroma of death to those who were perishing (2:15). Paul entered situations and engaged people with the gospel, fully aware that he hosted the very presence of Christ in his life, representing the integrity and sincerity of his ministry, and that is what made all the difference.

"Who is adequate for these things? For we do not market the word of God for profit like so many. On the contrary, we speak with sincerity in Christ, as from God and before God" (2:16-17). This mindset set the course for Paul's life and became the over-arching theme of all he taught throughout this letter. Everything came back to the presence and power of God in his life. It was God who was at work in his life, and in the lives of all whom he encountered. Paul's singular persuasion was borne of the miraculous transforming power of gospel. He was called to live it and proclaim it.

The gospel characterized Paul's life, witness, and work. By their own lives these Corinthian believers represented the fruit of Paul's loving labor among them, written on his heart. They testified to Paul's faithfulness because of their transformed hearts and lives, "not written with ink but with the Spirit of the living God – not on tablets of stone but on tablets of human hearts" (3:3).

Along with Paul, we marvel and celebrate the mystery of the gospel. Paul nailed it by comparing what we experience when we come to the Lord, with this high-water mark of the revelation of God's glory in the Old Testament. Though we can hardly fathom the glory Moses experienced on the mountain, and the glory of God in his face, how much more mysterious and awesome is the glory that rests upon us as believers in Christ! (3:7-18). "We all, with unveiled faces, are looking as in a mirror at the glory of the Lord and are being transformed into the same image from glory to glory; this is from the Lord who is the Spirit" (3:18).

As we experience God's glory in such a powerful, generative, and direct way, it puts things in right perspective. God has made us competent to be ministers of a new covenant, not of the letter, but of the Spirit (3:6, 17). Who indeed is sufficient for such a ministry (3:5)? There is nothing that we can do in our own capacity to effect the heart-transformation that so mysteriously and gloriously grips the lives of people who inherit salvation. This is the supernatural work of God in each soul.

Paul's ministry bore witness to the splendor of the gospel in his life. A veil may cover the hearts and minds of many. The god of this age may blind them. There may be overwhelming darkness. But Paul encourages us not to lose heart. "For God who said, 'Let light shine out of darkness,' has shone in our hearts to give the light of the knowledge of God's glory in the face of Jesus Christ" (4:6).

Paul described the gospel as this extraordinary power contained in "jars of clay," the salvation of God on display in his life (4:7), so that people would know this gospel came from God. Can we not identify with this? Isn't this good news, that the severity of our unworthiness is actually what God selects to house and display the splendor of the gospel, through our lives for all to see? This, too, is our testimony, our proclamation, that only by God's marvelous grace are we saved.

In so many ways we can agree with Paul, "We are afflicted in every way, but not crushed; perplexed, but not driven to despair; persecuted, but not forsaken; struck down, but not destroyed (4:8-9). We carry in our body the death of Jesus" (4:10). The life-giving power of the gospel on display through our affliction – as our mortal flesh is given over to death –

displays the life of Jesus in our lives and in the lives of those who receive the gospel from our witness. "For we who live are always being given over to death for Jesus's sake, so that Jesus's life may also be displayed in our mortal flesh. So then, death is at work in us, but life in you" (4:11-12).

Our fluency in the gospel among our lost neighbors, in the end, is really less about our persuasive eloquence and more about the vibrant and living testimony of the gospel on display in our lives. We believe in the simple familiar stories of the gospel because they represent changed lives, including our lives! It is a privilege to daily live out our faith before our lost neighbors so that they can witness the gospel at work in us, a tangible testimony to them. A coworker recently wrote,

> This week I met with Alev for coffee. I was able to share my testimony, after being interrupted several times, and talked about sacrifices and how Jesus is our ultimate sacrifice. I shared John 3:16-17 with her and told her that Jesus died for our sins. She quickly stopped me and said, "No, he died for your sins, but he didn't die for my sins."

One of the brothers in my church recently shared this response he received from his secular educated neighbor, "I can accept that God is love, but I cannot accept what they did to Jesus on the cross."

Comments and perspectives like these are common in our part of the world. When we confront our lost neighbors with the gospel, and appeal to them to be reconciled to Christ, they may be confounded, perhaps offended, or simply uninterested. What do we do with this? Do we give up, lose heart? No, we press on (4:1,16). We continue telling our lost neighbors the good news of Jesus. We continue entreating them to be reconciled to God.

Until our neighbors are drawn by God, through spiritual conviction, to come to the foot of the cross in repentance for their sins, they cannot understand the meaning of Jesus' sacrifice. Until their hearts turn from prideful offense toward abject poverty of soul, from indifference to sin, to godly grief (7:10-11) leading to overflowing thankfulness that God would look upon their unworthy state and save them, they cannot enter the Kingdom of Heaven.

Therefore, we persist in our appeal. God loves our neighbors. God loves Alev. I am thankful Alev heard the gospel and I pray she hears it again and repents. "He made the one who did not know sin to be sin for us, so that in him we might become the righteousness of God" (5: 21).

No other purpose compelled Paul to risk his life and suffer for the gospel among Gentiles throughout the Roman world than the love of Christ (5:14). God saved him, and changed him, completely. Paul staked his life on the life-giving power of the gospel (5:17). Paul's task was singular – to represent Christ. His appeal, simple – be reconciled to God (5:19-20). "See, now is the acceptable time; now is the day of salvation!" (6:2).

Paul presents himself to the Corinthians in a sincere effort to not be a stumbling block to anyone. He and his companions "commend themselves" (6:4), "opening their hearts" (6:11) with a deeply personal appeal, a whole-hearted testimony to how they have lived, witnessing to what they know to be true, displaying the transparent gospel with their very lives. It doesn't get any more personal than this:

> By great endurance, by afflictions, by hardships, by difficulties, by beatings, by imprisonments, by riots, by labors, by sleepless nights, by times of hunger, by purity, by knowledge, by patience, by kindness, by the

Holy Spirit, by sincere love, by the word of truth, by the power of God; through weapons of righteousness for the right hand and the left, through glory and dishonor, through slander and good report; regarded as deceivers, yet true; as unknown, yet recognized; as dying, yet see – we live; as being disciplined, yet not killed; as grieving, yet always rejoicing; as poor, yet enriching many; as having nothing, yet possessing everything (6:4-10).

Paul's open-hearted testimony is like a 360-degree view of the gospel – vibrant, pungently fragrant, obvious, and beautiful. It's the triumphal procession in Christ (2:14), Christ's aroma (2:15-16), the transformation from one degree of glory to another (3:18), the new creation (5:17). This is the gospel in Paul's life, at every turn, every angle, through all of his life's circumstances. Paul holds nothing back, he lays his life bare, and he testifies to the goodness of God. "We have spoken openly to you, Corinthians; our heart has been opened wide" (6:11).

Paul knows their hearts. He knows they are constrained by their own affections (6:12). He knows they need to give their hearts to the Lord. He speaks to them as his children, "widen your hearts also," with gentle and heart-felt appeal (6:13). Just as he had opened his heart them, he asks the Corinthians to do the same with him, to believe the gospel, to open their hearts to the Lord. Paul lived as one who reconciled people to God through the proclamation of the gospel alive in his heart.

This was the trajectory of Paul's life and ministry. In all areas of life, through all experience, he displayed the gospel, the personal life-changing, normal-defying, power of God in and through his life – a precious gift to the Corinthian church.

In the same way, our lost neighbors need to hear the gospel. They also need to see it lived out, through our lives and testimonies, as we invite them to God, through the heart-wrenching, life-giving power of the gospel found only in Jesus, the author of our salvation.

Our investment as cross-cultural ministers of the gospel most essentially is not in the outcomes, results, or completed strategies; rather, it is in the radical, life-changing, impossible-in-our-own-strength obedience to the simple and profound command: Go and make disciples of all peoples.

When I first met Sean and Kelly I learned that they were already fluent in another language, had willingly left a thriving ministry in the capable care of national partners, only to begin again from scratch in another part of the world, in a place few believers venture, among an unreached minority people.

The new language they had to learn was tough, with extensive dialectical differences between speakers from different cities, villages, and communities. Often mixed with other languages, just trying to communicate with people in their new language was like nothing they had previously experienced. Sean and Kelly confessed they had to constantly fight off a sense of failure. "We bring nothing to the table" (Sean and Kelly).

They pressed on faithfully. Every time I saw them, they would talk about visiting in neighbors' homes, drinking tea, and sharing the gospel. They talked about ways they were working on language, learning new stories, and sharing simple testimonies. It was obvious they were desperate to reach gospel fluency out of a deep love for the Lord, and a love for their neighbors. I thought of Paul's loving investment for his Corinthian children, "I will most gladly spend and be spent for you" (12:15).

I soon began hearing about some of these neighbors coming to Christ. Sean and Kelly continued learning, sharing, and pouring their lives into these new believers. As Paul invested his life in the Corinthian believers for the sake of the gospel, this is exactly how I saw Sean and Kelly spending their lives. Borne from a radical faith and hope in God, they lovingly and persistently invested in the lives of their neighbors, learned language, and faithfully shared the gospel with them. Fully aware that they came into this completely empty-handed, they personified what it meant to "die to self" and willingly gave themselves away for the sake of the gospel.

Gospel fluency therefore is not simply our ability to share the gospel in our new languages; it's really more about our faith, our faithfulness, and our willingness to die to ourselves.

When I think about Sean and Kelly, and so many others whom I've had the honor to know on this pilgrim journey, I think about my own father. Just as Paul said, "I am not seeking what is yours, but you" (12:14), my dad gladly spent his life on me. He trained me, coached me, counseled me, saved up for me, and swam a thousand seas for me. That's love.

Growing up in Southeast Asia, I had the incredible opportunity to closely watch my father pour his life into many other sons in the faith through the years. I think of Isaac, our neighbor, whom my dad discipled. Isaac eventually moved with his bride and infant daughter to live and share the gospel among the unreached villagers of northeast Borneo. Dad would often visit Isaac and Rosie. On one visit the tribal leader's wife passed away. She was a believer. At the funeral, Isaac and Dad reminded them that as followers of Christ we have eternal hope. What followed was a time of celebration and astonishment because, as the chief told Isaac and my dad, "We are honored that God has chosen one of us to populate heaven!"

Some of my best memories growing up are hearing Dad tell stories of the gospel like this one. My parents are pilgrims. They spent their lives among the unreached in "regions beyond" (10:16); they learned languages, and entrusted the gospel to many sons and daughters; they led people to faith, discipled new believers, counseled young couples, met in homes for prayer and worship, started churches, and did all of this wherever the Lord took them. And they had the joy of watching many of these disciples, just like Isaac and Rosie, take the gospel to regions beyond and disciple others (2 Timothy 2:2).

"Didn't we walk in the same spirit and in the same footsteps?" (2 Corinthians 12:18). Maybe this is what being pilgrims is all about; an unwavering assurance in our destination, and an insatiable desire to invite others – from the "nations of every language" (Zechariah 8:23) – to join us. "How beautiful are the feet of those who bring good news" (Isaiah 52:7, Romans 10:15). Anybody can be a nomad, traveling from place to place. It takes a deeper investment to be a pilgrim, to have ears that hear, eyes that see, and a heart that yields.

Reflect and Respond

1. *When we journey into new cultures and languages, our identities completely shift. Everything we are experiencing is new on the outside, and it feels like everything is changing on the inside.* How do you see yourself in your new language right now? How about a year from now? Be specific. [Example: I am sitting in a chai house in the evening with a neighbor talking about…]

2. What is one thing you can do right now that will move you toward this vision of your future language self?

3. Consider language learning and cross-cultural joys and struggles you have experienced, and the affect they may have had on your identity. What is one area in your life where you have experienced personal change?

4. *Paul departed from all he had known as a Jew and entered into the world of the Gentiles; barbaric, polytheistic, animistic, atheistic, unwelcoming, dangerous, unfriendly – in many ways, he was signing his own death warrant. Live or die, he was never the same person again.* Read 1 Corinthians 9:22. What is one adjustment you can make in your life where you can, like Paul, become all thing to all people, so that some of your neighbors might be saved? How would this adjustment effect your life choices, or perhaps even your identity?

Appendix 1

More from 2 Corinthians

We will never be weaker in our gospel proclamation ability than we are now. (Mel, first-year learner, to fellow learners)

We have a cultural perception that causes us to believe that dependence and vulnerability are weaknesses. On the contrary, the one who authenticates his life-message is the one whose strength lies in his willingness to be vulnerable. Jesus' willingness to go all the way to the cross is the supreme example of vulnerability being a strength.[72]

We often need to see things upside-down. (Ben, house church member)

We have great hope in Christ, especially as language learners and cross-cultural workers, as we consider our common pursuit to take the gospel to "lands beyond" (2 Corinthians 10:16). Paul brings us back to a strong and purposeful reminder, both to the church, and to us his readers, of his personal and profound insufficiency to pursue such a vision and task (2:16). We are completely and fully dependent on the power of Christ and the gospel as we consider any assignment to which God calls us.

"If boasting is necessary, I will boast about my weaknesses" (11:30). Paul enters into the final stretch of this letter reminding us of the overarching theme of his identity in Christ: a complete eradication of all personal commendation, with all boasting in the Lord, and all approval from the Lord (12:17-18).

Paul's life in many ways represented a paradox. When confronted with the need to validate his spiritual authority in his defense against false teachers (11:13), he could have boasted about as much. The sheer volume and intensity of meritorious experiences he endured is absolutely mind-blowing (11:23-33). We begin to understand just a little bit more what daily life must have been like for Paul – the intensity, the agony, the stress. Yet Paul did not boast in any of this, considering it all foolish (11:21).

Paul spoke of visions and revelations in the Lord, being caught up into the third heaven, "hearing inexpressible words, which a human being is not allowed to speak" (12:1-4). Again, Paul could have boasted in all of this. Rather, speaking about this experience in third person, Paul concluded, "I will boast about this person, but not about myself, except of my weaknesses" (12:6).

These verses provide us a deeper look at what seems to be core to Paul's pilgrim identity as he willingly entered into a position of weakness, a dynamic humility, reaching the end of himself, and his abilities; he put himself on the altar – his identity, dignity, honor, his sense of accomplishment – and fully trusted in Christ, depending on Christ's strength in all things. This position of weakness was the identity Paul willingly, actively, joyfully embraced. "Paul's own weakness in the work was part of God's design for the work" (David Platt).

And yet there's more. Paul points to something even more significant that happened to him in the wake of all the suffering, visions, and revelations that brought him to an even deeper and more profound awareness of who he really was in Christ: he was given a thorn in the flesh, a messenger of Satan, to afflict him. Paul pleaded with the Lord three times to be released from this suffering (12:7-8). Christ responded to him, grafting this message onto Paul's identity: "My grace is sufficient for you, for my power is perfected in weakness" (12:9) to which Paul concluded, "Therefore, I will most gladly boast all the more about my weaknesses, so that Christ's power may reside in me. So, I take pleasure in weaknesses, insults, hardships, persecutions, and in difficulties, for the sake of Christ. For when I am weak, then I am strong" (12:9-10).

So, then Paul rejoiced even more in his complete and utter weakness. For he understood that when he was weak, then he was strong. Paul embraced a life of complete faith and dependence on Christ's strength – even through suffering and pain – to bear the testimony of the gospel to the Gentiles. The strength of his testimony was not found in great and powerful revelations, rather in suffering and weakness; more specifically, in Christ's life-changing power and strength in and through personal weakness. This was the capstone of the gospel in Paul's life.

The paradox in all this is that Paul, already afflicted from the many trials of his life, asked repeatedly for this thorn in his flesh to be removed – something God could have so easily done – yet, it remained a source of pain and affliction, faith and humility, reminding Paul all the more of his weakness, of his complete dependence on the mercy and power of Christ. So Paul's perspective on life and success, crazy as it may seem at times, was not one of disappointment in his personal limitations, rather one of great hope in the power of God to work in and through the suffering and weakness of his life. "So let the one who boasts, boast in the Lord. For it is not the one commending himself who is approved, but the one the Lord commends" (10:17-18).

In light of that, consider Paul's defense of his weakness: God's strength was his strength. We should never consider our language learning pursuit a liability to the gospel. Our struggle may indeed be the very attitude and posture that God is forming in our souls for the ministry to which he has called us. Is it possible that God works his strength through our weakness for the sake of the gospel? We believe this, but when it comes to our basic communicative ability, it sounds strange, doesn't it? It just does not follow that the gospel can be clearly proclaimed when our language is weak. But the bottom line is, our language could always be stronger than it is, right? Is it possible that God actually is able to, and chooses to demonstrate his strength to us, in us, and through us for the sake of the gospel as we endure weak language ability?

I'm still trying to picture this: In what possible way could Paul exhibit strength through weakness? Or let's look at it more personally: how can we live this out when we experience the pain of weakness in our ministry? As cross-cultural workers we need to honestly admit to the reality of painful and exposing challenges we all face, including learning another language, often accompanied by extended debilitating seasons of struggle, doubt, and weakness, through which we may just find it hard to rejoice in the strength of the Lord. The reality is, we are weak; and yet, we are strong, because our hope is in Christ and in his promises. This paradox is one of the most confusing and yet most liberating promises in all of scripture and is particularly meaningful for us as we pursue gospel fluency across cultures.

Appendix 2

What Can I do in Church?

Learners often experience anxiety related to participation in local church. For some reason they feel like they need to be able to "do" everything at church that they did in their home language and location, even if those things are above their language level. I thought it could be helpful for them to see a list of proficiency-based activities[73] that they could reasonably expect to be able to do at each level and sub-level of ACTFL[74] proficiency in church. This takes the pressure off of them from doing things they aren't ready to do yet, as well as maybe push some of them who aren't really engaging as much as they could, considering their current language level. Here are some notes to help you get the most out of these activities:

- These activities are proficiency-focused (what you can do in the language right now, and how well you can do it), and based mostly on your growing ability to comfortably, spontaneously participate in the activities normally associated with being a part of church in your new language.

- These activities are contextual to my language and culture, so will need to be adapted to your language and culture.

- These activities do not include your ability to preach or teach, as those activities, even at the highest levels of proficiency, are not engaged in with full spontaneity, but rather with some level of preparation.

- Be on the lookout for nuanced changes as the levels progress. Some activities remain the same, while some change slightly to reflect advancement between the different levels. For example: An intermediate-low level learner can expect to be able to understand the general meaning of some prayer requests, while an intermediate-mid level learner can expect to be able to understand the general meaning of most prayer requests.

Novice

Low
- Greet everyone appropriately
- Follow and sing along with hymns
- Follow along with printed text or text on a screen (Scripture, prayers, etc.)
- Begin to recognize numbers as they are said (in hymn numbers, verse references, etc.)

Mid
- Greet everyone appropriately
- Be able to ask other church members 3-4 basic questions about themselves and their families (name, where they are from, family information, etc.)
- Be able to share 3-4 sentences of personal information with other church members (name, where you are from, family information, etc.)
- Follow and sing along with hymns
- Follow along with printed text or text on a screen (Scripture, prayers, etc.)
- Begin to recognize numbers and simple sentences
- Say simple, memorized words
- Examples:

- "Amen" after prayers and Scripture readings
- "Thank you" when receiving the Lord's Supper

High
- Greet everyone appropriately
- Expand on questions and conversations with other church members about topics such as daily life, family, and simple past events
- Follow and sing along with hymns
- Follow along with printed text or text on a screen (Scripture, prayers, etc.)
- Begin to recognize books of the Bible and more expansive sentences
- Expand on simple, memorized words and phrases
- Examples:
  - "Amen" after prayers and Scripture readings
  - "Thank you" when receiving the Lord's Supper
  - "Praise the Lord" after a praise or testimony is shared
  - "I am thankful for _____" as a simple addition to prayer time
- Read a short Bible verse or passage out loud
- Give encouragement to a church member from Scripture (showing them or reading to them a specific Scripture passage to encourage them)

Intermediate

All of the activities included in the Novice Level as well as the following:

Low
- Understand the general meaning of a few prayer requests
- Continue to engage other church members in basic conversation
- Give encouragement to a church member from Scripture and using simple creative expression related to the Scripture

- Share a simple, prepared prayer request
- Pray a pre-written prayer
- Read longer passages of Scripture aloud
- Understand the general direction of a sermon
- Ask and answer simple questions about the sermon or the passage being studied

Mid

- Understand the general meaning of most prayer requests
- Continue to engage other church members in more expansive conversation
- Give encouragement to a church member using Scripture and simple creative expression related to the Scripture, including simple personal testimony
- Share a simple, spontaneous prayer request
- Pray a simple spontaneous prayer
- Read longer passages of Scripture aloud
- Understand the main points of a sermon
- Engage in basic dialogue about the sermon or the passage being studied

High

- Understand the specific meaning of most prayer requests
- Continue to engage other church members in more expansive conversation
- Give encouragement to a church member using Scripture and simple creative expression related to the Scripture, including more detailed personal testimony
- Share a more detailed spontaneous prayer request
- Pray a simple spontaneous prayer
- Read longer passages of Scripture aloud
- Understand the main points and application points of a sermon
- Engage in basic dialogue about the sermon or the passage being studied

Advanced

All of the activities included in the Novice and Intermediate Levels as well as the following:

Low
- Understand all prayer requests
- Share a detailed personal testimony
- Narrate a familiar passage of Scripture in some detail using spontaneous expression
- Regularly pray a more complex spontaneous prayer about familiar topics
- Follow a sermon, including all of its main points and application points, and engage in more complex dialogue about it afterwards with other church members

Mid
- Understand all prayer requests
- Share a detailed personal testimony
- Narrate and explain a familiar passage of Scripture using spontaneous expression
- Regularly pray a more complex spontaneous prayer about familiar topics
- Follow a sermon, including all of its main points and application points, and engage in more complex dialogue about it afterwards with other church members
- Express opinions or feelings in a small group study

High
- Understand all prayer requests
- Share a detailed personal testimony
- Fluently explain and discuss persuasively many passages of Scripture with spontaneous expression
- Regularly pray a complex spontaneous prayer about almost any topic

- Follow a sermon, including all of its main points and application points, and give a summary of it to someone who had not attended
- Express opinions or feelings in a small group study and defend them
- Give advice to church members regarding their life, including your reasons for your advice
- Provide simple, summarizing translation for visitors

Superior

All of the activities included in the Novice, Intermediate, and Advanced Levels as well as the following:
- Give Biblical counsel in culturally appropriate manner
- Regularly pray freely and spontaneously
- Understand all interactions and presentations
- Participate fully in small-group studies
- Be able to debate an issue (not publicly) with confidence and grace
- Respond appropriately to perceived hostility, blaming, put downs, etc.
- Fluently explain and discuss persuasively most passages of Scripture with spontaneous expression
- Use illustrations and analogies effectively in conversation

Appendix 3

Language Portfolios

One of the best ways to demonstrate or showcase your personal creative expression in your new language is through the management of a language portfolio. Similar to the way portfolios are used in art, photography, writing, and other creative disciplines, a language portfolio can be used to track your language progress through the regular creation and submission of audio examples of whatever you are learning. I want to help you answer three questions:

>   What is a language portfolio?
>   Why should you create a language portfolio?
>   How do you create a language portfolio?

Specifically, a language portfolio for our purposes is a collection of audio pieces that describes or "showcases" what you have done in the language; in other words, what you *can do*. In short, you *can* make a portfolio in your new language. And you *should*. It's a great language practice, and as we'll see, a great gospel fluency practice.

A portfolio is an intentional collection of work guided by learning objectives. Whether art, photography, writing, or language, a portfolio is a collection of *your* work. In this case, your language work. It is your way of saying, "Here's what I can do."

Language portfolios comprise recordings and reflections of real-life simulations demonstrating your ability to handle events, tasks, topics, functions, interactions, activities, conversations, discussions, lessons, explanations, and descriptions in your new language.

So, *why* should you create and manage a personal language portfolio?

- Portfolios can help you to demonstrate and track your personal progress in the language. It's a great way to show those around (who need and want to know) how you are doing. To celebrate your progress with you. And to help guide you as you continue to make progress.

- Portfolios can help you to develop good learning habits. They should never be viewed as something extra to do that takes us away from our language learning. They are essential and best practices. Learn to do portfolios, and you'll learn the language better!

- Portfolios can help to give you confidence for formal language assessments. I don't know about you, but I don't like formal language assessments. Portfolios can help to mitigate the stress related to these tests in a lot of ways, and can even help to validate them.

- Portfolios can help you to sustain ongoing learning. Do you wonder why people often stop learning right about the time they complete formal required language? It's not always because they don't value ongoing learning and deeper ministry skills in the language, it's more often because they just don't know how to continue! Portfolios promote the kind of ongoing learning practices that will help give you the confidence, desire, and ability you need to keep our foot on the gas to never stop learning.

- Portfolios also can help you really get into the practice of gospel fluency in everyday conversations. How? Because you will intentionally add to your portfolio a growing repertoire of gospel content from scripture and from your testimony that relates to all the everyday life things you are learning to talk about.

- You'll be able to look back on what you were able to do just a few months ago and see the amazing progress you have made. Getting to gospel fluency is journey and creating and managing a portfolio can help you chart the journey with joy and confidence.

How do you create a language portfolio? I offer the following 10 steps which I list below and then discuss in more detail:

1. First of all, choose what you want to talk about.

2. Then, gather resources (stories, items, illustrations, texts, conversations, etc.)

3. To kick it off, you will need to get it started on your own and practice through it. Do this before you meet with a language partner. Have something ready to talk about. Even if it's unfinished. Actually, it should be unfinished because your main practice is with your language partner.

4. And this is exactly what you will do: Practice through it more with a language partner.

5. You'll want to get immediate feedback from your language partner.

6. Then, you'll record it with your Language Partner (5-15 minutes). Don't confusing this with having them do a recording as part of the feedback, which you can and should do as well. But, for our purposes in creating your portfolio, you need to record with them what you can do in the language on your chosen topic or task. Make it a dialogue with your language partner but be sure to feature your ability in the recording.

7. You need to write up a reflection of how you (and your partner) felt about it. Was it a good representation of your ability? What did your language partner think? This becomes an important part of your portfolio.

8. Then, send the recording and the reflection to your coach or colleagues. Do this at least once a month.

9. Feedback from your coach will help you ensure you are on track in your progress, plus will provide encouragement and further helpful tips. It's important that you sustain communication with your team and coach as you continue in language.

10. Finally, name it and store it within your portfolio. Make sure you work out a way that your coach or colleagues can help you keep track of your portfolio. This is a major way to show that you are making progress in the language. And that is an important part of the language assessment process.

What kind of topics or tasks can and should you choose for your language portfolio? Here are some ideas:

> Getting a haircut – something we all need to be able to do in our new language (with obvious successful or not-so-successful results!)

What's for breakfast? – this can be from a shared experience of having or making breakfast, or a verbal demonstration of the process of making breakfast (which in many parts of the world is an art-form itself!)

Making coffee – Where I live, the art of Turkish coffee or tea is truly an experience that everyone should know how to do, talk about, and fully live.

Talking with neighbors – Conversations define relationship and community, and we learn to talk about anything and everything – including the gospel – in the context of life on life interactions.

Whatever you choose to talk about, keep it simple, relevant, interesting, and understandable. Most important, practice it. Get help, correction, work on the dialogue, and then practice it again, and again.

Here's the key: practice it with your language partner. Come with something that needs work, so you can get input to improve it. You want to leave with something you can continue to work on. There just is no substitute for this kind of rich language learning experience. Your language partner's job is to give you great feedback. Your language partner should:

- Encourage you as much as possible, recognizing your effort and progress.

- Provide useful language tips – pronunciation, words, phrases, expression, grammar – anything that can help you improve expression.

- Provide useful culture tips – deeper understanding of things around you, idioms, illustrations, potential responses of different people – as you learn more and more not just how to *tell* the gospel story, but how to *converse* it with your neighbors in all scripts and contexts of life.

- Help you learn the topic or task through role play, dialogue, or some other engaging way.

- Record what you want to learn to say and talk about.

- Give you a few simple next steps you can intentionally work on.

Before you move on, make sure to record your portfolio piece. For example, it could be a 5-minute personal description, or a 15-minute dialogue or role play with your language partner. It does not have to be perfect. You may record some mistakes. That's OK. The point is to show that you've done it, and that you are on a path of making progress.

Be sure to reflect on what you just did. Ask yourself and answer these questions in a short write-up for your coach. Describe how you felt you did. Describe how you think your language partner felt you did. What did you learn? How did you feel you improved? What are your next steps? These are just examples of the kinds of questions you want to work through as you reflect on the experience of doing the portfolio piece.

Submit the audio and reflection to your coach for acknowledgement and feedback. Remember, this whole process will really help you, your coach, and your team to know how you are doing, and to encouraging you in your language progress.

Finally, be sure to name and save your recording and reflection to your personal portfolio. Your portfolio then becomes an important part of your language journey to gospel fluency.

You may not see a lot of progress from one month to the next, but over the course of several months you will see a big difference. It also gives you a lot of evidence to show the progress you are making, which is really important as a part of the assessment process. And this should encourage you. I promise you, as you do this it will also encourage your coach and your team, and probably your language partner, and national partners. This kind of practice really does put you on the path to gospel fluency.

Appendix 4

Twelve Weeks to Basic Conversational Fluency

Welcome to *Twelve Weeks to Basic Conversational Fluency*.[75] This program is designed to help learners be able to converse on many familiar topics and share simple familiar stories. The lessons are meant to be done with a language partner, recorded immediately, reviewed frequently, and practiced daily with neighbors.

Twelve Weeks to Basic Conversational Fluency includes 90 short lessons for the first six-week period, or the first half of the program. Each lesson should take about 20 minutes to work through, using selected methods. A summary of each lesson can then be recorded for further listening and study.

This first half of the 12-week program is designed for learners to be able to complete 15 lessons per week, or 3 per day, which would take between 1.5 to 2 hours per day, 5 days per week. Using this schedule, these 90 lessons should take six weeks to complete.

For the second six-week period, learners are given examples to follow, after which they create their own lessons based on the examples. Learners may choose to work through level-specific *Topics and Tasks* from the checklist we provide, or they may create their own topics and tasks for the lessons they create.

Definitions of the methods are provided. Further explanations for how each method can be used are provided as they are introduced in the lessons.

Dialogue is not a method per se, rather a means for getting the most out of each lesson using the selected method. Dialogue between learners and language partners, from the simplest "hello" to a full interview, is an essential component to each lesson.

A summary of the task or topic for each lesson should be provided by language partners at the end of each lesson, and learners should record these audio summaries. They provide good samples of intended expression for learners to listen to and work on during their personal study.

The lessons are divided into 6 two-weeks periods, each with specific intended outcomes. Learners should view these outcomes as 14-day goals to reach. For best results, learners should submit an audio for review demonstrating these outcomes in their personal speech and dialogue. This is a great way to demonstrate and track progress, and to receive helpful feedback. Here is a schedule of the lessons for each two-week period:

Schedule

Weeks 1-2: Survival expressions (30 lessons)
Weeks 3-4: Daily situations (30 lessons)
Weeks 5-6: Descriptions (30 lessons)
Weeks 7-8: Personal life events (example provided)
Weeks 9-10: Extended event descriptions (example provided)
Weeks 11-12: Simple familiar story narration (example provided)

Methods

These are the 9 methods used in these lessons, listed here in order of appearance, described in detail when first used in the lessons:

> *Dynamic Repetition* in which new words and phrases are repeated in multiple, varied, and memorable contexts for use in high frequency survival situations such as common greetings, basic life needs, etc.
>
> *Association* of new words with people, places, things, feelings, or situations to quickly learn vocabulary for daily situations and simple descriptions such as the names of common fruits and vegetables.
>
> *Role-play* new daily situations such as buying grocery items.
>
> *Total Physical Response* (TPR) to quickly learn actions and positions for daily situations by responding with understanding to instructions and descriptions such as "walk, run, stop, go back" or "my hand is on the book; my hand is beside the book.."
>
> *Substitution* of new words into pattern phrases or sentences to practice new forms such as "the *man* is eating…the *woman* is eating."
>
> *Picture description* for describing any scene with new words and expressions such as describing a photo.
>
> *Procedure* for describing a series or process of actions such as making tea.
>
> *Interview* to practice asking questions about a topic for language and culture exploration such as asking, "What did you do yesterday?"
>
> *Event description* for describing any event using new words and expressions such as answering, "What did you do yesterday?"
>
> *Story narration* for telling a complete simple familiar story using multiple and cohesive paragraphs.

Weeks 1-2 Sample Lessons

Simple Survival Expressions for Everyday Life (30 lessons)

Your 14-day goal is to meet people, survive, and learn as much as you can while using the language.

Lesson 1: Greetings and Introductions

Materials
Hello.
My name is [name]. What is your name?
I am happy to meet you. Where are you from?
Where do you live?
I have just arrived to [place].
This is all I can say.
Thank you for speaking with me.

Methods
Dynamic Repetition – Your language partner will say these or similar phrases in the language. These are phrases to memorize and use immediately for high frequency survival situations. Understand what they mean. Listen well. Repeat the phrases in many varied and memorable contexts. Receive correction. Try to pronounce them correctly.
Substitution – Form new phrases for more practice and association by substituting in new words (E.g. Where do you *live*? Where do you *work*? Where does *she* work?

Lesson 8: Numbers 1-12 (or 1-20) and Currency

Materials
A visual of the cardinal numbers
Examples of local currency

Methods

Association – Your language partner shows you one item from a group of around 20 items, saying it while pointing to it; then saying it and having you point to it, then adding more items following the same method, repeating often, correcting as needed, until you are able to correctly and quickly associate all the items when prompted.

TPR – Respond to demonstrations and instructions from your language partner about using currency. (E.g. Give me 20 Lira, take 5 Lira from here, put 10 Lira on top of this 5 Lira...)

Weeks 3-4 Sample Lessons

Daily Life Situations (30 lessons)

Your 14-day goal is to learn to understand and talk about daily life situations using the language.

Lesson 38: Describe a Simple Familiar Picture

Materials
A picture that is simple and familiar to you

Methods
Picture description – Describe a picture to your language partner. Your partner may ask questions to help you with the description. Have your partner describe it back to you.

Lesson 53: Making Tea or Coffee

Materials
Real or pretend utensils and ingredients for making coffee or tea

Methods

Role Play – Pretend to make and serve tea to your language partner. Include appropriate phrases and dialogue. Reverse roles and do it again.

Procedure – Using real or pretend utensils and ingredients describe the series or process of making tea or coffee. (E.g. First grind the beans, then boil the water…). Your language partner may ask questions to help you. Your partner can then describe it back to you.

Weeks 5-6 Sample Lessons

Descriptions (30 lessons)

Your 14-day goal is to learn to understand and give simple descriptions using the language.

Lesson 71: Talk about what you prefer

Materials
Pictures or examples of things you prefer
Hobbies
Clothes

Methods
Interview – your language partner asks you questions about what you prefer. Then you ask your language partner about what she prefers.

Lesson 87: What did you do yesterday?

Materials
Journal notes in the language about your day

Methods

Interview – Your language partner asks you questions about what you did yesterday.

Event description – Describe what you did yesterday.

Below are instructions and examples provided for the second half of the program. Individual lessons are not provided, rather, examples of lessons that learners may use to create their own lessons from topics or tasks on the checklist, or from their own life experiences. The idea is for learners to learn how to generate their own lessons for language they need to learn from daily life events and experiences. In the end, we want learners to be able to understand and tell a simple familiar story in the language. We will take a look at the familiar passage in Mark 2:1-12 to see how this is done.

Weeks 7-12 Sample Lessons

Events and Stories

Read through each section below and examine your 14-day goals. Using the examples provided, you are responsible for creating your own lessons from topics and tasks in the checklist or from your own life experiences. When you complete each two-week period of learning (8, 10, and 12 weeks, respectively), submit up-to a 15-minute audio recording for review. You may use notes. In the recording, you should also include any *dialogue* you have with your language partner.

Weeks 7-8

Simple Event Description

Your 14-day goal is to learn to describe topics or tasks from the checklist, or from personal events in your life. These lessons will take some time to prepare and up to two hours to work through with your language partner. Here is an example.

Personal Life Event

Time: 2 hours

Outcomes
Understand and learn how to talk about simple life events in your new language.

Materials
Personal journal
Props such as photos or videos of the event to help you with the description.

Methods
Journal about a recent event in your life that would be interesting to talk about. Simplify this in your new language. Present it extemporaneously to your language partner. Have your partner offer some improvements in grammar, vocabulary, and overall expression. For further listening practice, have your partner reword and record what you have said, as much as possible saying what you intend to communicate. Practice describing this event in conversations with friends and neighbors.

My son and the bully (example)
Yesterday when my son came home from school, he told me what happened at school. There is a big boy at school who has no friends. This boy has no friends because he likes to hit and push other children. He is

lonely. My son played with him today. While they were playing the other children laughed at them. But then other children started to play with them. The big boy had fun. He did not push or hit any of the children. They laughed and played together. They enjoyed playing together. I asked my son, "Why did you play with the big boy?" He said, "Because Jesus loves him and I want to be like Jesus." I was happy to hear this.

Weeks 9-10

Extended Event Description

Your 14-day goal is to learn to describe a series of events using topics or tasks from the checklist, or from your own life experiences. These lessons will take some time to prepare and up to two hours to work through with your language partner. Here is an example.

Personal Life Event

Time: 2 hours

Outcomes
Understand and learn how to talk about extended life events in your new language.

Materials
Personal journal
Props such as photos or videos of the event to help you with the description.

Methods
Talk about a recent experience that involved several events.

Have your partner listen to your description and help you improve it.

Installing a wood stove (example)
Our first home in the city used natural gas for heating. Then we moved outside of the city. Our neighbors all asked us how we were going to heat our home. It was just May. We asked them how they heated their homes. They said that some homes used radiators with diesel generators, but most homes used wood stoves. Our neighbors described the process for setting up and operating a stove. We decided to get a stove. So, then our neighbors helped us get a stove and install it. The piping system was complicated and went throughout the house. We also had to raise the chimney. One of our neighbors used bricks to raise the chimney. After that, our neighbors helped us get wood and coal. We got coal from the store. We got wood from the village. They recommended that we burn a mixture of olive and oak. We had to find a place to store it for the winter. Our neighbors helped us build a small woodshed to keep it dry from rain. We were thankful for our neighbors.

Weeks 11-12

Simple Familiar Story Narration

Your 14-day goal is to learn to tell a simple familiar story using a topic or task from the checklist, or from your personal selection. These lessons will take time to prepare and up to two hours to work through with your language partner. Here is an example.

Bible story

Time: 2 hours

Outcomes
Learn to tell a simple familiar story from scripture to proclaim the gospel.
Demonstrate devotion to the Bible as God's word.
Learn to narrate in paragraphs that come together as a story.

Materials
Scripture text
Sketch or drawing of the event (optional)

Methods
I want to be able to share the gospel from the Bible. I decided to try to learn to tell a simple familiar story with straightforward action, characters, and dialogue, one that would clearly communicate the gospel to my neighbors. In the story of Jesus healing the paralytic from Mark 2:1-12 (also found in Luke 5:17- 26 and Matthew 9:1-8), Jesus forgives a paralyzed man of his sins, and then he heals him. I live among people who believe Jesus as a miracle-performing prophet, but they do not consider him God. They do not believe he can forgive sins. In this passage, Jesus confronts the disbelief of the religious leaders who watch him forgive and heal the paralytic. I wanted to be able to tell this story. I want my friends and neighbors to hear this story. I want them to understand that Jesus can forgive their sins and heal them. I also chose this passage because it is simple, and I was familiar with it. It has relatively few characters, a simple plot, and few complicated events.

Jesus heals the paralytic Mark 2:1-12 (example)

When he entered Capernaum again after some days, it was reported that he was at home. So many people gathered together that there was no more room, not even in the doorway, and he was speaking the word to them. They came to him bringing a paralytic, carried by four of them. Since they were not able to bring him to Jesus because of the crowd, they removed the roof above him, and after digging through it, they lowered the mat on which the paralytic was lying. Seeing their faith, Jesus told the paralytic, "Son, your sins are forgiven."

But some of the scribes were sitting there, questioning in their hearts: "Why does he speak like this? He's blaspheming! Who can forgive sins but God alone?"

Right away Jesus perceived in his spirit that they were thinking like this within themselves and said to them, "Why are you thinking these things in your hearts? Which is easier: to say to the paralytic, 'Your sins are forgiven,' or to say, 'Get up, take your mat, and walk'? But so that you may know that the Son of Man has authority on earth to forgive sins"- he told the paralytic – "I tell you: get up, take your mat, and go home."

Immediately he got up, took the mat, and went out in front of everyone. As a result, they were all astounded and gave glory to God, saying, "We have never seen anything like this!" (Mark 2:1-12)

I read the story first in English, and outlined it with notes by listing characters, events, and parts that were not events but were important to the story. I then read the story in my new language, took notes, and made an outline.

I made notes as an outline because I wanted something to refer to specific words, phrases, and transitions as I told the story so I would not get stuck. But I also did not want to read the story or tell it from memory.

I simplified the story from the text. For example, instead of saying, "And Jesus, knowing their thoughts, said..." I worked on, "Jesus knew their thoughts. Jesus said..." This exposed me to new grammar but also enabled me to simplify the story using the grammar and vocabulary that I already knew, while still communicating the gospel message.

The characters in the story were: Jesus, the Pharisees, other people in the house, friends of the paralytic, and the paralyzed man. The story breaks down into events which are active, and parenthetically reported, which illustrate a significant verb distinction in my new language. This is only one of many ways the story can be outlined. I used these notes when I retold the story:

> Jesus was teaching – the people came – (the Pharisees and people were sitting) – (the power of God was present) – men came with a paralytic – they tried to enter the house – (they could not enter because it was crowded) – they went to the roof, dug a hole, and lowered their friend – Jesus said, "Your sins are forgiven" – the Pharisees thought, "No one can do this except God alone!" – Jesus knew their thoughts... Jesus said, "Which is easier to say – your sins are forgiven or get up?" – So, he said to the paralytic, "Get up..." – immediately, he stood, took his bed, and went home praising God – everyone was amazed and praised God.

I presented this extemporaneously to my language partner. I referred to the outline while I spoke. He helped me say it better. I had my language partner say the story back to me in his own words while recorded it. I listened to the recording several times, and then re-told the story to some neighbors.

These 12-weeks of lessons with a language partner represent only a portion of our learning during this time. Doing these lessons with a language partner provides us with a great controlled setting to get focused language input and output practice on basic life topics and tasks. When combined with grammar and fluency practice, working through this program should help learners reach *basic conversational fluency* within 12 weeks.

Appendix 5

Learning Zone Exercise

Language barriers and learning zone practices described in Chapter 8 are reproduced and listed (below) for you to look over. Read the directions and work through the following exercise designed to help you operate more and more in your language learning zone.

10 Barriers

    1. Lack of Vision ☐

    2. Part-time Learner Mindset ☐

    3. English-dominant Identity ☐

    4. Criticism or Ridicule from Nationals or Colleagues ☐

    5. Lack of Team Support (or no place to share our cool stories) ☐

    6. No Close Relationships with Nationals ☐

    7. Excessive Social Media and Virtual Ghettos ☐

    8. Intangible Destabilizers ☐

9. Family Considerations and Challenges ☐

10. Getting Stuck on the Mediocre Plateau ☐

10 Learning Zone Practices

1. The Familiar Discomfort of Immersion ☐

2. Making Space for Creative Expression ☐

3. The Art of Failing and Getting Immediate Feedback ☐

4. Expanding the Language We Need ☐

5. Scaffolding ☐

6. Dual-Investment ☐

7. Minimizing and Optimizing ☐

8. The Rhythm of Endurance ☐

9. Demystifying Progress ☐

10. Envisioning ☐

Directions

1. Go through each list mentally asking yourself, "I avoid..." for each barrier, and "I practice..." for each learning zone practice. Check off each item to demonstrate your positive progress. Great job and keep it up!

2. Think about how you want to improve. What is one item you can choose from either of these lists – either a barrier you want to avoid or stop doing, or a learning zone practice you want to improve or start doing – as a positive next step for you in your language?

3. Describe how you plan to take your next step (to avoid or stop a barrier to your learning, and to improve or start a learning zone practice).

4. Share your plan with someone.

Acknowledgements

Many have contributed to this book in incalculable ways. Lonna Dickerson, Greg Holden, and Carol Orwig coached me in these principles and practices for over 20 years. Josiah Daniels and Thor Sawin shared their insatiable joy and brilliance on our many cross-cultural adventures together. Eric Schmidt provided amazing technical and creative support for this project. Lonna, James, Lisa, Frank, and Jackie edited and improved my writing. Many others have been an integral part of my personal "1000 cups" journey, especially my dear parents, sister, and brother. Thanks to my Journeyman colleagues, as well as those from Mission Arlington, Crosspoint, International Celebration, World Relief, Cottonwood Church, MTI, ICCT, LLEC, ICLL, and the IMB; to the amazing "A-Team" we had the honor to lead in the late 90s who first showed me what it meant to live the gospel fluently among the most unreached; and to our many amazing national and international partners throughout Asia and around the world who continue to daily proclaim the gospel among all peoples, and teach others to do likewise. Most of all, thanks to Jenn and our three boys: you inspire me, and I love each of you with all my heart! Jenn, I agree with Mike, "When I look at you, I see Jesus."

Endnotes

[1] Josiah Daniels, Certified Bilingual Educator, MA Ed., Former Communication Resource Specialist, IMB; decades-long colleague in cross-cultural ministry.

[2] Carol Orwig, SIL International; long-term mentor and colleague in coaching second language acquisition for Christian workers.

[3] H. and G. Taylor, *Hudson Taylor's Spiritual Secret,* (Moody Press, Chicago, 1987), 192. I received this little book as a gift in 1987 (and have carted it with me ever since) while listening to Hudson Taylor III appeal to churches in Singapore to take the gospel into China. It made a lasting impression that he preached in Chinese, and his Chinese colleague interpreted into English.

[4] Taylor, *Hudson Taylor's Spiritual Secret,* 135-75.

[5] Taylor, *Hudson Taylor's Spiritual Secret,* 152.

[6] https://www.desiringgod.org/messages/the-ministry-of-hudson-taylor-as-life-in-christ

[7] Taylor, *Hudson Taylor's Spiritual Secret,* 230.

[8] https://www.desiringgod.org/messages/the-ministry-of-hudson-taylor-as-life-in-christ

[9] James Hudson Taylor (2012-05-12). *A Ribband of Blue And Other Bible Studies* (Kindle Locations 246-249). Kindle Edition.

[10] Taylor, *Hudson Taylor's Spiritual Secret,* 235.

[11] Taylor, *Hudson Taylor's Spiritual Secret,* 247.

[12] Taylor, *Hudson Taylor's Spiritual Secret,* 192.

[13] Thomas E. Brewster, 1983. Language Learning and Mission. A LEARN! Video seminar for YWAM participants, Unpublished transcription Buchloe, Switzerland. 192. Found in Brewster, Dan. 1997. *Only Paralyzed From the Neck Down.* William Carey Library. Pasadena, CA. 131.

[14] https://www.actfl.org

[15] New Hope, https://www.multiplyhealing.org

[16] https://www.language180.com

[17] https://www.language180.com

[18] Jared Wilson, *The Imperfect Disciple* (Baker, 2017) EPUB-ebook, 96.

[19] John Piper, "How to Drink Orange Juice to the Glory of God," *Pierced by the Word: Thirty-One Meditations for Your Soul* (Multomah, 2013), 10.

[20] C.S. Lewis, *The Weight of Glory* (Harper-Collins, 2001).

[21] Nik Ripken, *The Insanity Of God* (B&H, 2013), 86.

[22] New Hope, https://www.multiplyhealing.org.

[23] Andy Reese, Jennifer Barnett, *Freedom Tools, Overcoming Life's Tough Problems* (Baker 2015), 105.

[24] Bruce Privatsky, *Muslim Turkistan: Kazak Religion and Collective Memory*. Surrey: Curzon Press. 2001. This book helped me sort out a basic understanding of concepts and beliefs about metaphysical power and evil in our part of the world.

[25] I adapted these ten questions in 2000 from their original form found in David Penny's Question-Approach-Index (1999) and have used them as a tool for language learning and gospel engagement.

[26] Mike Shipman, *Any-3: Anyone, Anywhere, Anytime* (Wigtake, 2013).

[27] David and Paul Watson, *Contagious Disciple Making: Leading Others on a Journey of Discovery* (Thomas Nelson, 2014).

[28] New Hope, Multiply Healing, https://www.multiplyhealing.org.

[29] Brewster, 1983. 45. Found in Brewster. 1997. 131.

[30] Mark Zuckerberg included "The Hacker Way" in his Letter to Prospective Facebook Investors Feb 1, 2012.

[31] Charles Kraft, 1973. *Introductory Hausa*. Berkeley and Los Angeles: University of California Press. Found in Brewster, Dan. 1997. *Only Paralyzed From the Neck Down*. William Carey Library. Pasadena, CA. 104.

[32] Complete lessons for the first twelve weeks of learning can be found at https://www.language180.com/lessons.

[33] L. Davachi and I. Dobbins, *Declarative Memory*, (Current Directions Psychological Sciences 17-2, 2008) 112-118 as cited in Roy V. H. Pollock, Andy Jefferson, Calhoun W. Wick, *The Six Disciplines of Breakthrough Learning: How to Turn Training and Development into Business Results*, EPUB-ebook (Pfeiffer; 3rd edition, 2015), 122-124.

[34] D. Sousa, *How the Brain Learns* (Corwin, 2011) 134 as cited in Pollock, Jefferson, Wick, *The Six Disciplines of Breakthrough Learning*, 127.

35 Thor Sawin, Drawn from personal notes during our survey trip with teams engaging Central Asians in three urban diaspora contexts, October 2018.

36 Ibid.

37 Ibid.

38 Ibid.

39 Ibid.

40 Ibid.

41 Brewster, 1983. 45. Found in Brewster. 1997. 97-8.

42 Lloyd Kwast, 1981. *Understanding Culture*. In Winter et al. 397-399. At https://www.worldchristians.info/wp-content/uploads/2012/03/lesson_10.pdf.

43 M. Imai, *Kaizen: The Key to Japan's Competitive Success*. (McGraw-Hill, 1986) as cited in Pollock, Jefferson, Wick, *The Six Disciplines of Breakthrough Learning*, 275.

44 Sawin, survey notes, 2018.

45 Ibid.

46 Ibid.

47 Ibid.

48 Ibid.

49 This famous quote I'll attribute to Denise F, a good friend who coached the 2008 Para-Olympic team representing our beloved host country. She taught me much about learning, teaching, and living well as a cross-cultural witness for Christ in all walks of life among our host communities. A more complete description of teach-backs can be found at http://www.teachbacktraining.org/.

50 Sawin, survey notes, 2018.

51 Ibid.

52 Joshua Foer, *Moonwalking with Einstein: The Art and Science of Remembering Everything* (New York: Penguin Press, 2011).

53 *Interval training* is designed to improve performance through high-intensity workouts interspersed with lower-intensity workouts and rest to help to manage fatigue. Interval training, as a healthy rhythm of training, can be applied to many disciplines for improved results, including language learning. Studies indicate we can optimize intense learning activities by

keeping them between 1.5 to 2 hours in duration, with plenty of rest in-between. We need to find a rhythm of learning that works within a time-frame of optimal intensity. When we finish a task, we should have a good idea about what we need to do next. Do we need to get out and converse with neighbors? Do we need to study more? Do we need some intense practice with a language partner? Intentionally thinking about what we need next, in a given day, week, or month, will help us work toward discovering a learning rhythm that works for us as we learn language. We may need to aim for a new stride requiring some mental conditioning we are not accustomed to. We may also need to adjust our schedule and level of intensity for different seasons of life and learning.

[54] Our bodies are designed to withstand a certain amount of stress, which elite athletes leverage to push against their training limits without exceeding them. This is the principle of *overload* or *over-reach*. Athletes practicing over-reach may push just beyond their optimal limit and begin to experience fatigue. When athletes experience the onset of fatigue, they are wise to plan for a de-load immediately following intense training. In most physical training this means reducing volume and intensity by up to 60% of the maximum for one week. This overall process is called *phase-based training*. Athletes who stay within this spectrum of intensity and recovery by practicing phase-based training generally experience improved performance without the risk of over-fatigue. Principles of phase-based training can be applied toward creating healthy language learning rhythms. How can we manage the intensity and stress of our learning, especially those aspects which require a lot of focused energy on our part? Deliberately managed stress can promote fantastic language growth, as long as we are also aware that stress can also accumulate and potentially lead to fatigue and burnout.

[55] Stephen Curry, https://www.masterclass.com/classes/stephen-curry-teaches-shooting-ball-handling-and-scoring.

[56] Athletes who consistently over-train are highly motivated, but perhaps blind to pain (or simply ignore it), and may need to rework their programming. Over-training allows fatigue to accumulate, and without sufficient rest and recovery, this can lead to over-fatigue. This often happens due to a failure to properly recover and adapt to the training. Athletes who over-train may experience a severe decline in performance and risk poor long-term recovery. Again, this principle can be applied to any discipline or practice we seriously pursue, including language learning. We need certain amounts of stress in our learning in order to reach our potential, but we also need to monitor it to avoid risks of over-fatigue and burnout.

⁵⁷ Rick Warren, *Bible Study Methods* (Zondervan, 2006), 38.

⁵⁸ Andrew Murray, *The Secret of Adoration*, Introduction.

⁵⁹ David Matthis, https://www.desiringGod.org/articles/twelve-gospel-passages-to-soak-in.

⁶⁰ Brewster, 1983. 31-2. Found in Brewster. 1997. 270-1.

⁶¹ Jim's Pathfinder's Guide draws from Paul Nation's *The Four Strands* (2008) which states in the abstract: "The activities in a language course can be classified into the four strands of meaning-focused input, meaning-focused output, language-focused learning and fluency development. In a well-designed course there should be an even balance of these strands with roughly equal amounts of time given to each strand." (https://www.doi.org/10.2167/illt039.0).

⁶² Zedeke Zemduken, Personal Letter to Author. YWAM. Nicosia, Cyprus, October 23. Found in Brewster, Dan. 1997. Only Paralyzed From the Neck Down. William Carey Library. Pasadena, CA. 269.

⁶³ C.H. Spurgeon, *The Treasury of David: Spurgeon's Classic Work on the Psalms* (Kregel Academics, 2004), 649.

⁶⁴ Paul Miller, *A Praying Life: Connecting with God in a Distracting World* (NavPress, 2017).

⁶⁵ In response to a film chronicling the amazing work of God and his kingdom around the world, Bill Johnson reminds us of the greater journey.

⁶⁶ John Bunyan, *Pilgrim's Progress* (first published 1678).

⁶⁷ Les and Jeannette Maxwell quoted Jimmy Evans over tea one day as we were praying together about their recent trip to see us. See also https://www.gateway-people.com.

⁶⁸ Elfrieda Lepp-Kaethler and Zoltán Dörnyei, The Role of Sacred Texts in Enhancing Motivation and Living the Vision in Second Language Acquisition, chapter 11 of *Christian Faith and English Language Teaching and Learning* (Mary Shepard Wong, Carolyn Kristjansson, Zoltan Dornyei, ed., Routledge, NY, 2013).

⁶⁹ Zemduken, 1986.Found in Brewster, Dan. 1997. *Only Paralyzed From the Neck Down*. William Carey Library. Pasadena, CA. 270.

⁷⁰ Andrew Murray, *Humility*, (first published March 9th 1895).

⁷¹ Paul Miller, *A Praying Life*.

[72] T and E Brewster, *On Listening to Christ*. 1984. Unpublished Notes. Found in Brewster, Dan. 1997. *Only Paralyzed From the Neck Down*. William Carey Library. Pasadena, CA. 128.

[73] Amy Morrison created these activities from "task and topic" lists I adapted from ACTFL "can do" statements.

[74] https://www.actfl.org.

[75] Twelve Weeks to Basic Conversational Fluency. Complete lessons for the first twelve weeks of learning can be found at https://www.language180.com/lessons.

Made in the USA
Columbia, SC
01 December 2022